Improving the Relevance of Search Results

DENGYA ZHU

Improving the Relevance of Search Results

Search-term Disambiguation and Ontological Filtering

VDM Verlag Dr. Müller

Impressum/Imprint (nur für Deutschland/ only for Germany)
Bibliografische Information der Deutschen Nationalbibliothek: Die Deutsche Nationalbibliothek
verzeichnet diese Publikation in der Deutschen Nationalbibliografie; detaillierte bibliografische
Daten sind im Internet über http://dnb.d-nb.de abrufbar.
Alle in diesem Buch genannten Marken und Produktnamen unterliegen warenzeichen-, marken-
oder patentrechtlichem Schutz bzw. sind Warenzeichen oder eingetragene Warenzeichen der
jeweiligen Inhaber. Die Wiedergabe von Marken, Produktnamen, Gebrauchsnamen,
Handelsnamen, Warenbezeichnungen u.s.w. in diesem Werk berechtigt auch ohne besondere
Kennzeichnung nicht zu der Annahme, dass solche Namen im Sinne der Warenzeichen- und
Markenschutzgesetzgebung als frei zu betrachten wären und daher von jedermann benutzt
werden dürften.

Coverbild: www.purestockx.com

Verlag: VDM Verlag Dr. Müller Aktiengesellschaft & Co. KG
Dudweiler Landstr. 99, 66123 Saarbrücken, Deutschland
Telefon +49 681 9100-698, Telefax +49 681 9100-988, Email: info@vdm-verlag.de
Zugl.: Curtin University of Technology, Diss, 2007

Herstellung in Deutschland:
Schaltungsdienst Lange o.H.G., Berlin
Books on Demand GmbH, Norderstedt
Reha GmbH, Saarbrücken
Amazon Distribution GmbH, Leipzig
ISBN: 978-3-639-14085-9

Imprint (only for USA, GB)
Bibliographic information published by the Deutsche Nationalbibliothek: The Deutsche
Nationalbibliothek lists this publication in the Deutsche Nationalbibliografie; detailed
bibliographic data are available in the Internet at http://dnb.d-nb.de.
Any brand names and product names mentioned in this book are subject to trademark, brand or
patent protection and are trademarks or registered trademarks of their respective holders. The use
of brand names, product names, common names, trade names, product descriptions etc. even
without a particular marking in this works is in no way to be construed to mean that such names
may be regarded as unrestricted in respect of trademark and brand protection legislation and
could thus be used by anyone.

Cover image: www.purestockx.com

Publisher:
VDM Verlag Dr. Müller Aktiengesellschaft & Co. KG
Dudweiler Landstr. 99, 66123 Saarbrücken, Germany
Phone +49 681 9100-698, Fax +49 681 9100-988, Email: info@vdm-publishing.com
Curtin University of Technology, Diss, 2007

Printed in the U.S.A.
Printed in the U.K. by (see last page)
ISBN: 978-3-639-14085-9

Acknowledgements

I would like to express my sincere thanks and gratitude to my supervisor, Prof. Dr. Heinz Dreher for giving me the opportunity to research in the field of Information Retrieval. Thanks for his generous support, guidance, and advice through this research project. His knowledge and experience in academic research and his attention to detail have proved to be very valuable in the completion of this research.

I would also like to express my deep thanks to Prof. Elizabeth Chang for her encouragement, help, extensive knowledge, and advice during this project.

Thanks to Prof. Dr. Christian Gütl for his support, advice and assistance.

My special thanks to Mr. Christopher Jones for implementing the programming job of the ODP semantic characteristics extraction.

Thanks to all of the staff who generously consented to take part in the relevance judgment experiment.

Finally, I would to like to express my gratitude to my wife and my son for their support and understanding during my research course. Thanks to my parents for their encouragement.

Table of Contents

Table of Contents iii

List of Figures vii

List of Tables...xi

Chapter 1.   Problem Statement 1

1.1 Introduction 1

1.2 Information Overload of Search Engines – What does 63 million Returned Items Mean?.......4

1.3 Mismatch of Search Results of Search Engines – High Recall, Low Precision 8

1.4 Missing Relevant Documents of Search Engines – Low Recall.............................9

1.5 Poorly Organized Search Results of Search Engines...12

1.6 Mismatching Human Mental Model of Clustering Engines 13

1.7 Low Recall of Web Navigating..14

1.8 Research Objectives 15

1.9 Research Methodology..16

1.10 Summary 16

Chapter 2.   Previous Work and Literature Review...19

2.1 Introduction 19

2.2 Information Retrieval Models 23

2.3 Web Information Retrieval and Search Engines 32

2.4 Text Clustering...38

2.5 Text Categorization 40

2.6 Ontology-Based Information Classification...49

2.7 Research Significance 51

2.8 Summary 53

Chapter 3.   Conceptual Solution...55

3.1 Introduction 55

3.2 An Interactive Information Retrieval Model 56

3.3 Using Web Services APIs to Retrieve Information from the Web 63

3.4 Semantic Characteristics Extraction from the ODP 65

3.5 Indexing the ODP Data 72

3.6 Using Vector Space Model as a Classifier to Categorize Search Results 72

3.7 Filtering Search Results Based on the ODP Lightweight Ontology 74

3.8 An Example to Illustrate VSM as a Classifier 75

3.9 Design Principle and Alternatives 75

3.10 Summary 76

Chapter 4.   Implementation 77

4.1 Introduction 77

4.2 System Structure 77

4.3 Extracting Semantic Characteristics from the ODP by JAXP 80

4.4 Using Lucene to Index the Semantic ODP Data 87

4.5 Using a Tree to Represent the ODP Lightweight Ontology 93

4.6 Using Lucene Searcher to Classify Search Results 95

4.7 Ontologically Filtering Search Results 99

4.8 Summary 107

Chapter 5.   Special Search-browser Performance Evaluation 109

5.1 The Objectives of the Evaluation 109

5.2 The Testing Strategy 110

5. 3 Measuring Search Effectiveness 112

5.4 Evaluation Procedure 115

5.5 Relevance Judgment of Search Results 117

5.6 Special Search-browser Evaluation 124

5.7 Limitation and Discussion 131

5.8 Summary 135

Chapter 6.   Conclusion and Future Work 137

6.1 Probabilistic Model as a Classifier 137

6.2 Machine Learning... 138

6.3 Ontology-Based Information Retrieval 140

6.4 Combining Categorization and Clustering to Improve Categorization Quality.... 141

6.5 Larger Scale Experiment 141

6.6 Conclusion.. 142

6.7 Summary 143

References 145

Appendices 157

Appendix 1: Abbreviation List... 157

Appendix 2: Stop Word List of Wikipedia 158

Appendix 3: Search Results of the Five Queries.. 159

Appendix 4: The First Two Levels of the ODP Categories 173

Appendix 5: Index Structure of Lucene 175

Appendix 6: Consent Form 179

Appendix 7: Information Form 180

Appendix 8: Relevance Judgment Survey Form... 181

Appendix 9: Statistical Results of the Five Judges 185

Appendix 10: Classified Search Results of "Clinton".. 196

Appendix 11: Classified Search Results of "Ford" 199

Appendix 12: Classified Search Results of "health" 201

Appendix 13: Classified Search Results of "jaguar".. 206

Appendix 14: Classified Search Results of "UPS" 208

Appendix 15: An Example to Illustrate VSM as a Classifier.. 211

Appendix 16: A Sample Survey Result... 221

List of Figures

Figure 1-1 Search results of "jaguar" returned from Google 5

Figure 1-2 Search results of "George Washington" returned from Google 6

Figure 1-3 Search results of "Wei Liu" returned from Google 7

Figure 1-4 Search results of "laptop" returned from Google 11

Figure 1-5 Search results of "notebook" returned from Google 12

Figure 1-6 Search results of "jaguar" of Clusty.com 14

Figure 2-1 A typical IR system 21

Figure 2-2 Broad outline of an information retrieval system 21

Figure 2-3 The process of retrieving information 22

Figure 2-4 General search engine architecture 22

Figure 2-5 A taxonomy of IR models 24

Figure 2-6 Index file and linked list 29

Figure 2-7 Illustration of precision and recall Precision = |Ra| / |A|, Recall = |Ra| / |R| 31

Figure 2-8 High level Google architecture 34

Figure 2-9 Meta-search software component architecture 35

Figure 3-1 Main components of the system 56

Figure 3-2 A simplified standard model of the information access process 57

Figure 3-3 Generative Conceptualisation 58

Figure 3-4 Gyroidal Web searching procedure 60

Figure 3-5 An interactive information retrieval and categorization system architecture 61

Figure 3-6 The first page returned by Google when searching for "ups" 63

Figure 3-7 The hierarchical structure of the ODP 67

Figure 3-8 The 15 + 1 first level categories of the ODP 67

Figure 3-9 Subcategories of the category "Society" in the ODP 69

Figure 3-10 FAQ screenshot of "Science: Biology: Flora_and_Fauna: Animalia" 70

Figure 3-11 Screenshot of category "Flora and Fauna" 71

Figure 3-12 Screenshot of "Description" of category "Flora and Fauna" 71

Figure 3-13 Demonstration of Majority Voting 74

Figure 4-1 System structure of the special search-browser 78

Figure 4-2 ODP semantic data extraction 79

Figure 4-3 Screenshot of category "Kids and Teens" 81

Figure 4-4 Screenshot of "Description" of category "Kids and Teens" 81

Figure 4-5 Format of the ODP kt-structure.rdf 82

Figure 4-6 Screenshot of category "Pre-School" 83

Figure 4-7 Format of the ODP kt-content.rdf 84

Figure 4-8 Links (resources) under category "Kids and Teens/Pre-School" 85

Figure 4-9 Lucene indexing 88

Figure 4-10 Lucene index structure 89

Figure 4-11 Source code for indexing the created category-document 92

Figure 4-12 An interface screenshot of the special search-browser 94

Figure 4-13 Categorization processing flowchart 100

Figure 4-14 Detailed categorizing process 101

Figure 4-15 Majority Voting processing flowchart 102

Figure 4-16 Implementation of Majority Voting class 103

Figure 4-17 Relationship among classes FirstLevelNode, ExTreeNode and RetResults 105

Figure 4-18 Flowchart of search results filtering 106

Figure 5-1 An example of precision-recall curve 114

Figure 5-2 Categorized search results of "Clinton" 115

Figure 5-3 Categorized search results of "Clinton" under category "Society" 116

Figure 5-4 Average percentage of relevance judgment of the five judges 122

Figure 5-5 Precision-Recall curve of the search results of Yahoo! 125

Figure 5-6 Recall-precision curves of search-term "Clinton" 126

Figure 5-7 Recall-precision curves of search-term "Ford" 127

Figure 5-8 Recall-precision curves of search-term "health" 127

Figure 5-9 Recall-precision curves of search-term "jaguar" 128

Figure 5-10 *Recall-precision* curves of search-term "UPS" (1) 129

Figure 5-11 Recall-precision curves of search-term "UPS" (2) 129

Figure 5-12 Average recall-precision curves of Yahoo! search results and categorized search results over the five search-terms 130

Figure 5-13 Relationship between precision improvement and relevance judgment convergent degree 134

Figure A5-1 Lucene index format 177

List of Tables

Table 2-1 Comparison of IR models 25

Table 2-2 Typical term-weighting formulas 27

Table 2-3 Term-weighting usage recommendations 28

Table 2-4Table 2-4 Training set and test set 41

Table 2-5 A contingency table 46

Table 2-6 Comparison of relative work and the special search-browser 53

Table 3-1 Query-formulation → Find → Re-formulation (QFR) 58

Table 3-2 A gyroidal Web searching procedure 62

Table 4-1 The 15 first level categories of the ODP and the number of their subcategories 93

Table 4-2 Factors in cosine similarity score calculation 97

Table 4-3 Brief description of Query and its subclasses 99

Table 5-1 Search-terms used in the experiment 110

Table 5-2 Relevance judgment score 120

Table 5-3 Summary of relevance judgments of the five judges (50 results for each query) 121

Table 5-4 Judgment overlap of judge pairs (number of agreement) 123

Table 5-5 Summary of pairwise agreement comparison 123

Table 5-6 Aggregation of pairwise judgments by judge 124

Table 5-7 Precisions at different cut-off levels of the 50 search results of Yahoo! (%) 125

Table 5-8 P@5 and P@10 of Yahoo! and categorized search results (%) 131

Table 5-9 Recall of categories 131

Table 5-10 Relevance judgment convergent degrees of the five search-terms 133

Table 6-1 Machine learning in IR 140

Chapter 1.   Problem Statement

This chapter is composed of three parts. The first part (section 1.1) introduces some basic concepts and characteristics of Web information retrieval; the second part of this chapter discusses some problems that face search engines. The problems, namely, information overload, mismatch of search results, missing relevant documents, poorly organized search results, mismatch of human mental model, and low *recall* of Web navigation are discussed in section 1.2 to 1.7 respectively. The last part (section 1.8 and 1.9) of this chapter presents the objectives of the research, and a summary of this chapter.

1.1 Introduction

Information Retrieval (IR, see Appendix 1 for abbreviation and acronym list), as pointed out by Voorhees (2005b, p. 1), "is concerned with locating information that will satisfy a user's information need." However, according to Chowdhury (2004, pp. 193-194), information need *per se* is a vague, dynamic, individual-dependent, and environment-dependent concept, and often results in some unsolved problems. Information needs arise in the following circumstances: 1) user's current state of knowledge is insufficient to cope with the task at hand; 2) to resolve conflicts in a subject area; and 3) to fill a void in some area of knowledge. Furthermore, information needs are hard to measure and usually remain unexpressed or poorly expressed. Baeza-Yates and Ribeiro-Neto (1999, p. 1) propose "information retrieval (IR) deals with the representation, storage, organization of, and access to information items. The representation and organization of the information items should provide the user with easy access to the information in which he is interested." In brief, IR is an information analysis and interactive process aimed at satisfying user information needs.

Jacobs and Walsh (2004, p. 1) from the World Wide Web Consortium (W3C, http://www.w3.org) define the Web as "The World Wide Web (WWW, or simply Web) is an information space in which the items of interest, referred to as resources, are identified by global identifiers called Uniform Resource Identifiers (URI)." Chowdhury (2004, p. 330) suggests "the web is a massive collection of web pages stored on the millions of computers across the world that are linked by the Internet."

Search engines (Chapter 2, section 2.3.2) are the most widely used tools to retrieve information on the Web. A search engine uses a crawler to download Web pages from the Internet, the contents of the Web pages (some pages are downloaded by search engines) are treated as documents (the term Web page and document are thus used interchangeably in this book), and terms in the documents are indexed. When a user submits a query (search-terms or search-term) to a search engine, it will first estimate the similarities between the query and the indexed Web pages (documents); then a set of search results is selected and ranked according to the *authority*[1] (Kleinberg 1999) of each Web page. Search results are also referred to as search items or information snippets. Each of the returned search results usually includes the address of the Web page (URL), the title of the page, and a snippet of the page which contains the search-terms submitted for searching.

With the rapid growth of the Web, IR research communities are facing challenges, because compared with the traditional text retrieval, Web information retrieval has four typical characteristics.

First, the Web information with distributed structure is huge, dynamic, and expanding. Web information is distributed all over the world. No one knows exactly how much information is available on the Web now, and how many computers with which the Web resources created are interconnected by the Internet. However, the fact is that the Web information is growing exponentially. For example, the number of websites is estimated to have grown from 2,851,000 in 1998 to 9,040,000 in 2002[2]; more than threefold within four years. Meanwhile, the content of Web pages changes frequently; and they may also be moved or deleted (Chowdhury 2004, p. 331).

Second, the quality of Web information differs dramatically. Nowadays, any person, even a primary school student can have a Blog[3] and publish articles freely on it. On the other hand, many very important articles are also digitalized and published on the Web; many e-journals, digital libraries are also available on the Web. Therefore, much effort is needed to deal with controlled and uncontrolled information resources and to assess the quality of information resources.

The third characteristic of Web information retrieval is that more and more people, such as children, people with disabilities and aging population, begin to use the Internet as the main approach to get information needed (Olson & Olson 2003). Web information searchers may be anyone located anywhere in the world, with multiple languages. At the same time, Baeza-Yates and Ribeiro-Neto (1999, p. 69) point out that users are not good at expressing their information needs by search-term format, notwithstanding this format is preferred by most information seekers.

---

[1] The notion of authority is an algorithmic formulation "based on the relationship between a set of relevant authoritative pages and the set of "hub pages" that join them together in the link structure. (Kleinberg 1999) Simply speaking, "Authority pages are those most likely to be relevant to a particular query." (Arasu et al. 2001, p. 34)

[2] Yahoo! announced it has indexed 20 billion Web pages in 2006; it is estimated that the hide Web pages is 2-500 times big than the indexed pages (http://www.cse.lehigh.edu/~brian/course/sem/notes/searchengines.pdf). Based on this figure, the number of Web pages now is around 40-10,000 billion.

[3] A website that displays in chronological order the postings by one or more individuals, and usually has links to comments on specific postings (http://www.answers.com/blog&r=67).

The last characteristic is that people's information needs are diverse; different people need different kinds of information expressed in different formats (Chowdhury 2004, pp. 192-195). People may publish anything on the Web; people may also want to retrieve this information in return. In brief, people want information providers who can provide high quality information services to satisfy their information needs.

The information explosion and the demands of high quality information services enlarge the gap between information retrieval services provided by search engines, and information consumptions requested by the ever increasingly large population of miscellaneous Web users. The inherent problems of polysemy and synonymy of information retrieval make the situation worse. Almeida and Almeida (2004), Gauch et al. (2003), Glover et al. (2001), Pitkow et al. (2002), Shah et al. (2002), and many others indicate that 50 per cent of search results of search engines are irrelevant; users' individual information needs are neglected and thus make the research results less value.

Numerous efforts have been devoted to improve the relevance of search results to satisfy users' information needs such as using different IR models and their variations, relevance feedback, information clustering/re-organization, personalization, semantic web, ontology-based IR, question-and-answer systems, and so on. Some featured search engines, for instance, Clusty.com (http://www.clusty.com),   Answers.com   (http://www.answers.com),   MagPortal (http://www.magportal.com), and visualized meta-search engine Kartoo (http://www.karto.com) are becoming popular now. As the result of the continuous endeavours of the information retrieval community, the problems facing the Web search engines are somewhat alleviated. However, the situation of effectively searching relevant information on the Web is still not optimistic.

Among the techniques mentioned above, the promising one is the information clustering/classification. Search engines usually return a list of thousands or even millions of retrieved items that are ranked according to their relevance to the search-terms. The plain list of such a large number of search items without proper organization will frustrate information seekers. Clusty.com (http://www.clusty.com) uses information clustering techniques to re-organize the retrieved items according to the subjects/topics formed by the different groups of the search results. Answers.com (http://www.answers.com) also clusters search results in some circumstances, while its main concern is to provide an accurate definition of the search-term.

The initial, and the ultimate, purpose of information retrieval is to provide information seekers with relevant information needed. However, many information seekers' information needs are usually not definite at the very beginning and tend to change as the searching procedure goes on (Chowdhury 2004, p. 194). Information retrieval is therefore believed to be an inherently interactive procedure through which the user's feedback should be adapted by the Information Retrieval System (IRS) to refine the search results (Cool & Spink 2002).

The major focus of the research is to dynamically re-organize search results under a socially constructed hierarchical knowledge structure, and consequently to facilitate information seekers to access and manipulate the retrieved search results, and finally to improve the relevance of search results.

1.2 Information Overload of Search Engines – What does 63 million Returned Items Mean?

Search engines now tend to return thousands, even millions, of search results for the short queries (less than three words) preferred by most users (Gauch et al. 2003, Rocha et al. 2004). Google claims it has indexed more than eight billion Web pages (http://www.google.com), and Yahoo! announced recently that 20 billion Web pages have been indexed (Cohn & Herring 2005). While these figures may indicate that the search engines have the potential ability to return more search results, surveys (Chowdhury 2004, pp. 347-349; Jansen & Spink 2006; Spink et al. 2002) show that Web information seeker's concern is mainly about how to retrieve relevant information effectively; and only a minority will review more than ten relevant search results. Searching for information about the animal "jaguar" by Google results in 63,500,000 search items returned, and among the top ten search results on the first returned page, only the last (tenth) search item is not irrelevant (Figure 1-1, retrieved on December 11, 2006). Searching for the first American president, "George Washington", by Google, there are more than 28 million (28,300,000) search results returned (Figure 1-2, retrieved on December 11, 2006).

Searching for a person's name by search engines is sometimes very frustrating. When searching for the American president, "George Washington", Google returns a large number of search result; most of the search results in the first few returned pages are related to this president, except for some irrelevant results such as George Washington University, and George Washington Bridge. However, if one is trying to find some information about the boxing trainer George Washington, not one search result within the first ten pages is about this boxing trainer. Searching for a popular Chinese name, such as "Wei Liu", the first ten search results of Google are about ten different people (Figure 1-3, retrieved on December 11, 2006). Especially the case when the person's name is also a factory, or a company name, for example "Ford", it may indicate a person Henry Ford who is the American founder of the Ford Motor Company, or a Ford car, and any person who's last name is Ford.

Figure 1-1 Search results of "jaguar" returned from Google
Adaption of: *www.google.com*, retrieved on December 11, 2006

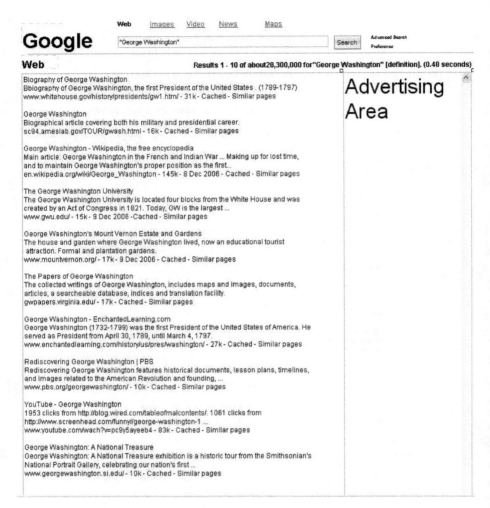

Figure 1-2 Search results of "George Washington" returned from Google
Adaption of: *www.google.com*, retrieved on December 11, 2006

The huge amount of search results, such as the 63 million returned search items, is no doubt an information overload. Users have to select amongst relevant information from this huge number of returned search results. Antoniou and Harmelen (2004) argue that the term information retrieval is somewhat misleading, because extracting the relevant information from the result lists is actually a location finding procedure. Thus the term location finder is more appropriate in the Internet search context. Information overload easily brings on valuable information being overlooked; information overlook easily results in opportunity costs.

Google

Web   Images   Video   News   Maps

"Wei Liu"   Search   Advanced Search
                                                                  Preference

Web   Results 1 - 10 of about 315,000 for "Wei Liu" (0.14 seconds)

Wei Liu's Homepage
Wei Liu received his B.S. and Ph.D. in Computer Science from Tsinghua University...[MICRO'06],
Shan Lu, Pin Zhou, Wei Liu, Yuanyuan Zhou and Josep Torrellas...
www.uiuc.edu/~liuwei/ - 14k - Cached - Similar pages

Unique Wei LIU's Homepage
Wei LIU 刘威. Supervisor: Prof. Xiaoou Tang - Curriculum Vitae, Multimedia Laboratory
Department of Information Engineering...
mmlab.ie.cuhk.edu.hk/~face/ - 10k - Cached - Similar pages

Wei Liu's ---home page at UWA
Welcome to Wei Liu's homepage. I am a lecturer in the School of Computer Science and ...
Page created by: Wei Liu Last Modified: 16:01:46 Friday July 16, 2004.
www.csse.uwa.edu.au/~wei/ - 6k - Cached - Similar pages

          Information for Wei Liu
          Dr Wei Liu MEng HUST, China, PhD Newc. Lecturer ... email. Dr Wei Liu School of
          Computer Science & Software Engineering The University of Western Australia ...
          www.csse.uwa.edu.au/people/info.php?name=wei - 8k - Cached - Similar pages

DBLP: Wei Liu
24 Wei Liu, Chris Westrup: ICTs and Organizational Control Across Cultures: The Case of a
UK Multinational Operating in China. ...
www.infomatik.uni-trier.de/~ley/db/indices/a-tree/l/Liu:Wei.html - 86k -
Cached - Similar pages

Dr. Wei LIU's Homepage
Dr. Wei LIU. School of Mathematics · University of Southampton Southampton, SO17 1BJ,
United Kingdom Office: Building 54, Room 6013 ...
www.maths.soton.ac.uk/~wl - 2k - Cached - Similar pages

Liu Wei - Free Artist Portfolio at absolutearts.com
Liu Wei contemporary art presents at absolutearts.com.
w.absolutearts.com/portfolios/l/liuwei/ - 15k - Cached - Similar pages

Wei Liu's Homepage
Wei Liu. I am a PhD candidate at the Department of Physics, Stanford University, Currently I
am working with Professor Vahé Petrosian (see the group home...
sun.stanford.edu/~weiliu/ - 7k - Cached - Similar pages

Wei Liu
Mr. Liu is pursuing his Ph.D Degree at the School of Electronic and Computer
Science, University of Southampton since October 2003.
www-mobile.ecs.soton.ac.uk/comms/_private/wl03r.htm - 2k - Cached - Similar pages

The Mathematics Genealogy Project - Wei Liu
Wei Liu Ph.D University of California, Santa Barbara 1992. United States. Dissertation: On
the Sensitivity and Stability of Posterior Quantities...

Figure 1-3 Search results of "Wei Liu" returned from Google
Adaption of: www.google.com, retrieved on December 11, 2006

1.3 Mismatch of Search Results of Search Engines – High Recall, Low Precision

Two fundamental performance measurements of an IR system are *recall* and *precision*. For a given query, suppose |A| is the total number of documents returned, |R| is the total number of relevant documents in the IR system, and |Ra| is the number of relevant documents returned. Then, the definition of the two measures is: *recall* = |Ra| / |R| and *precision* = |Ra| / |A| (Chapter 2, section 2.2.5). *Recall* is the percentage of relevant documents retrieved, and *precision* is the percentage of documents retrieved that are relevant (Baeza-Yates & Ribeiro-Neto 1999, p. 75). When a user performs a search by using a search-term like "jaguar", Google returns 63,500,000 search items; each of them contains the term "jaguar", no matter whether the documents are about the animal jaguar; a jaguar car; the operating system named jaguar; or anything that is referred to by the term "jaguar". Therefore, the search results have a very high *recall*, because there are as many as 63,500,000 items that contain the search-term "jaguar" returned (a huge number of search results returned compared with the total documents which contain the term "jaguar"). However, from the user's perspective, the *precision* of the search results is very low, because among the answer set most of the search results are not related to the animal jaguar.

Low *precision* high *recall* problem may be caused by the following three reasons. The first reason is the inherent polysemy characteristic of natural languages – the same term can refer to different matters. Polysemy problems may cause a very big number of returned search results, that is, the |A| is very big. Based on the definition of *precision*, for the same |Ra|, when |A| is getting bigger, the *precision* is getting smaller. For example, because the search-term "jaguar" may refer to different things, it is very difficult, or impossible, for a search engine to return only relevant search results for an individual seeker. One searcher may want to retrieve some information about the animal jaguar; another seeker may want to search where to buy a jaguar car. Without interaction with the individual user, it is unreasonable for a search engine to return only information concerned with a jaguar car; or only to return search results related to the animal jaguar. Therefore, for a search engine, there is no choice but to try its best to return all the documents that contain the term "jaguar". However, for a given user, the animal jaguar may be the only concern; thus from this user's perspective, the *precision* of the search results is very low, because many of the search results are not relevant to the user's information need.

Another reason is that the information retrieval model that most search engines employ is based on the term-weighting strategy which relies on the idea of "taking words as they stand" and "counting their stances" (Jones 2003). This implies that search engines perform only syntactic comparison between search-terms and indexed terms of document repositories (Arasu et al. 2001, Kobayashi & Takeda 2000); semantic characteristics of the search-terms and the documents are ignored.

A third reason is users' search habit of using very short search-terms. Research (Jansen & Spink 2006, Jansen et al. 2005) shows that more than 70 per cent of queries are composed of one, two, or three terms. However, in many situations, using more than one word as a search-term allows search engines to return more relevant search results than just using only a single word as a search-term. For example, when searching for information about the boxing trainer, "George Washington", if the search-terms are "George Washington" + boxing, the returned search results are mainly related to the boxing trainer, George Washington. Training users to select proper search-terms is out the scope of this research.

These three reasons are the sources of the high *recall*, low *precision* problem of search engines.

1.4 Missing Relevant Documents of Search Engines – Low Recall

Despite of millions of research results returned, the issue of missing relevant documents is still facing search engines in some circumstances. The problem of low *recall* of search results may be caused by both the polysemy and synonymy characteristics of natural languages; another reason is that searching information for one category usually would not get information of its subcategories.

The polysemy feature of natural languages may cause relevant documents to be missed. As discussed in the previous section, when performing a search by using a search-term "George Washington" to retrieve information about the boxing trainer, George Washington, most of the search results are about the first American president, George Washington, or George Washington University, or George Washington Bridge. Seldom search results are about the boxing trainer (not one returned result within the top 100 ranked documents relates to the boxing trainer).

Search results returned by search engines are mainly decided by two calculated factors, one is a syntactic similarity comparison between documents (Web pages) indexed by search Engines and the search-terms; another is the *authority* of the Web page (Chapter 2, section 2.3). The search results are then ranked according to the calculated similarities and their authorities. If the similarity and *authority* of a Web page is higher than a so-called *threshold*[4], the Web page is to be returned as a search result; otherwise, it will not be considered relevant to the search-term and will not appear in the list of search results. Compared with the Web pages about the first American president George Washington, George Washington University, or George Washington Bridge, the *authority* of Web pages about the boxing trainer George Washington is obviously relatively low. Therefore these documents are ranked after the Web pages about the present George Washington and other more *authority* Web pages as mentioned above. In this circumstance, although there are millions of

---

[4] Threshold is also called cut-off. In IR, matching function of search-terms and documents "is given a suitable threshold, retrieving the documents above the threshold and discarding the ones below. If T is the threshold, then the retrieved set B is the set $\{Di \mid M(Q, Di) > T\}$."(Rijsbergen 1979, p.76)

search results, some of the relevant documents are still not included in the search results set; the *recall* is thus very low because IRaI is very small.

The inherent synonymy problem of natural languages is another reason for missing relevant search results. For example, "laptop" and "notebook" are two synonymies. Both refer to a very small portable computer that can be used on one's lap (notebook is usually believed smaller than a laptop). When searching for "laptop", Google returns 121,000,000 search results (retrieved on December 11, 2006), as shown in Figure 1-4. When searching for "notebook", however, Google returns 132,000,000 search results (retrieved on December 11, 2006), as shown in Figure 1-5. As can be seen from the two figures, the search results of the two synonymies are different, although many of the returned Web pages of both search result sets are about "a portable, usu. battery-powered microcomputer small enough to rest on the user's lap" (http://dictionary.reference.com/search?r=8&q=laptop).

Using acronyms or abbreviations of some search-terms also causes search engines to return different search results. "AI" is an acronym of "Artificial Intelligence". Using "Artificial Intelligence" as a search-term, Google returns 81,400,000 search results (retrieved on October 12, 2006); when using "AI" as a search-term, there are 576,000,000 returned items (retrieved on October 12, 2006). Among the first 20 top ranked search results of the two search-terms, only eleven returned items are common for both search-terms.

Using a thesaurus or WordNet (http://wordnet.princeton.edu) can alleviate the problem caused by synonymy of natural languages (Ramakrishnanan & Bhattacharyya 2003). However, some synonymies may further introduce polysemy problems. In the example of "notebook" and "laptop" above, except for having a similar meaning to "laptop", the term "notebook" also represents a film named "notebook", an "electronic notebook of Google" and, of course, the commonsense meaning , according to Wikipedia (http://en.wikipedia.org/wiki/Notebook), "a virgin book of paper on which notes may be written." Therefore, among the first 20 retrieved search results of "notebook", only five of them have a similar meaning to "laptop". Using "notebook" as a synonym may improve *recall* of search results; however, the *precision* of the search results may further be deteriorated.

Searching for information relevant to one category usually will not obtain documents relevant to its subcategories. For example, when searching for "machine learning", the search results will not contain "genetic programming", a subcategory of machine learning and artificial intelligence. This is because the IR model utilized by search engines only matches documents that are syntactically similar to search-terms, and no semantic factors are considered (Chapter 2, section 2.2.1, section 2.3.2). As a result, in the situation when searching for information about one category, search engines usually do not return information of its subcategories, and the *recall* of the search results is thus very low.

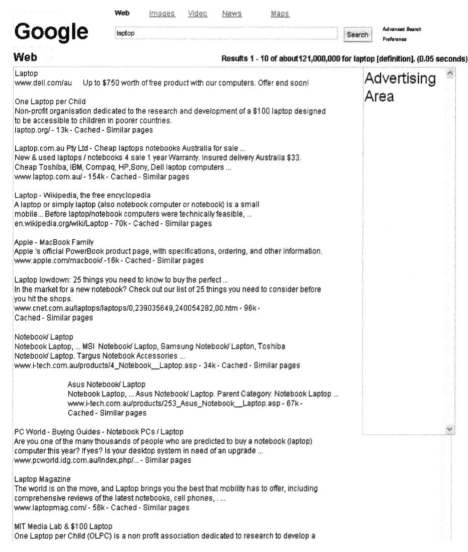

Figure 1-4 Search results of "laptop" returned from Google
Adaption of: www.google.com, retrieved on December 11, 2006

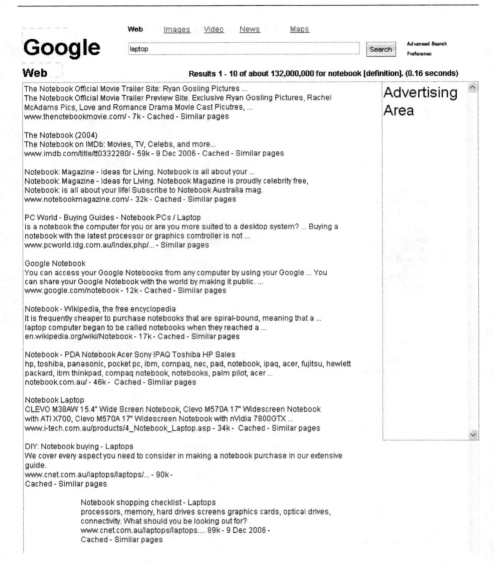

Figure 1-5 Search results of "notebook" returned from Google
Adaption of: *www.google.com*, retrieved on December 11, 2006

1.5 Poorly Organized Search Results of Search Engines

Most search engines arrange search results according to ranking algorithms that rank documents in

higher priority according to the document's literal similarities to the given query (Arasu et al. 2001,

Kobayashi & Takeda, 2000). Ranked documents are considered relevant to a user's query in

descending order, that is, the first several documents are more relevant to the user's query than the rest of the search results. However, because of the problems of information overload, mismatch of search results, missing relevant documents, and search engines frequently returning thousands or even millions of search results in a plain format list as shown in Figure 1-1 to Figure 1-5, a user may have to check hundreds of items to pick up useful information. Finding a relevant document among the returned Web search results is like finding a needle in a haystack (Baeza-Yates and Ribeiro-Neto 1999, pp. 389-390).

A plain list of search results also delivers no information about knowledge structure related to the returned search results; searched items are isolated from each other and presented to the user independently. A plain list format of search results is appropriate when the returned items are less than 50 (relevant documents reviewed per session are around ten or fewer, Chowdhury 2004, p. 348). Therefore, the thousands, or even millions of search results returned need to be re-organized to facilitate Web information seekers to locate relevant information efficiently.

1.6 Mismatching Human Mental Model of Clustering Engines

One approach to re-organize the long list of search results is to cluster the search results based on the cluster hypothesis that relevant documents tend to be more similar to each other than to non-relevant documents (Hearst & Pedersen 1996). There are already many researchers attempting to deal with this problem (Hearst & Pederson 1996; Zamir & Etzioni 1998), and some search engines that cluster search results have been developed. The main problem of clustering search result is that sometimes search results are not properly clustered. For example, Clusty (http://www.clusty.com), ranked number four of the top 20 search engines by SquirrelNet (http://www.SquirrelNet.com), is a *cluster engine* which organizes search results into folders that group similar items together. When using this search engine searching for "jaguar", the search results are illustrated in Figure 1-6.

Search results are clustered and organized in a hierarchical structure and presented in groups with subjects/topics. However, from the point of view of knowledge structure of human beings, the arrangement of the search results is mental model confusion. For instance, cars, parts, and models are all arranged in the first level of the hierarchy, whereas the well-known fact for people is that a car has parts and different models. The arrangement of panthera onca and animal has the same problem, because panthera onca is only a kind of animal and should be arranged as a subcategory of animal. Furthermore, within the cluster of animal, there is another panthera onca as the sub-cluster of animal, and within the category panthera onca, there is a category of animal. Clustering search results and entitling the groups with the extracted topic/subjects usually do not reflect the hierarchical knowledge structure; and this approach thus tends to lead to a mismatch between the human mental model of persons searching and the formed clusters.

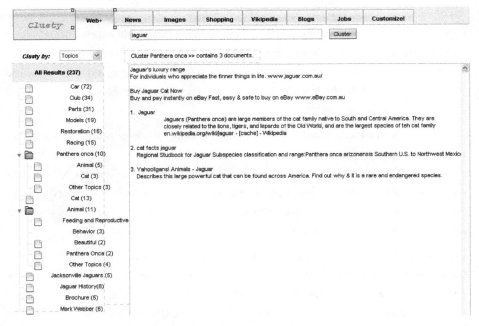

Figure 1-6 Search results of "jaguar" of Clusty.com
Adaption of: *www.clusty.com*, retrieved July 10, 2006

1.7 Low Recall of Web Navigating

Another approach to obtain Web information is browsing or navigating a Web directory, such as *Yahoo! Web Directory* (http://dir.yahoo.com/) or Open Directory Project (ODP) (http://www.dmoz.org), by following its hierarchical structure of categories. These Web directories will, like a map, instruct an information searcher where to go to find the relevant information. For example, *Yahoo! Web Directory* has 14 first level categories: Arts & Humanities; Business & Economy; Computers & Internet; Education; Entertainment; Government; Health; News & Media; Recreation & Sports; Reference; Regional; Science; Social Science; and Society & Culture. If one wants to find some information about a soccer player, a clear route is: Recreation → Sports → (Type of Sports) Soccer → Players → Men, where a list of male soccer players is presented. If one is interested in *Zidane*, the famous French soccer player, it is easy to find there are six Web sites that are all about the player. By this approach, one can find a place where nearly all the Web pages are relevant. The *precision* of the results is almost as high as 100 per cent[5].

---

[5] The *precision* may be as high as 100 per cent. However, because relevance judgment is subjective, it is therefore improper to claim the *precision* is absolutely 100 per cent. Refer to chapter 5, section 5.2

However, one serious problem of this approach is the extremely low *recall* of the retrieved results – only six results are given by *Yahoo! Web Directory*. If the term "Zidane" is submitted as a query to Google, there are 21,400,000 search results returned, and Yahoo! returns 10,800,000 search results (retrieved on July 10, 2006). Compared with the six Web sites given by *Yahoo! Web Directory*, one conclusion easily drawn is that the *recall* of search results of *Yahoo! Web Directory* is much lower than that of Google or Yahoo!'s Web searching. This example also reveals one reason why more and more people are using searching instead of navigating to retrieve information from the Web. *Yahoo! Web Directory* is maintained by a small group of experts, no matter how hard they work, their edit speed can not keep up with the increasing growth of the Web. *Yahoo! Web Directory* used to be an essential feature of Yahoo!; however, it is getting farther and farther from the Web information seeker's interest centre.

1.8 Research Objectives

The above discussions indicate that information overload, caused by the polysemy characteristic of natural languages, is still a challenge facing search engines. Search results clustering tries to re-organize search results into groups according to the similarities among the returned results; however, the hierarchical structure of these formed clusters usually mismatches the human mental model. The focus of this research is consequently to improve the relevance of search results by utilizing a socially constructed hierarchical knowledge structure, like the ODP, as an ontology to classify the search results, and with the interaction of users, to disambiguate search-terms and ontologically filter search results. A special search-browser will be developed, and its retrieval effectiveness will be estimated based on the two widely accepted measures of an information retrieval system[6], *recall* and *precision* (Chapter 2, section 2.2.5)

Therefore, the objectives of this research are to:

1) Model the thematic content of the Web in a structured hierarchy by utilizing the categories of the ODP;

2) Develop a special search-browser to integrate search results of search engine and the ODP-based ontology using a navigation metaphor;

3) Categorize the search results returned by search engines (Yahoo!/Google) according to the ontological filter based on the structured hierarchy of ODP - from objects one and two above. Improving the relevance of Web search

4) Evaluate the retrieval effectiveness of the developed search-browser by calculating the *precision* and *recall* of the search results after successive (three or four) search/re-search iterations.

---

[6] A number of studies have been conducted on evaluation criteria for information systems, such as *learnability* and *efficiency of use* proposed by Nielsen (1993, pp. 192-194) from a perspective of *usability engineering*. Section 2.2.5 presents a detailed discussion on evaluation criteria for the more specific area, information retrieval systems.

1.9 Research Methodology

Association for Information Systems (http://www.isworld.org) classifies research methodologies into three categories: quantitative, qualitative and design research. Quantitative research emphasises quantitative data collection and analysis and uses a positivist philosophy that assumes a theory should be induced rather than be based on observation (Straub et al. 2005). Qualitative research uses qualitative data (interviews, documents, and participant observation data) to inform and explain social phenomena (Myers 2005). Design research, according to Vaishnavi and Kuechler (2005), aims to explain, understand and improve on the behavioural of aspects of Information Systems by analysing the use and performance of designed artefacts, such as algorithm (e.g. for information retrieval), Human Computer Interface, and so on.

The main purpose of the research is to improve the relevance of search results by utilizing ODP as an ontological filter to disambiguate search queries. To achieve objective one, design research is to be employed because it explains and analyzes the semantic characteristics of the ODP category and consequently constructs a *category-document* (Section 3.4.3) set – the designed product. To implement objective two and objective three, the design research approach is to be utilized again – because a special search-browser is designed and developed. The special search-browser will integrate search results of search engine (*Yahoo! Search Web Services API*) and the ODP-based ontology using a navigation metaphor. Ontological filtering process is performed by providing a user interface with a tree like Web knowledge structure which enables users to interact with the special search-browser. The last objective is corresponding to the evaluation phase of design research method (Vaishnavi & Kuechler, 2005). Experimental data is collected and analyzed to evaluate the performance of the designed and developed special search-browser, and conclusion is finally reached.

To achieve the ultimate purpose – to improve the relevance of search results, a special search-browser is to be designed and developed. Therefore, the design research methodology is to be employed in this research, because according to Vaishnavi and Kuechler (2005), design research involves the analysis of the use and performance of designed artefacts (proposed special search-browser) to understand, explain and very frequently to improve on the behavior of aspects (precision) of Information Systems (Information Retrieval Systems).

Qualitative and quantitative research methods are not suitable for this research purpose and thus not used.

1.10 Summary

With the explosion of the Internet, information on the WWW is also increasing exponentially. Classic IR techniques are facing challenges in the aspects of: 1) Web information is huge, dynamic and constantly increasing; 2) the quality of Web information differs dramatically; 3) Web information seeker may be anyone located anywhere in the world but not good at expressing their information needs in search-term format; and 4) the users' information needs are diverse and miscellaneous. While search engines are trying to deal with these issues, other problems are emerging, such as information overload, mismatch of search results and users' information needs, missing relevant documents, poorly organized search results, mismatching the human mental model of formed clusters, and low *recall* of Web navigation. The main purpose of this research is thus to improve the relevance of search results via search-term disambiguation and ontologically filtering the search results. A search-browser is to be developed where the ODP is utilized as an ontology with which the search results are categorized. The categorized search results are expected to help Web information searchers to retrieve relevant documents more easily. Next chapter, basic concepts and related words are reviewed.

Chapter 2.   Previous Work and Literature Review

This chapter reviews the most relevant research that has been undertaken in Web information retrieval that is related to this project. Section 2.1 focuses on the definition of information retrieval and information retrieval systems. Section 2.2 presents information retrieval model and related techniques. Section 2.3 discusses Web information retrieval and structure and algorithms utilized by search engines. Discussions of text clustering and text categorization are presented in section 2.4 and section 2.5 respectively. While section 2.6 reviews literature on ontology-based information classification, section 2.7 presents the significance of this research. Finally, section 2.8 provides a summary of this literature review.

2.1 Introduction

2.1.1 Definition of Information Retrieval

The advent of computers and the WWW triggered two waves of IR research. From the 1950s to the late 1980s, various IR models were developed and these new models/techniques were experimentally proven to be effective on small text collection (Singhal 2001). Researchers at this time tried to utilize computers to achieve automatic document indexing, sorting and retrieving. This period represents the first wave of IR research. The second wave is, as pointed out by Singhal (2001), from the middle of 1990s to the present, with the rapid development of the Web. The researchers at this time concentrate mainly on the large, dynamic text collections and multimedia information, and on providing information services for the huge number and diversity of information consumers.

With the explosion of information in modern society, the definition of IR is also changing. An early definition given by Lancaster (cited in Rijsbergen 1979, p. 1) is:

> An information retrieval system does not inform (i.e. change the knowledge of) the user on the subject of his inquiry. It merely informs on the existence (or non-existence) and whereabouts of documents relating to his request.

This definition is obviously too narrow and not suitable for information retrieval on the Web.

Baeza-Yates and Ribeiro-Neto (1999, p. 1) define IR as:

> Information Retrieval (IR) deals with the representation, storage, organization of, and access to information items. The representation and organization of the information items should provide the user with easy access to the information in which he is interested.

This definition emphasizes not only information access, but also information representation, storage and organization; it also does not confine IR to only text documents retrieval; it uses "information items" to make the definition more comprehensive. This definition expresses the IR researcher's point of view.

Chowdhury (2004, p. 1) presents a similar definition to that of Baeza-Yates and Ribeiro-Neto's: "Modern information retrieval deals with storage, organization and access to text, as well as multimedia information resources".

Voorhees (2005b, pp. 1-2) claims that IR "is concerned with locating information that will satisfy a user's information need ... regardless of the medium that happens to contain that information." He points out that the traditional concept of document can be interpreted as any information unit such as a MEDLINE[7] record, a Web page, or an email message. This definition of IR is from the user's point of view.

A definition recently given by Manning et al. (2006, p. 3) is,

> *Information retrieval is finding material (usually documents) of an unstructured nature (usually text) that satisfy an information need from within large collections (usually on local computer servers or on the Internet).*

Material of an unstructured nature and large collections reveal the characteristics of the information on the Web; and this definition is given based on the information seeker's perspective.

In the researcher's opinion, IR has three properties. First, information retrieval is an information analysis and process procedure. It involves information analysis, organization, storage and finally effective information searching to satisfy users' information needs. Second, information itself is in diverse forms such as text documents or multimedia material, and usually has an unstructured nature. However, the information should be digitalized (processable by computers), and the collection of the information is huge – more than hundreds of millions or even billions of information items. Third, information retrieval is an interactive process; users' information needs are satisfied by the interaction between the users and the IR system. In brief, **IR is an information analysis and interactive process aimed at satisfying user information needs.**

2.1.2 Information Retrieval System

A very direct and simple definition of an IR system is the one given by Rijsbergen (1979,   p. 4) as shown in Figure 2-1. The figure shows *Input, Processor* and *Output* are the three main parts of an IR system. Feedback implies the interactive property of information retrieval.

Chowdhury (2004, p. 4) believes an IR system is comprised of three parts (Figure 2-2): *information items*; *users' queries* and *matching* of these queries with the document database. It is designed to retrieve the documents or information required by the user community. It is a bridge that connects the creators or generators of information with the users who have the need for that information.

---

[7] The world's most comprehensive source of life sciences and biomedical bibliographic information, with nearly eleven million records. http://medline.cos.com/

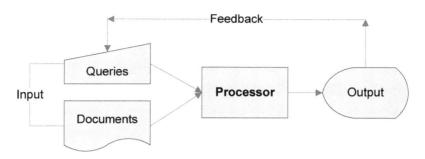

Figure 2-1 A typical IR system
Adaption of: Rijsbergen 1979, p. 4

Tasks in Figure 2-2 can be divided into two groups: subject/content analysis; and search/retrieval. The former group deals with analysis, organization and storage of information, and the latter's tasks include analyzing users' queries, creation of search formulas, and the actual searching and retrieving of information. However, the interaction aspect of IR is not manifested in this figure.

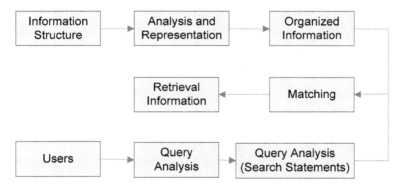

Figure 2-2 Broad outline of an information retrieval system
Adaption of: Chowdhury 2004, p. 4

Baeza-Yates and Ribeiro-Neto (1999, pp. 9-10) illustrate the retrieval process of an IR system in Figure 2-3. Text documents are stored in the Text Database which is managed by the DB Manager Model. The user's information need is pre-processed with text operators, and represented by a proper query which is compared with the indexed items of a document collection. The retrieved documents are ranked based on ranking algorithms, and the ranked list is delivered to the user. The user inspects the ranked list and determines which documents are relevant and which are not. According to the user's relevance feedback (Salton & Buckley 1990), the query is re-constructed and more relevant documents are expected to be returned by using the new query. This figure demonstrates and emphasizes that IR is inherently an interactive process.

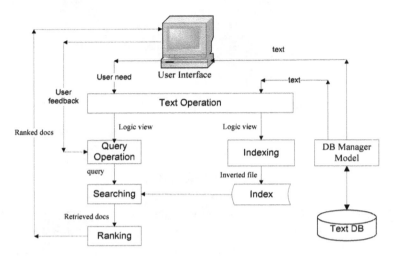

Figure 2-3 The process of retrieving information
Adaption of: Baeza-Yates and Ribeiro-Neto 1999, p. 10

A search engine is also an IR system with additional components. In addition to the components in Figure 2-3, a search engine also includes a crawler which crawls the Web sites and indexes the crawled Web pages to build a page repository. Figure 2-4 is a general search engine structure presented by Arasu et al. (2001). Chapter 2 section 2.3 presents a more detailed discussion on Web IR and search engines.

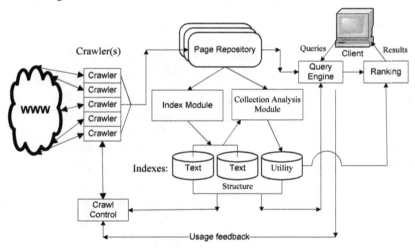

Figure 2-4 General search engine architecture
Adaption of: Arasu et al. 2001, p. 4

2.1.3 Information Retrieval versus Data Retrieval

Information retrieval differs from database searching. In the context of database searching, an exact match is the main concern. This approach is obviously not suitable for text document retrieval because data retrieval systems only return a list of documents if—and only if—they contain the exact search-term (query), and without concern about how to satisfy users' information needs. Database retrieval languages (such as SQL) aim at searching all objects which match clearly defined conditions like those in an algebraic expression. Any mismatching among thousands of objects is thus an error. However, an IR system is more tolerant to this kind of inaccurate matching error. This is mainly because an IR system usually deals with natural language text which is not always well structured and could be semantically ambiguous (Baeza-Yates & Ribeiro-Neto 1999, pp. 1-2).

Another difference between IR and data retrieval is that an IR system is always trying to retrieve information about a subject topic. To be effective in trying to satisfy users' information needs, an IR system tries somewhat to interpret the contents of the text objects in a collection, and ranks the retrieved results according to their degree of relevance to the search-terms. This interpreting process involves extracting both syntactic and semantic characteristics from the text objects and using the extracted information to match the user information needs. In an IR system the concern is not only the syntactic interpretation of search-terms and text objects, but also the relevance of an object to the user information needs (Baeza-Yates & Ribeiro-Neto 1999, pp. 1-2). However, *relevance judgment* (Chapter 5, section 5.5) *per se* is a nontrivial issue.

2.2 Information Retrieval Models

Traditional IR uses index terms to index and retrieve documents. An index term is usually a keyword or keywords that represent some meaning in a document in which it appears. Although this retrieval strategy enables a simplified retrieval process, semantics of both documents and user query are lost when the content of documents are replaced with a set of indexed terms (words). Semantic loss caused by the retrieval strategy easily results in irrelevant search results (Problems of mismatch of search results and missing relevant documents in Chapter 1). Therefore, predicting which documents are relevant or not is a central issue of modern IR (Baeza-Yates & Ribeiro-Neto 1999, p. 19). Another issue of modern information retrieval is that an IR system has to deal with a huge amount of documents (Problem of information overload in Chapter 1). Many "old" techniques have to be modified and new techniques are being developed to perform effective retrieval over large collections (Singhal 2001). Researchers in IR models try to alleviate these problems.

In a broad sense, information retrieval models can be classified into two groups: user-centred (cognitive) models and system-centred models (Chowdhury 2004, p. 171). The discussion of information retrieval models in this book refers only to system-centred models.

2.2.1 Information Retrieval Models

There are three main classic models in IR (Baeza-Yates & Ribeiro-Neto 1999, pp. 20-21, Chowdhury 2004, pp. 171-180). Figure 2-5 is a taxonomy of IR models presented by Baeza-Yates and Ribeiro-Neto (1999, p. 21). Table 2-1 shows the comparison of the three models mentioned in Figure 2-5 above.

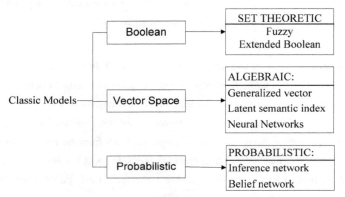

Figure 2-5 A taxonomy of IR models
Adaption of: Baeza-Yates and Ribeiro-Neto 1999, p. 21

As pointed out by Baeza-Yates and Ribeiro-Neto (1999, p. 30), the vector space model (VSM), although very simple, is a resilient ranking scheme with general document collections. Compared with other ranking strategies, experiments demonstrate that the VSM is either superior or almost as good as the known alternatives, and is fast. Therefore, the VSM is employed in this research.

2.2.2 The Vector Space Model

The content of a document can be represented by a set of indexed terms t_i (i = 1, 2, ..., t), or a term vector $d_j = (t_1, t_2, ..., t_t)$, where an indexed term "is simply a (document) word whose semantics helps in remembering the document's main themes)". (Baeza-Yates & Ribeiro-Neto 1999, p. 24) However, not all terms are equally important to describe the content of a document. *Term-frequency - inverse document frequency* (tf-idf)[8] is the most popular way to weight the terms in a document (Baeza-Yates & Ribeiro-Neto 1999, pp. 29-30, Salton & Buckley 1988, Salton et al. 1996). By using the tf-idf strategy, a document d_j is represented by a t-dimensional vector $d_j = (w_{1,j}, w_{2,j}, ...,$

---

[8] A term weighting scheme based on statistical information regarding occurrence of indexing terms in the document space

$w_{t,j}$), a query is also represented as a t-dimensional vector $\mathbf{q} = (w_{1,q}, w_{2,q}, ..., w_{t,q})$. The document collection X can therefore be represented by a term vector T multiples a document matrix D: $X = T \times D$, where $T = \{t_1, t_2, ..., t_t\}$ and $D = \{d_1, d_2, ..., d_N\}$, where t is the dimensionality of the term vector, and N is the total number of documents in the IR system.

Table 2-1 Comparison of IR models

Model	Advantages	Disadvantages
Boolean Model	1) Simplicity; 2) Clean formalism.	1) Exact matching leads to too many or too few search results; 2) No ranking mechanism 3) Users are often confused by the operators of AND, OR, NOT.
Vector Space Model	1) Term-weighting scheme improves retrieval performance; 2) Partial matching allows retrieving documents that approximate the query conditions; 3) Provide cosine ranking strategy.	1) Theoretically, index terms are assumed to be mutually independent (however, in practice, this is not a disadvantage).
Probabilistic Model	1) Theoretically, documents are ranked in decreasing order of their probability of being relevant.	1) The need to guess the initial separation of documents into relevant and non-relevant sets; 2) Term frequency is not considered (binary weights schema); 3) The adoption of the independence assumption for index terms.

Adaption of: Baeza-Yates & Ribeiro-Neto 1999, pp. 24-34, Chowdhury 2004, pp. 171-180

The degree of similarity between documents, or between a query and a document can be measured by the cosine value of the angle between these two vectors (Salton & Buckley 1988). According to the definition of dot product of two vectors in a vector space, $\mathbf{A} \bullet \mathbf{B} = |\mathbf{A}| \times |\mathbf{B}| \cos(\theta)$, there is:

$$sim(\mathbf{d_j}, \mathbf{q}) = \cos(\theta)$$

$$= \frac{\mathbf{d_j} \bullet \mathbf{q}}{|\mathbf{d_j}| \times |\mathbf{q}|}$$

$$= \frac{\sum_{i=1...N} W_{i,j} \times W_{i,q}}{\sqrt{\sum_{i=1...N} W_{i,j}^2 \times \sum_{i=1...N} W_{i,q}^2}}$$

2.2.3 Term Weighting Strategy – tf-idf

Just as Jones (2003) suggested, there are two very simple ideas that pervade modern IR systems. One of these ideas is taking words as they stand. The other is counting their stances. The Boolean model is criticized because it only considers if a term occurs in a document and neglects how many times it appears. The VSM, on the other hand, measures not only the frequency of a term (tf) appearing on a document but, furthermore, it considers the inverse document frequency (idf) as well.

Salton and Buckley (1988) present a detailed discussion of the term weighting approaches in IR. They suggest that term weighting strategy addresses enhancement of retrieval effectiveness which is determined by two factors: one is that items likely to be relevant to the user's information needs must be retrieved; another factor is that items likely to be extraneous must be rejected. In other words, the two factors are: what are the features which better describe the document which are relevant; and what are the features which better distinguish the relevant documents from the remaining documents (Baeza-Yates & Ribeiro-Neto 1999, p. 29). *Recall* and *precision* (section 2.2.5) are two measures used to assess the above two factors. To improve *recall*, highly frequent terms that appear in many documents of the collection can be used, because such terms tend to pull out many documents, including many of the relevant documents. On the other hand, to improve *precision*, narrow, highly specific terms may be expected to isolate the few documents from the mass of non-relevant ones. Both high *recall* and *precision* are preferable, but in practice, a reasonable compromise is made by using terms broad enough to yield a high *recall* without meanwhile producing unreasonably low *precision*.

Term weighting factors that contain both *recall* and *precision* enhancing components can be combined together to satisfy the different *recall* and *precision* requirements. Three components appear important in this scenario. The first one is "terms that are frequently mentioned in individual documents, or document excerpts, appear to be useful as *recall* enhancing devices." (Salton & Buckley 1988, p. 516) Thus, term frequency (tf) can be used as a part of the term weighting system measuring the frequency of occurrence of the terms in the document or query texts (Salton & Buckley 1988). This factor is also named intra-document characterization (Baeza-Yates & Ribeiro-Neto 1999, p. 29).

The second factor, inverse document frequency (idf), is document-dependent that favours terms concentrated in a few documents of a collection. This factor varies inversely with the number of documents n to which a term appearing in a collection of N documents. idf is usually calculated by $log(N/n)$.

Robertson (2004) proves that there are good theoretical justifications of both the idf and tf-idf in traditional probabilistic mode of information retrieval.

Term discrimination implies that "the best terms for document content identification are those able to distinguish certain individual documents from the remainder of the collection." (Salton &

Buckley 1988, p. 516) This means the best terms should have the properties of high tf and high idf. The product of tf and idf can therefore be used to measure the term importance.

The third factor is the normalization factor. Short documents tend to be represented by short vectors whereas longer documents are assigned larger term sets. When a document is represented by a large number of terms, the chance of term matches between queries and documents is high. Normalization of term weighting formula will give all documents, no matter how long are the documents, the same opportunity when calculating the similarity between documents and queries. The final term weight is defined as (Salton & Buckley 1988)

$$w / \sum_{\text{vector}\,i} w_i \quad or \quad w / \sqrt{\sum_{\text{vector}\,i} (w_i)^2}$$

Salton and Buckley (1988) present some typical term-weighting formulas (Table 2-2) and some suggestions (Table 2-3) of when these formulas are used.

Table 2-2 Typical term-weighting formulas

Weighting System	Document Term Weight	Query Term Weight
Best full weighted system	$tf \bullet \log(N/n) / \sqrt{\sum_{\text{vector}} (tf_i \bullet \log(N/n_i))^2}$	$\left(0.5 + \dfrac{0.5tf}{\max tf}\right) \bullet \log \dfrac{N}{n}$
Best weighted probabilistic weight	$0.5 + \dfrac{0.5tf}{\max tf}$	$\log \dfrac{N-n}{n}$
Classical idf weight	$\log (N/n)$	$\log(N/n)$
Standard tf weight	$\dfrac{tf}{\sqrt{\sum_{\text{vector}} (tf_i)^2}}$	tf

Adaption of: Salton & Buckley 1988, p. 518

Note: N is the total number of documents in the repository; n is the number of documents in which the term i appears; max tf is the maximum term frequency of a document.

Almost all the information retrieval systems include search engines are now using if-idf strategy to weight indexed terms for its proven effectiveness and efficiency. This strategy is employed in this research as well.

Table 2-3 Term-weighting usage recommendations

	Query Vectors	Document Vectors
tf component	For short query vector, $0.5 + \dfrac{0.5tf}{\max tf}$ For long query vector, tf	For technical vocabulary and meaningful terms, use $0.5 + \dfrac{0.5tf}{\max tf}$ For more varied vocabulary, use tf For short document vectors possibly based on controlled vocabulary, use binary weighting strategy
idf component	$\log(N/n)$	Normally use log (N/n) For dynamic collections with many changes in the document collection makeup, use 1.0
Normalization component	Query normalization does not affect query-document ranking or overall performance, 1.0	When the deviation in vector lengths is large, use $\dfrac{1}{\sqrt{\displaystyle\sum_{vector}(tf_i)^2}}$ For short document vectors of homogeneous length, use 1.0

Source Salton & Buckley 1988, p. 518

2.2.4 Index File Structure

As pointed out by Manning et al. (2006, p. 3) IR is finding materials of an unstructured nature (the opposite of structured data which can be processed by database technology). Materials with unstructured nature refer to "data which does not have clear, semantically overt, easy-for-a-computer structure" (Manning et al. 2006, p. 3). Therefore, IR system employs specific IR models as discussed above and special data structures as discussed below to enhance the effectiveness and efficiency of the system constructed.

One common index file structure used in IR is inverted file. The idea comes from the back-of-the-book index. When one wants to locate a particular term or phrase, for example, "computer" or "information retrieval", from a book, one can start from the first line in the first page and continue up to the last line in the last page of the book. Another approach is to look up the index in the back of the book. The back-of-the-book index is a simple alphabetical list of all the potential index terms, drawn from the text of the book, each having a pointer showing the occurrences of the terms. If a file serves the same purpose as that of the back-of-the-book index, the file is an inverted file. To do a search, the inverted file is first consulted; the inverted file then leads to the main document collection where document records are stored (Chowdhury 2004, p. 97).

The inverted file is actually organized into two files, one is the index file (or dictionary), another one is the postings list (linked list). The dictionary is a list of all the index terms of the IR system, frequency of occurrence of the terms; and a pointer points to the corresponding postings list. The postings list is usually a singly linked list; each element in the linked list contains the address and other related information of those documents that contains the search-term (Baeza-Yates & Ribeiro-Neto 1999, pp. 192-194, Chowdhury 2004, pp. 96-101, Manning et al. 2006, pp. 6-10). Figure 2-6 is an example of a dictionary and postings list.

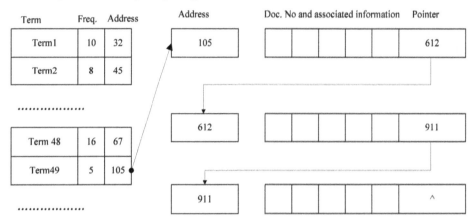

Figure 2-6 Index file and linked list
Adaption of: Chowdhury 2004, p. 100

The other two index organizations are suffix trees/suffix arrays[9], and signature files. Suffix trees/suffix arrays allow an IR system to answer complex queries more efficiently. However, the construction process is costly and the text must be readily available at query time. Signature files are word-oriented index structures based on hashing; it can produce relatively small index files, at the cost of forcing a sequential search over the index, and thus makes the technique suitable for not very large document collections. Experiments demonstrate that inverted files outperform the above file structure in most circumstances (Baeza-Yates & Ribeiro-Neto 1999, pp. 204-205). No matter what index structure is utilized, maximum performance and minimum resource utilization is the goal of index file design (Gospodnetić & Hatcher 2005, p. 394).

Appendix 5 is a case study of index structure of Lucene (Gospodnetić and Hatcher 2005,   pp. 393-407) and shows how the index file structure is implemented.

---

[9] "Text indices based on a lexicographical arrangement of all the text suffixes." (Baeza-Yates & Ribeiro-Neto 1999, p. 452)

2.2.5 Retrieval Evaluation

The evaluation criteria to be considered depend on the objectives of an information retrieval system. There are two types of information retrieval system evaluation, *performance evaluation* which focuses on time and space factors, and *retrieval performance evaluation* which evaluates how precise is the answer (Baeza-Yates and Ribeiro-Neto 1999, p. 73). Chowdhury (2004, p. 246) points out that effectiveness and efficiency are two basic parameters for measuring the performance of a system. In the field of IR, effectiveness indicates how far an IR system can retrieve relevant information while withholding non-relevant information; efficiency can be measured by such factors as at what minimum cost does the system function effectively. Some of the factors are: time taken by the system to provide an answer; the time and effort needed by a user to interact with the system and analyze the output retrieved in order to get the correct information. Other factors include the form of representation of the search output which affects the user's ability to make use of the retrieved items and collection coverage (Chowdhury 2004, p. 246).

Although they have been criticized and many other criteria have been proposed, *precision* and *recall* are still the two most widely accepted and used measurements of the retrieval performances of an IR system. *Recall* is a criterion to measure the ability of an IR system to retrieve all relevant documents; *precision* measures the ability of an IR system to retrieve only relevant material (Rasmussen 2003, Voorhees 2005b). The following definition is presented by Baeza-Yates and Ribeiro-Neto (1999, p. 75).

> *Consider an example information query I (of a test reference collection) and its set R of relevant documents. Let |R| be the number of documents in this set. Assume that a given retrieval strategy (which is being evaluated) processes the information request I and generates a document answer set A. Let |A| be the number of documents in this set. Further, let |Ra| be the number of documents in the intersection of the sets R and A (that is, |Ra| is the number of relevant documents in the intersection of the sets R and A). Figure 2-7 illustrates these sets. The* **recall** *and* **precision** *measures are defined as follows:*
> **Recall** *is the fraction of the relevant documents (the set R) which has been retrieved,*
> $$Recall = |Ra| / |R|$$
> **Precision** *is the fraction of the retrieved documents (the set A) which is relevant,*
>
> $$Precision = |Ra| / |A|$$

The computation of *precision* and *recall* is very simple. However, the premise is that exhaustive relevance judgments are available for each document for each search request, and all the relevant documents are linearly ranked (Salton & Lesk 1968). This scenario has only happened in laboratory environments in which many variables are controlled: the document collection is static and relatively small (hundreds of documents); queries are provided in a standard form; and the documents that are relevant to the query are known a priori[10]. In modern IR system, especially for Web IR, not only does the collection of documents (Web pages) always change, but there are also large variations in the number of Web pages covered among search engines (Rasmussen 2003).

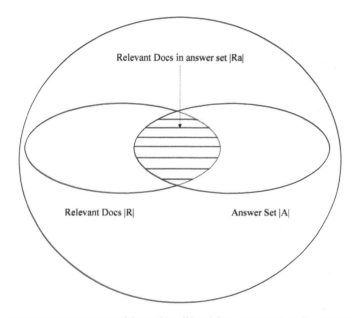

Figure 2-7 Illustration of precision and recall Precision = |Ra| / |A|, Recall = |Ra| / |R|
Adaption of: Baeza-Yates and Ribeiro-Neto 1999, p. 75

Just because of the impossibility of calculation of *recall* for each query in modern IR system, some quantitative studies of Web performance now measure *precision* alone (Rasmussen 2003), and the *precision* is measured at certain cut-off levels (Hawking et al. 2001, Leighton & Srivastava 1999, Voorhees 2005b). Recently, a Web track was introduced into the Text REtrieval Conference [11](TREC http://trec.nist.gov) experiments to build a text collection that imitate the Web retrieval environment (Hawking et al. 1999). By using this static Web test collection, problems inherent in experimentation on the dynamic Web can be eliminated, and the impact of the Web crawler from the assessment of the text retrieval system can be also be removed (Rasmussen 2003).

---

[10] However, relevance and relevant judgment is a nontrivial topic, because relevance is inherently considered subjective. Relevance judgments usually differ between judges and for the same judge at different times (Voorhees 2005). See discussion in Chapter 5, section 5.2

[11] The Text REtrieval Conference (TREC), co-sponsored by the National Institute of Standards and Technology (NIST) and U.S. Department of Defense, was started in 1992 as part of the TIPSTER Text program. Its purpose was to support research within the information retrieval community by providing the infrastructure necessary for large-scale evaluation of text retrieval methodologies. http://trec.nist.gov

2.3 Web Information Retrieval and Search Engines

"The Web is becoming all things to all people, totally oblivious to nation/country/continent boundaries, promising mostly free information to all, and quickly growing into a repository in all languages and all cultures"(Ozsoyoglu & Al-Hamdani 2003, p. 9). The WWW has also brought significant changes in the way people access information. The exponential growth information on the Web triggers the need for efficient tools to manage, retrieve, and filter information from this huge Web database (Baeza-Yates & Ribeiro-Neto 1999, p. 367). To efficiently access information on the Web, traditional IR techniques that have been developed over the last 40 years had to be tested and modified to suit this new scenario (Chowdhury 2004, p. 330), and new techniques need to be developed also to deal with problems (Section 2.3.1 and Chapter 1, section 1.2 to section 1.7) facing the IR research society.

2.3.1 Information Retrieval on the Web

Web IR has many different characteristics from the traditional IR. Baeza-Yates and Ribeiro-Neto (1999, pp. 368-369) classify these features into two types, features of data itself and features relating to users. The characteristics related to the data are (Baeza-Yates & Ribeiro-Neto 1999, pp. 368-369, Brin & Page 1998, Chowdhury 2004, pp. 331-332, Rasmussen 2003):

  1) distributed nature of the Web data;
  2) large size and growth of the Web;
  3) unstructured and redundant data;
  4) heterogeneous data type;
  5) high percentage of volatile data;
  6) massive resource requirements.

Users of the Web are also increasing tremendously. Traditional IR system is usually designed to meet the information needs of a particular user group. Today, users of an information resource on the Web may be anyone, located anywhere in the world (Chowdhury 2004, p. 332). From a user's perspective, as Baeza-Yates and Ribeiro-Neto (1999, p. 369) point out, the challenges facing an IR system are:

  1) how to specify a query;
  2) how to interpret the answer provided by the Web IR system.

A longitudinal study (Jansen & Spink 2006, Spink et al. 2002, and Wolfram et al. 2001) from 1997 to 2002 reveals some important features of Web users regarding Web pages viewed per session, query length, usage of Boolean operators, how may queries performed per session, and frequency of topic changes.

1) Users are viewing fewer result pages, and at least half of them only view the first page of search results.

2) Users prefer shorter queries (more than 30 per cent are single query sessions).

3) Queries that include Boolean operators are in the minority (less than 20 per cent).

4) More than 50 per cent retrieval activities are single-query sessions.

5) Web searching topics are changing. The overall trend is towards using the Web as a tool for information or commerce. Rather than entertainment, they are using the Web for an increasing variety of information tasks.

2.3.2 Search Engines

According to Answers.com (www.answers.com), a *search engine* is:

1) a software that searches a database and gathers and reports information that contains or is related to specified terms;

2) a website whose primary function is providing a search engine for gathering and reporting information available on the Internet or a portion of the Internet.

This definition indicates that the Web search engine, or simply search engine, is an information retrieval system which helps users search and retrieve information from the Web (Chowhury 2004, p. 335). Furthermore, definition of search engine given by Wikipedia (http://www.wikipedia.org) is "a program designed to help find information stored on a computer system such as the World Wide Web, inside a corporate or proprietary network or a personal computer". This definition expands the information source from the Internet to intranet and personal computer.

2.3.2.1 Search Engine Structure

Brin and Page (1998) present an overall architecture of Google as shown in Figure 2-8; compare this architecture with the one illustrated in Figure 2-4, it can be found that *PageRank* and *Anchors* are two characteristics of the Google search engine.

According to Brin and Page (1998), crawlers receive a list of URLs to be fetched from an *URLServer*; Web pages extracted from the crawlers are temporarily stored in the *store server* where they are compressed and then passed to *repository* to store. To identify the crawled Web pages, an associated ID number called *docID* is assigned whenever a new URL is passed out of a Web page. *The indexer* reads from the *repository* the stored Web pages and performs indexing processing; index files are stored in *barrels*. The *indexer* also parses out all the links in every Web page and stores important information about them in an *anchors' file*, which includes the information needed to determine where each links point from and to, and the text content of the link. *The anchor's file* is dispatched to the *URLServer* where relative URLs are converted into absolute URLs, and in turn, into *docIDs*. The link information in the *anchor file* is also represented by pairs of *docIDs* which are stored in a *links database*. The link information is essential to calculate the *PageRanks* for all the documents (Chapter 2, section 2.3.2.4). The *searcher* uses data from *barrels*, the *Doc index*, *PageRank*, and *Lexicon* to answer queries.

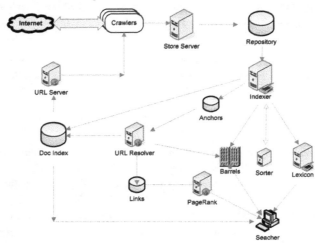

Figure 2-8 High level Google architecture
Adaption of: Brin and Page 1998, p. 111

Another kind of search engine is called meta-search engine (Baeza-Yates & Ribeiro-Neto 1999, p. 387, Chowdhury 2004, p. 339), which is defined by Meng et al. (2002, p. 49) as "a system that provides unified access to multiple existing search engines." They point out that the introduction of a meta-search engine is mainly based on the following three reasons:

1) A single search engine's processing power may not scale to the tremendous, increasing and virtually unlimited amount of data;

2) It is hard or even impossible for a single search engine to gather all the data on the Web and keep it up-to-date;

3) Some "deep web"[12] (Bergman 2001) may not allow their documents to be crawled by external websites, but allow the documents to be accessed by their own search engine only.

Figure 2-9 illustrates a conceptual architecture of a meta-search engine. Users' queries are first analyzed and a set of suitable databases (search engines) are selected by the *database selector*. *Document selector* decides either the number of documents that should be retrieved from the component search engines, or a local similarity *threshold* is used to limit the document retrieved from the component search engine. *Query dispatcher* establishes a connection with the server of each selected search engine and passes the query to it. The returned search results from the selected

---

[12] Deep Web differs from the ordinary Web because pages in deep Web do no exist until they are created dynamically as a result of a specific search; where ordinary Web pages are static and linked to other Web pages (Bergman 2001)

component search engines are merged by *results merger*, which combines all the results into a single ranked list and presents it to the user (Meng et al. 2002). However, because few meta-search engines are allowed to access the largest, most useful search engine databases (Barker 2006), meta-search engines are not as widely used as the general search engines such as Google, Yahoo! or MSN.

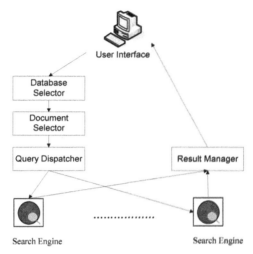

Figure 2-9 Meta-search software component architecture
Adaption of: Meng et al. 2002, p. 55

2.3.2.2 Crawler

"A crawler is a program that downloads and stores Web pages, often for a Web search engine." (Cho & Garcia-Molina 2002, p. 124) A crawler is also called a *robot*, a *spider*, a *worm*, a *bot*, or an *ant*. As can be seen from Figure 2-4 and Figure 2-8, crawlers are at the front end of a search engine and play a vital role in the system. Generally, a crawler starts off with an initial set of URLs which are placed in a queue where all URLs to be retrieved are kept and prioritized. From this queue, the crawler gets a URL based on some ordering strategies, downloads the page, extracts URLs in the downloaded page, and put the new URLs in the queue. This process is repeated until the crawler decides to stop (Arasu et al. 2001, Cho & Garcia-Molina 2002).

Many challenges are facing crawlers due to the huge size, complexity and rapid growth of the Web. Arasu et al. (2001) summarized the following four issues:

1) What pages should the crawler download so that the fraction of the Web that is visited (and kept up-to-date) is more meaningful?

2) How should the crawler refresh pages in order to detect changes and refresh the downloaded collection?

3) How should the load on the visited Web sites be minimized to avoid complaints from the Web sites, which sometimes completely block access by the crawler?

4) How should the crawling process be parallelized so that different crawlers do not visit the same Web site multiple times, and so they communicate with each other effectively to avoid significant communication overhead?[13]

Cho and Garcia-Molina (2002) conducted a comprehensive study on how to design an effective parallel crawler. Based on the proposed multiple architectures for a parallel crawler and to identify fundamental issues related to parallel crawling, matrices to evaluate a parallel crawler are suggested. According to the results of a comparison of the proposed architectures using 40 million pages collected from the Web, a guideline on when to adopt which architecture is proposed.

2.3.2.3 Indexer

The *indexer module* and *collection analysis module,* as shown in Figure 2-4 of a search engine, build a variety of indexes on the collected pages. A *Structure* (or *Link index*) is created by *indexer module.* To build a link index, the crawled portion of the Web is modelled as a directed graph. Each Web page is represented by a node in the graph, and a directed edge from node A to node B represents a hypertext link in page A that points to page B. With the directed graph, the neighbourhood information can be used by search algorithms to retrieve the set of pages pointed to by the given page P (outward links), or the set of pages pointing to P (incoming links) (Arasu et al. 2001).

Text index is also created by *indexer module.* As pointed out by Baeza-Yates and Ribeiro-Neto (1999, p. 383), most indexes use variants of the inverted file (see section 2.2.4). Arasu et al. (2001, p. 21) express a similar point of view. They point out that text-based retrieval (that is, searching for Web pages containing some keywords) at present continues to be the primary approach for identifying pages relevant to a given query, even though link-based techniques are utilized to enhance the quality and relevance of search results. "Indexes to support such text-based retrieval can be implemented using any of the access methods traditionally used to search over text document collection."

Utility indexes are created by the *collection analysis module* based on the features of a search engine. If a search engine allows restriction on a specific site or domain (such as www.curtin.edu.au), a site index can be built that maps each domain name to a list of pages belonging to that domain (Arasu et al. 2001).

---

[13] The original term used by Arasu et al. is "communication overhead"; the term overload seems more appropriate.

2.3.2.4 Ranking

Ranking strategies employed by search engines are different from that adopted by traditional IR system. Kobayashi and Takeda (2000) claim that detailed information regarding ranking algorithms used by major search engines is not publicly available. Baeza-Yates and Ribeiro-Neto (1999, p. 380) argue that "most search engines use variations of the Boolean or vector model to do ranking." However, Baeza-Yates and Ribeiro-Neto (1999, p. 380) also suggest that some of the new ranking algorithms also use hyperlink information to enhance the ranking performance, and this is an important difference between the Web and normal IR database. Arasu et al. (2001) indicate that traditional IR techniques may not be effective enough in ranking query results for the following two reasons:

1) Many Web pages that contain the search-terms may be of poor quality or not be relevant, because of the great variation in the amount, quality, and the type of information in Web pages;

2) Many Web pages are not sufficiently self-descriptive, so the IR techniques that examine the contents of a page alone may not work well. For example, many principal search engines do not contain the term "search engine". Furthermore, many pages contain some misleading terms (or repeat some key terms) to increase their ranking. Ranking techniques based on the content of pages alone are easy to manipulate.

Among various Web ranking algorithms, HITS (Hypertext Induced Topic Search) and PageRank are two famous ranking strategies which explore the hyperlink information (Arasu et al. 2001, Baeza-Yates & Ribeiro-Neto 1999, pp. 380-382, Manning et al. 2006, Rasmussen 2003). HITS (Kleinberg 1999) is a query-dependent ranking technique which considers the set of pages S that point to or are pointed to by pages in the answer set. *Authority pages* are those most likely to be relevant to a particular query, that is, pages that have many links pointing to them in S. The *hub* pages are pages that are not necessarily authorities themselves but point to several *authority* pages, that is, pages that have many outgoing links (they should point to similar content). A positive mutually reinforcing relationship exists between the *hubs* and *authorities*: higher *authority* pages come from incoming edges from good *hubs*; and good *hub* pages come from outgoing edges to high *authorities*. This intuition leads to the HITS algorithms (Arasu et al. 2001, Kleinberg 1999).

Page et al. (1998) argue that instead of simple citation counting, PageRank takes advantage of the link structure of the Web to produce a global importance ranking of every Web page. The first intuitive description of PageRank is: "a page has high rank if the sum of the ranks of its backlinks is high. This covers both the case when a page has many backlinks and when a page has a few highly ranked backlinks." (Page et al. 1998, p. 3) Another assumption is there is a "random surfer" who is given a Web page at random and simply keeps clicking on successive links; never hitting "back", and jumping to some other page when eventually getting bored.

The famous PageRank is defined as (Brin & Page 1998, pp. 109-110):

> *We assume page A has pages T1...Tn which point to it (i.e., are citations). The parameter d is a damping factor which can be set between 0 and 1. We usually set d to 0.85. There are more details about d in the next section. Also C(A) is defined as the number of links going out of page A. The PageRank of a page A is given as follows:*

$$PR(A) = (1-d) + d\ (PR(T1)/C(T1) + ... + PR(Tn)/C(Tn)$$

> *Note that the PageRanks form a probability distribution over web pages, so the sum of all web pages' PageRanks will be one.*

Both HITS and PageRank algorithms leverage the linked structure of the Web to enhance the relevance of search results, despite the fact that the TREC experiments have not demonstrated the usefulness of hyperlinks for IR (Picard & Savoy 2003). In addition to PageRank, Google also utilizes standard IR measures, proximity, anchor text to rank search results (Page et al. 1998). However, the polysemy problem of IR, as described in Chapter 1 section 1.3 and section 1.4, is still a challenge facing most search engines today.

2.4 Text Clustering

2.4.1 Definition of Text Clustering

According to Sebastiani (2006), *text clustering* indicates there are only desired number of groups (or clusters) known in advance, and no semantics indication is given as input. Text clustering aims at assembling together documents which are related among themselves and satisfy a set of common properties. It can be used to expand a user query with new and related index terms (Baeza-Yates & Ribeiro-Neto 1999, p. 173), and facilitate a user quickly browsing through search results (Zeng et al. 2004). Initially, clustering was suggested both for efficiency and as a way to categorize or classify documents. As a consequence, clustering experiments have always assumed clustering is performed over the entire collection in advance, independent of the user's query (Hearst and Pedersen 1996). Much effort has been devoted to this field since late 1970s, and some commercial (such as http://www.clusty.coom) so-called "cluster engines" have been developed to cluster the search results of principal search engines.

2.4.2 Clustering Instances

Hearst and Pedersen (1996) developed Scatter/Gather project, "a cluster-based document browsing method, as an alternative to ranked titles for the organization and viewing of retrieval results." The importance of their work is that their experiment provides evidence validating the cluster hypothesis (Rijsbergen 1979, pp. 30-31): **relevant documents tend to be more similar to each other than to non-relevant documents**. Not relying on predefined clusters, clustering in Scatter/Gather is dynamic, and the clustered results are actually a consequence of which documents were retrieved in response to the query. They utilize *Fractionation*, a non-hierarchical partitioning clustering algorithm, to cluster n documents into k groups in $O(kn)$[14] time; and cosine values between document vectors is to utilized to measure the similarities among the documents. In addition, their experiment also supports another assumption about clustering: **the same set of documents may behave differently in different contexts.** Despite the simplicity of algorithms adopted, this research was one of the first search results clustering software packages.

Hotho et al. (2001) proposed ontology-based text clustering approach in order to apply background knowledge during pre-processing to improve the quality of clustering results and allow selecting clustered results based on the ontology. They argue that current text clustering approaches suffer from three main problems. The first is that text clustering is mostly taken as an objective method, which delivers one clearly defined result, which needs to be optimal in some way. This, however, runs contrary to the second assumption given by Hearst and Pedersen (1996). Subjective criteria are therefore needed that allow diverse views from which to look at the clustering task. The second problem is that clustering in a high dimensional space, typical for most clustering algorithms, has been shown to be very difficult because every data point tends to have the same distance from all other data points. Lastly, without an explanation of why particular texts were categorized onto a particular cluster, text clustering *per se* is often rather useless. The ability of current text clustering approaches to provide an explanation again suffers from the high number of features chosen for computing clusters. They consequently build various views basing their selection of text features on an ontology, and compute multiple clustering results using K-Means[15] clustering algorithm; the results thus can be distinguished and explained by the corresponding selection of concepts in the ontology. However, their approach still needs to be tested over a large document collection.

Zeng et al. (2004) propose that clustering problems can be dealt with as a salient phrase ranking problem. With a given query and a list of ranked titles and snippets returned by a search engine, salient phrases can be extracted and ranked as candidate cluster names, based on a regression model learned from human labelled training data. The documents are assigned to relevant salient phrases to form candidate clusters, and the final clusters are generated by merging these candidate clusters. Experiments reveal that correct clusters with short names can be produced. The main shortcoming of their approach is that the clusters formed by their approach are flat, and lack hierarchical structure.

---

[14] Big O notation is used in algorithm analysis to describe the asymptotic behaviour of functions. http://en.wikipedia.org/wiki/Big_O_notation

[15] "An algorithms to cluster objects based on attributes into k partitions." http://en.wikipedia.org/wiki/K-means

The *Lingo* algorithm suggested by Osiński and Weiss (2005) combines common phrase discovery and latent semantic indexing techniques (LSI, Deerwester et al. 1990) to separate search results into meaningful groups. It aims at looking for meaningful phrases to use as cluster labels and then assigns documents to labels to form groups. The Lingo algorithm first extracts frequent phrases by using a variant of suffix arrays and identifies all frequent complete phrases. It then identifies the abstract concepts that best describe the input snippet collection and uses frequent phrases to construct a human-readable representation of these concepts. From Lingo's point of view, a limited number of orthogonal factors of LSI represent a set of abstract concepts which are perfect candidates for cluster labels, and each of these concepts conveys some idea common to a subset of the input collection. After determination of the relationship between LSI and the frequent phrases, which is called cluster-label induction, Lingo uses VSM to allocate returned snippets to corresponding clusters (cluster-content allocation). Experiments demonstrate that Lingo can create significantly purer clusters than the suffix tree clustering algorithm. The drawback of Lingo is that sometimes it assigns incorrect documents to a cluster because VSM is phrase-unaware.

WebRat (Granitzer et al. 2003, Sabol et al. 2002) is a lightweight, web-based retrieval, clustering and visualization framework. Search results are dynamically clustered thematically and then visualized. The system organizes search results by clustering, rather than by mapping them into a predefined ontology. They use a sampling-accelerated force-directed placement algorithm with a cosine similarity coefficient to reduce the high feature space, but without revealing the details of the algorithms. The system is found very helpful when users deal with an unfamiliar knowledge domain.

As one of the successful commercial clustering engines, Vivisimo (http://www.vivisimo.com) utilize their proprietary algorithm to put documents together based on textual similarity of Web pages. It suggests that *concise, understandable, accurate* and *distinctive* are four criteria for a high quality cluster descriptions. Another feature of Vivisimo is that the same documents may be placed in different clusters at the same time. This is in accordance with Hearst and Pedersen's (1996) second assumption.

Two challenges in text clustering research, as stated in Chapter 1 section 1.5 and section 1.6 are: 1) how to create clusters with hierarchical structure which are in accord with the human mental model; and 2) to provide high quality cluster description.

2.5 Text Categorization

2.5.1 Definition of Text Categorization

According to Webster's online dictionary (http://www.websters-online-dictionary.org/), the noun

"*categorization*" indicates:

> *1) a group of people or things arranged by class or category;*
> *2) the basic cognitive process of arranging into classes or categories;*
> *3) the grouping of things into classes or categories.*

Mitchell (1997) defines classification as a task to classify examples into one of a discrete set of possible categories. Yang (1999) states that text categorization is the problem of automatically assigning predefined categories to free documents. A formal definition of Text Categorization (TC) is given by Sebastiani (2005):

> *TC may be formalized as the task of approximating the unknown target function $\Phi : D \times C \rightarrow \{T,F\}$ (that describes how documents ought to be classified, according to a supposedly authoritative expert) by means of a function $\bar{\Phi} : D \times C \rightarrow \{T,F\}$ called the classifier, where $C = \{c_1, \ldots, c_{|C|}\}$ is a predefined set of categories and D is a (possibly infinite) set of documents. If $\Phi(d_j, c_i) = T$, then d_j is called a positive example (or a member) of c_i, while if $\Phi(d_j, c_i) = F$ it is called a negative example of c_i.*

Text categorization can be used in many fields, such as automatic indexing for Boolean IR system, document organisation, document filtering, word sense disambiguation, Yahoo!-style search space categorization, e-mail routing, spam filtering, and authorship attribution. Since early 1990s, machine learning approaches have gained prominence and eventually become the dominant approaches to construct automatic document classifiers. However, the basic mechanism of IR is still the core of machine learning approaches. As pointed by Sebastiani (1999, 2006), text categorization includes three essential parts: 1) indexing and dimensionality reduction; 2) construction of classifier; and 3) IR-style evaluation. Among the three parts, the first and the last part are IR-based techniques.

2.5.2 Training Set and Test Set

Suppose $C0 = \{\bar{d}_1, \ldots, \bar{d}_t\}$ is an initial document corpus previously categorized by experts under a set of categories $C = \{c1, \ldots, cm\}$. This can be expressed as a decision matrix shown on Table 2-4.

Table 2-4Table 2-4 Training set and test set

	Training Set				Test Set			
	$\bar{d}_1$	$\cdots$	$\cdots$	$\bar{d}_g$	$\bar{d}_{g+1}$	$\cdots$	$\cdots$	$\bar{d}_t$
c_1	ca_{11}	$\cdots$	$\cdots$	ca_{1g}	$ca_{1(g+1)}$	$\cdots$	$\cdots$	ca_{1t}
$\cdots$	$\cdots$	$\cdots$	$\cdots$	$\cdots$	$\cdots$	$\cdots$	$\cdots$	$\cdots$
c_i	ca_{i1}	$\cdots$	$\cdots$	ca_{ig}	$ca_{i(g+1)}$	$\cdots$	$\cdots$	ca_{it}
$\cdots$	$\cdots$	$\cdots$	$\cdots$	$\cdots$	$\cdots$	$\cdots$	$\cdots$	$\cdots$
c_m	ca_{m1}	$\cdots$	$\cdots$	ca_{mg}	$ca_{m(g+1)}$	$\cdots$	$\cdots$	ca_{mt}

Adaption of: Sebastinni 1999, p. 7

2.5.3 Feature Selection and Extraction

Nearly all categorization classifiers utilize a bag-of-words approach to represent documents, that is, terms are used as feature to represent documents. The tf-idf (Chapter 2, section 2.2.3) strategy is the most popular and effective term weighting scheme (Salton & Buckley 1988, Baeza-Yates & Ribeiro-Neto 1999, pp. 29-30). As the amount of documents is increasing exponentially, the original feature space is becoming very huge, *Term Space Reduction* (TSR) is thus needed to remove non-informative words from documents, to reduce the overfitting (overtraining) in classifier construction, to suit for some sophisticated algorithms, and to improve the computation efficiency (Sebastiani 1999, Yang 1999).

There are two types of TSR approaches. The first one is the *Dimensionality reduction by feature selection* approach which tries to reduce feature space by choosing a subset of the original features; another one is the *dimensionality reduction by feature extraction* approach which purports to create a set of new features that maximize the obtained effectiveness from the original feature set (Caropreso et al. 2001, Li & Jain 1998, Sebastiani 1999, Sebastiani 2002, Sebastiani 2006, Yang & Pedersen 1997).

2.5.3.1 Feature Selection

Dimensionality reduction by feature selection techniques are usually encoded by the intuition that the best terms for classification purposes are the ones that are distributed most differently across the different categories. Statistics and information theories are employed to construct *feature selection function*, which selects a small portion of the "best" words that are expected to have the greatest impact on the accuracy of the constructed classifier (Sebastiani 2006).

Yang and Pedersen (1997) studied five frequently used feature selection techniques, namely, document frequency, Information Gain (IG), mutual information, χ^2 test and term strength. They found that information gain, χ^2 test, and also document frequency performed excellently in their experiments. "Using IG thresholding with a k-nearest neighbour classifier on the Reuters corpus[16], removal of up to 98 per cent removal of unique terms actually yielded an improved classification accuracy (measured by average *precision*)." (Yang and Pedersen 1997, p. 412) They also indicate document frequency thresholding performed similarly with information gain and χ^2 test. However, document frequency thresholding is the simplest technique and it can easily scale to very large corpora with a computational complexity approximately linear in the number of training documents.

---

[16]   also   known   as   Routers   Collection,   refer   to   http://www.daviddlewis.com/resources/testcollections/rcv1/,   and
http://about.reuters.com/researchandstandards/corpus/

Debole and Sebastiani (2003) believe that information on the membership of training documents to categories can also be used to determine term weights; they therefore proposed a *supervised term weighting* approach which leverages on the training data by weighting a term according to how different its distribution is in the positive and negative training examples. Their experiment on Reuters corpus demonstrates that an average ten per cent F_1[17] (See section 2.5.5) improvement can be achieved when applied for classifier of Support Vector Machines (SVM) (Joachims 1998) and k-Nearest Neighbours (k-NN) (Yang 1994).

2.5.3.2 Feature Extraction

Feature extraction attempts to generate a set of "synthetic" terms (a reduced vector space) from the original term set to maximize the categorization effectiveness. In the new extracted vector space, each dimension is a combination of some (or all) of the original dimensions. Feature extraction usually reduces not only the dimensionality of the original vector, but also the overall stochastic dependence among dimensions. Latent Semantic Indexing (LSI) (Deerwester et al. 1990) and term clustering (Li & Jain 1998) are two main approaches of feature extraction.

LSI is originally developed for automatic indexing and information retrieval. LSI uses Singular-Value Decomposition (SVD) to compress document vectors into vectors of a lower-dimensional space by trying to extract their "semantic structure" (Deerwester et al. 1990). By utilizing this semantic structure, LSI judges the dependence among the original terms of a document collection and then wires these dependences into new independent dimensions. The data in the newly obtained vector with a lower dimensionality are hard to be interpreted because after the SVD process, the original term by *document matrix* (see section 2.2.2) is decomposed into three matrices, each with linearly independent components. Experiments demonstrate LSI performs at least as good as the most effective feature selection techniques in text classification. A drawback of LSI is that if some terms are particularly distinctive to a category, the power of this discrimination may be lost in LSI (Sebastiani 2002).

2.5.4 Classifier Construction

Sebastiani (1999, 2002) systematically studies a wide spectrum of approaches of the inductive construction of a text classifier and discusses a general form of text classifier. Roughly, to inductively construct a classifier for a category $c_i \in C$, a function which returns a so-called *categorization status value* (CSVi), is to be defined with a value field of [0, 1]. CSVi : D → [0, 1] represents the evidence for the fact that $d_j \in c_i$. Documents are then ranked according to their

---

[17] F_1 is a measurement of effectiveness of information retrieval systems based on precision and recall.

CSVi value. According to the learning method used, the CSVi function takes up different meanings, for instance, it may be defined in terms of probability, or a measure of similarity between vectors in a high dimensional space. Then, a definition of *threshold* τ_i is needed such that CSVi($\mathbf{d}$) > τ_i is interpreted as a decision to categorize document $\mathbf{d}$ under category c_i; otherwise as a decision not to categorize $\mathbf{d}$ under c_i. If a classifier provides a binary judgment, that is, CSVi : D → {true, false}, the τ_i is trivial in this case.

2.5.4.1 tf-idf Classifier

tf-idf classifier, also called Rocchio method, is an IR technique-based text categorization approach (Joachims 1997, Sebastiani 1999, Sebastiani 2002). Term frequency and reverse document frequency (Chapter 2, section 2.2.3) is first calculated. Learning process is achieved by adding training document vectors into a prototype vector $\vec{c}_i$ for each $\vec{c}_i \in C$. That is, a classifier $\vec{c}_i$ = <w_{1i}, …w_{ti}> is trained by calculating each of elements in classifier $\vec{c}_i$ (Sebastiani 2002, p. 26):

$$w_{ki} = \alpha \cdot \sum_{d_j \in POS_i} \frac{w_{kj}}{|POS_i|} - \beta \cdot \sum_{d_j \in NEG_i} \frac{w_{kj}}{|NEG_i|}$$

Here, w_{kj} is the weight of term t_k in document d_j, $POS_i = \{d_j \in Tr \mid \check{\Phi}(d_j, c_i) = T\}$, and $NEG_i = \{d_j \in Tr \mid \check{\Phi}(d_j, c_i) = F\}$. Note that α and β are two control parameters that adjust the relative impact of positive and negative training example. When set $\alpha = 1$ and $\beta = 0$, the profile of $\vec{c}_i$ is the centroid of its positive training examples.

Classifier $\vec{c}_i$ = <w_{1i}, …, w_{ti}> can be represented in another approach as described by Jachims (1997),

$$\vec{c}_i = \alpha \frac{1}{|C_i|} \sum_{d \in C_i} \frac{\vec{d}}{\|\vec{d}\|} - \beta \frac{1}{|D - C_i|} \sum_{d \in D - C_i} \frac{\vec{d}}{\|\vec{d}\|}$$

Classifier $\vec{c}_i$ is referred to prototype vector for each class C_i, $\vec{d}$ represent document, $\|\vec{d}\|$ denotes the Euclidian length of a vector $\vec{d}$. The elements of each $\vec{d}$ are the tf-idf weight of the corresponding terms in the vector space. The resulting set of prototype vectors, where each vector represents each class, is the learned model, which can then used to classify a new document. The cosine value of the new document $\vec{d}'$ between each prototype vectors $\vec{c}_i$ is calculated, and $\vec{d}'$ is assigned to the class with which the cosine value is the highest.

The tf-idf classifier is easy to implement and quite efficient. However, if the documents in the category tend to occur in disjointed clusters, the centroid of these documents may fall outside all of these clusters. In this frequently occurring scenario, this classifier prefers poorly (Joachims 1997, Sebastiani 2002).

2.5.4.2 Naive Bayes Classifier

In probability and statistics, the Bayes' rule (Mendenhall et al. 2006, pp. 158-161) is expressed as:

Let C_1, C_2, ..., C_k represent k mutually exclusive and exhaustive subpopulations with prior probabilities $P(C_1)$, $P(C_2)$, ...,$P(C_k)$. If an event D occurs, the posterior probability of C_i given D is the conditional probability

$$P(C_i \mid D) = \frac{P(C_i)P(D \mid C_i)}{\sum_{j=1}^{k} P(C_j)P(D \mid C_j)} \dots\dots\dots\dots\dots\dots\dots\dots Formula\ 2\text{-}1$$

for i = 1, 2, ..., k.

In the context of text categorization, C is a random variable whose values are those classes $c_i \in C = \{c_1, c_2, ..., c_k\}$, k is the total number of classes. D is a vector random variable whose values are vectors of feature values, $d \in D = \{d_1, d_2, ..., d_{|D|}\}$, $|D|$ is the total number of training document available, one vector for each document, $d_j = \{w_{1j}, w_{2j}, ... w_{|T|j}\}$, w_{ij} is the term weight; $|T|$ is the total number of selected features. Assumption is made that all possible events (in case of Text categorization, documents) fall into exactly one of the classes of C and words are to occur independently of the other words in the document (Joachims 1997, Lewis 1998).

Probabilistic classifiers $CSVi(\overline{d}_j)$ can be constructed by estimating the probability of $P(c_i \mid \overline{d}_j)$, the probability of document $\overline{d}_j$ belongs to a class c_i (Joachims 1997, Lewis 1998, Sebastiani 2002). According to Bayes' rule, the highest classification accuracy is achieved when $\overline{d}_j$ is assigned to the class c_i which maximizes $P(ci \mid \overline{d}_j)$. The posterior probability $P(ci \mid \overline{d}_j)$, according to Bayes' rule, is represented as *Formula 2-1*.

Different classifiers have been developed regarding how to calculate components in *Formula 2-1* based on different assumptions (Joachims 1997, Lewis 1998, Mitchell 1997, pp. 177-190, Sebastiani 2002). Although the Naive Bayes model has been remarkably successful in IR (Lewis 1998), it seems that the results in text categorization are not inspiring; it performs equally as the tf-idf classifier (Sebastiani 2002).

2.5.4.3 Other Classifiers

Sebastiani (1999, 2002) presents a comprehensive review of different classifiers such as *decision tree, decision rule, regression methods, on-line methods, neural networks, example-based classifier, support vector machines, boosting* and *classifier committees*. Sebastiani (2006) also pointed out experiments so far have shown that use of external resources (such as lexicons, thesauri, or ontologies) in text categorization have obtained no substantial benefits. In recent years, *support vector machines* (Joachims 1998) and *boosting* (Schapire et al. 1998) are two dominant learning methods in text categorization; these two approaches have strong justification in terms of computational learning theory, and outperformed all other competing text categorization algorithms. They are both free for research purposes now (http://svmlight.joachims.org, http://www.cs.princeton.edu/~schapire/).

2.5.5 IR-Style Measurement for Text Categorization

To evaluate the performance (effectiveness) of a classifier, IR-style measurement, *recall* and *precision* are introduced in text categorization (Yang 1997, Yang 1999, Yang & Pedersen 1999). Suppose a classifier takes a document as input, at a particular *threshold*, it outputs a list of ranked categories the document is to be assigned to, then:

$$\text{Recall} = \frac{\text{categories found and correct}}{\text{total categories correct}}$$

$$\text{Precision} = \frac{\text{categories found and correct}}{\text{total category found}}$$

where "categories found" indicates that the categories are above a given score *threshold*. For a document collection, the *precision* and *recall* are measured for each document and then they are averaged. The conventional interpolated 11-point average *precision* is used to evaluate the performance of a classifier on a specific document collection.

According to Yang (1999), the classifiers introduced above are called binary classifiers because for a given document, these classifiers make a YES/NO decision for each category, independently from their decisions on other classifiers. For binary classifiers, the performance can be measured by a two-way contingency table as shown in Table 2-5 for each category (Sebastiani 2002, Yang 1999).

Table 2-5 A contingency table

	YES is correct	NO is correct
Assigned YES	a	b
Assigned NO	c	d

Adaption of: Yang 1999, p. 75

a: counts the documents correctly assigned to this category; *true positive* of classifier c_i(TPi).

b: counts the documents incorrectly assigned to this category; *false positive* of classifier c_i(FPi).

c: counts the documents incorrectly rejected from this category; *false negative* of classifier c_i(FNi).

d: counts the documents correctly rejected from this category; *true negative* of classifier c_i(TNi).

Based on these counts, *recall* (*r*), *precision* (p), *fallout* (*f*), *accuracy* (*Acc*) and *error* (*Err*) is defined as (Yang 1999, p. 75):

r = a / (a + c) suppose a + c > 0; otherwise undefined;
p = b / (a + b) suppose a + b > 0; otherwise undefined;
f = b / (b + d) suppose b + d > 0; otherwise undefined;
Acc = (a + d) / n where n = a + b + c + d > 0
Err = (b + c) / n where n = a + b + c + d > 0

Another common measure of a classifier is referred to as *F-measure*, defined as (Yang 1999):

$$F_\beta(r,p) = \frac{(\beta^2 + 1)pr}{\beta^2 p + r}$$ .... Formula 2-2

β is used to differentiate p and r. When β takes value 1, that is, *recall* and *precision* is weighted equally, the Formula 2-2 is simplified to F_1 measurement.

$$F_1(r,p) = \frac{2pr}{p + r}$$

2.5.6 Categorization of Web Search Results in a Hierarchical Structure

With the exponential growth of the Internet and intranet, to effectively manage the huge searching results, hierarchically categorizing Web pages is needed. However, the categorization models introduced above are flat, non-hierarchical models which, as mentioned by Sebastiani (2006), do not delivery high accuracy in all applicative contexts, such as classification of Web pages.

Mladenic (1998) uses *Yahoo! Web Directory* as an automatic Web-page classifier. For each of the top level Yahoo! categories, a separate Naive Bayesian classifier is constructed and trained for both positive and negative examples. Documents are represented as feature vectors using the bag-of-words method. In addition, up to five words occurring in a document as a sequence are also selected as features. The influence of different numbers of features is observed, the best performance is achieved when only a small number (the author does not provide what the figure is) of features is used. Generally speaking, about 50 per cent of the testing examples ranked one or two are assigned to the correct category.

Klas and Fuhr (2000) use tf-idf weighting scheme and probabilistic retrieval model to classify Web documents under the hierarchical structure of *Yahoo! Web Directory*. They downloaded all the Web pages in each of the categories in *Yahoo! Web Directory*; the texts of all documents belonging to a category are concatenated to form a so-called megadocument. The terms in the megadocuments are weighted by tf-idf technique. To classify a document, the first n best terms (according to their idf values) are selected as a query vector. The similarity search is based on a probabilistic model and a document is assigned to the category (represented by megadocument) with the highest similarity. Their experiments demonstrate that their approach achieves relatively good results with Web documents, whereas classical approaches perform badly for these collections. When applied to Reuters collection, the approach proposed is comparable to the average of other classical text categorization methods.

Frommholz (2001) argues that most text categorization algorithms lack the consideration of an underlying hierarchical structure, and thus suggests the knowledge about the hierarchy like *Yahoo! Web Directory* be used to gain better categorization results in terms of effectiveness. The proposed approach by him can theoretically deal with all hierarchies by taking them as an acyclic graph, and documents can be inserted to not only leaf nodes, but also the inner category. He first uses a non-hierarchical classifier, like the one proposed by Klas and Fuhr (2000), to assign weights to every category in the category scheme. Then he uses hierarchical information to calculate a new weight for each category, the document d is thus assigned to the category with the highest weight. Experiments on Yahoo! Computers & Internet category show a marginal improvement can be achieved compared with the approach proposed by Klas and Fuhr (2000). However, the cost is the computational complexity.

Dumais and Chen (2000) propose a SVM-based classifier which was trained by using the hierarchical structure such as Looksmart Web Directory (http://search.looksmart.com/) and *Yahoo! Web Directory*. They focus on only the top two levels of the hierarchies because they believe many search results can be disambiguated at this level. LookSmart Web Directory is used as a pre-defined hierarchical structure in their research. In pre-processing phase, plain text is extracted from each Web page. The title, description and keyword fields from the META tag, and the ALT field from the IMG tag[18] were also extracted if they existed. A summary of each Web page is also created for evaluation purpose. Their approach uses a binary vector to represent each Web page. The reason is that good performance can be achieved when binary vector is used in SVMs, and this representation improves efficiency. To reduce the feature space, words that appear in only a single document are eliminated; 1000 words with highest mutual information with each category are then selected as features. The hierarchical structure is exploited by first choosing a class among the top level, and then at the lower level, a more specific distinction is made. The experiments show small advantages in the F_1 accuracy score for the hierarchical model, compared with the flat, non-hierarchical models.

The work of Dumais and Chen (2000) is very interesting because they explore the hierarchical structure to classify the Web search results dynamically. The LookSmart Web Directory used in their research consisted of 13 top categories, a total 171,713 categories and 370,597 Web pages. Compared with over 590,000 total categories and 5,274, 288 Web pages of the ODP, how to use

---

[18] META tag, ALT field and IMG tag are all elements of HTML, the predominant markup language for the creation of Web pages

this enriched information and reduce the computation complexity to improve efficiency are some factors that need to be considered; especially the search results returned by search engines need to be categorized dynamically. Furthermore, enhancing the interactivity between user and an IR system and filtering search results are also issues needed to be addressed.

Northern Light search engine (http://www.northernlight.com) provides Custom Folders to organize search results. The folders are automatically created according to the four dimensions. The first one is *subject folders* that use a hierarchy of over 200,000 subject terms created by the librarians on Northern Light's staff. It seems that Northern Light uses word occurrences in each page and matches by keyword to the subject terminology, and it does not reliably identify the subject of all Web pages. It is a rough approximation. *Source folders* can be one specific publication. This type of folder is only available for search results from the special collections database (e.g., commercial sites, personal Web pages, magazines, encyclopaedias, databases). The third is the *type folders*. Some examples of this kind of folder are press releases, product reviews, and resumes. The last kind of folders is *language folders*. There is no global information provided about the category structure or about the distribution of search results across categories (Allan & Raghavan 2002, Dumais et al. 2001, Notess 1998). Each folder is a one or two words label; documents that contain the label are organized under the label. However, Northern Light does not reveal the approach how to create the folders (Zamir & Etzioni 1998).

The developed special search-browser is different from the Northern Light Search Engine (NL) in the following four aspects. First, NL **clusters** search results, the special search-browser **categorizes** search results; second, NL uses labels (syntactic) to arrange retrieved documents, the special search-browser uses semantics of categories to categorize search results; the third difference is that NL uses a **proprietary hierarchy** similar to the *Yahoo! Web Directory*, created by a small group of experts. This kind of hierarchy is hardly likely to keep pace with the development of the WWW. Yahoo! it seems now does not emphasis *Yahoo! Web Directory* any more. The special search-browser uses ODP which is a **"social"** category contributed by millions of editors all over the world. Lastly, NL is a **proprietary product;** the special search-browser's algorithm is public.

2.6 Ontology-Based Information Classification

2.6.1 Definition of Ontology

The widely accepted definition of ontology is the one given by Gruber (1993, p. 908) as "an ontology is a formal, explicit specification of a conceptualisation". Conceptualisation is defined as an abstracted, simplified view of the world that we wish to represent for some purpose. Bruijn (2003), Uschold and Gruninger (1996) indicate that according to their expressiveness, ontologies can be classified as, for example: *thesaurus* - relations between terms, such as synonyms; *informal taxonomy* - there is an explicit hierarchy but there is no strict inheritance; *formal taxonomy* - there is strict inheritance; *general logic constraints* - values may be constrained by logical or mathematical formulas using values from other properties, and so on. Bruijn (2003) points out ontologies can be simply equated with taxonomic hierarchies of classes.

A formal definition of ontology is given by Hotho et al. (2001):

> A ***core ontology*** *is a sign system* $O := (L, F, C, H, ROOT)$ *which consists of*
> A ***lexicon****: The lexicon* L *contains a set of terms*
> A *set of* ***concepts*** C
> The ***reference function*** F *with* $F: 2^L \mapsto 2^C$. F *links sets of terms* $\{Li\} \subset L$ *to the sets of concepts they refer to.*
> A ***heterarchy*** H: *concepts are taxonomically related by the directed, acyclic, transitive, reflexive relation* H, $(H \subset C \times C)$.
> A *top concept* $ROOT \in C$. *For all* $C \in C$ *it holds:* $H(C, ROOT)$.

If an ontology is taken as a taxonomic hierarchy of classes, the element of reference function can be removed from the definition above; for example, when ODP is regarded as an ontology in this study.

2.6.2 Ontology in Text Categorization

Labrou and Finin (1999) believe that categories like *Yahoo! Web Directory* offer a standardized and universal way for referring to or describing the nature of real world objects, activities, documents, and so on, and thus suitable to semantically characterize the content of documents. They proposed using Yahoo! categories as an ontology to automatically describe Web documents by an n-gram-based classifier. The title of each category, especially a brief description, which is provided either by the human indexers or by the creator of the Web page when the page is submitted to Yahoo!, are actually the *semantic content* and can be taken advantage of. The research reveals that the description of Yahoo! categorized entries help their n-gram-based classifier to produce better results. Experiments also reveal some of the top matches might not be the Yahoo! official match, but may be useful for providing some sort of semantic information about the content of the Web pages.

Luca and Nürnberger (2004) present an approach to classify search results by combining indexing and ontology-based IR technique which intended to exploit the fact that every word conveys a certain meaning that can be made accessible and available using ontologies. They believe that the domain within which the search-terms occur plays an important role for word sense disambiguation. Multiwordnet (http://multiwordnet.itc.it/english/home.php), an expanded version of the WordNet (http://wordnet.princeton.edu/online/) is used as an ontology. The first step of their approach is to construct a so-called "sense folder" by extracting the concepts from the ontology for a given search-term. The concept vectors in the sense folder consists of the hypernyms (the superordinate word), the hyponyms (the subordinate word) and the belonging glosses (human readable description of the words). These derived concepts can form a concept hierarchical structure. The second step is to get the search results from search engines. Lastly, all the returned search results and the concepts in the sense folder are represented by tf-idf weighted term vectors; VSM is used to calculate the cosine similarity between each search result and concept vectors. A search result is assigned to a concept if the similarity between them is the highest. However, further experiment is needed to evaluate their approach proposed.

Kunz (2003) indicates that although browsing a Web directory and using Google style searching are two main approaches to get Web information, the two approaches are still separate jobs and many principal search engines do not provide a user interface to combine them. Using a Web directory for browsing Web pages is not only time consuming but also tends to lead users to lose the overview of the topic structure. Search engines, on the other hand, tend to return millions of irrelevant search results. SERGIO, a user browser aims at supporting users understanding their information needs, providing an overview of the structure and relationships of the information spaces, and facilitating users with effective mechanisms for accessing information with a specific context. SERGIO combines semantic Web techniques with keyword-based search engines and text categorisation into the visualisation interface. By applying ontologies to conventional retrieval techniques, refined search can be supported through thematic category, and users can also easily be aware of their own information needs and the structure of the information space. The main four parts of SERGIO are: *visualisation and user interface*; *query and inference service*, which deals with user queries and generates the appropriate visualisation on ontological information; *indexer* analyzes the information and creates a textual representation in form of word vectors; *categorizer* "applies relations between information resources and from information objects to corresponding thematic categories in the ontology." (p. 579) However, using an adjacency matrix to represent a Web hierarchical structure is hard to understand for most users and further experiments are also needed to evaluate the system proposed.

The ontologies used in this section are also called "light-weight ontologies" (Bruijn 2003, p. 8), that is, they are actually *thesaurus* or *informal taxonomy*. Research introduced in section 2.5.6 also utilizes light-weight ontologies as a knowledge structure to re-organize search results, and they may also be introduced in this section. However, if machine learning algorithm is the focus of that research, it is to be classified under section 2.5.6; on the other hand, if the research mainly concentrates on how to exploit the semantic characteristics of an ontology, the research is to be introduced in this section.

2.7 Research Significance

The study is significant for the following four reasons. Firstly, by enhancing interaction of the search process, search-term disambiguation can be achieved accurately, simply and efficiently. By excluding the irrelevant categories from the search results directly by users, more relevant results will be presented. The problems of high *recall*, low *precision* search results of search engines are expected to be alleviated.

Next, the results of this study are expected to help users acquire an overview of the knowledge structure especially for unfamiliar knowledge domains. Search result locus and relationship to other knowledge domains within an overall framework of knowledge can be presented – to the best knowledge of the author; this has not been done before. It can also present the searchers where the position of the search results is in the hierarchy of the whole Web directory, and the relationships between other knowledge domains.

Thirdly, a combination of information navigation and search-term querying in a special search-browser will facilitate both novice and expert information searchers for a given knowledge domain. Search-term query interface is not appropriate for novice searchers, because it is hard for them to find a proper Search-term for searching, which has been proven a key factor for the relevance of search results. ODP-based ontology can present a general concept map as a starting point for the searchers. In addition, to the best of my knowledge, this is the first project using the ODP as a pre-defined category to categorize Web search results. Chirita et al. (2005) employ the ODP as an ontology to personalize search. They rank Web pages by calculating the distance between a user-profile defined using ODP topics and the set of the ODP topics.

Fourthly, toward categorization issues, the machine learning approach is dominant at present, but needs firstly a training set to train the learning algorithms (Sebastiani 1999, Sebastiani 2002). Much human labour and effort is demanded to create the training set to ensure the learning algorithms to be properly trained. This research proposes and implements an innovative approach to extract semantic characteristics of the ODP data to represent the informative and subject matters about the categories in the ODP. When these categories are taken as the features of the Web category, the extracted semantic characteristics can therefore be utilized as training data.

Lastly, there is an absence of such an interface as proposed here (see research objective, stage 2 Chapter 1, section 1.8). Some systems try to improve relevance by clustering search results (Granitzer et al. 2003, Kunz 2003, www.vivisimo.com, Notess 1998, http://www.northernlight.com). Some systems use *Yahoo! Web Directory* as categories for an ontology to describe the contents of Web pages (Labrou & Finin 1999). However, these differ from using ODP as an ontology to classify search results and to disambiguate search-terms.

Table 2-6 is a comparison of the related work and this research - the special search-browser. Comments are also provided for the related work.

Table 2-6 Comparison of relative work and the special search-browser

RESEARCH	S	O	J	C	COMMENTS
Clusty.com	N	Y	N/A	Proprietary	It clusters but not categorizes search results, refer to Chapter 1 section 1.6
Dumais and Chen 2000	Y	Y	N	SVMs	They use exactly 1000 word to represent each category and no convincing explanation is given; relevance judgment is not considered in their experiment.
Frommholz 2001	N	Y	N/A	Probabilistic Model	While using acyclic graph can describe more complex hierarch, the computational cost is also very high. Experimental results also reveals the high computational cost is not rewarded by high performance
Klas and Fuhr 2000	N	Y	N/A	Probabilistic Model	Why they select 10 or 50 words to represent a document to be classified is not clearly explained. Also, their experiment is only based on one first level category of Yahoo, "Computers & Internet"
Luca and Nurnberger 2004	N	Y	N	VSM	Experiment is needed to demonstrate their approach, using only one search term and made relevance judgment by the author themselves is the main limitation in their research.
Northern Light	N	N	N/A	Proprietary	Refer to the last two paragraphs of Section 2.5.6
SERGIO	N	Y	N	Don't know	Using adjacency matrix to represent a knowledge structure is hard understood. A further experiment is also needed to evaluate the system.
Special search-browser	Y	Y	Y	VSM	

Note: S=Socially constructed knowledge structure; C=Categorization technique utilized in the research; O=Only categorize into one category; J=Judges employed when doing experiments;

2.8 Summary

This chapter briefly reviewed the main concepts, and some research, related to information clustering and categorization. IR is an information (can be digitalized) analysis and stepwise interactive process. To alleviate the two inherent problems – caused by the polysemy and synonym features of natural language – facing IR, many different IR models have been developed; for example, the Vector Space Model, probabilistic model, and Boolean model. Researchers also utilize text categorization and text clustering to organize the research results, where traditional IR techniques and machine learning techniques are utilized.

With the advent, and the rocket growth of the Internet, information on the Web is growing exponentially as well. While search engines try to present more and more search results, how to reorganize these millions of search items is becoming more and more prominence. Facing the huge and dynamic search results from search engines, an effective and efficient categorization approach will to some extent alleviate the problems as mentioned in Chapter 1, section 1.2 to section 1.7. In the following chapter, a conceptual solution is proposed which addresses the issues mentioned above.

Chapter 3.   Conceptual Solution

This chapter proposes an approach to improve the relevance of search results returned by search engines. The skeleton of the proposed IR system is presented in section 3.1. An interactive IR model is depicted in section 3.2. *Yahoo! Search Web Services API*, which is used to retrieve the Web pages directly from the Yahoo! indexed text database, is introduced in section 3.3. Section 3.4 provides a detailed description of the structure and the data in the ODP. This is followed by section 3.5 that describes indexing of the semantic characteristics of the ODP data. Using VSM as a classifier to categorize the returned search results is discussed in section 3.6. With the interaction of users, filtering search results based on the ODP is consequently presented in section 3.7. Section 3.8 presents an example with detailed calculation to demonstrate the proposed approach. Finally, section 3.9 summarizes this chapter.

3.1 Introduction

The focus of this study is to ontologically disambiguate search-terms by categorizing Web search results returned from search engines. To achieve the objective, a special search-browser is to be developed which combines search engine results, the ODP-based ontology as a navigator, and search results categorization. The special search-browser utilizes *Yahoo! Search Web Services APIs* to support search-term searching. Socially constructed hierarchical categories of the ODP are taken as a predefined ontology, and VSM is employed to calculate the similarities between retrieved items from Yahoo! and concepts represented by the ODP categories. With the interaction of users, the proposed search-browser filters the irrelevant search results, and only the results under the selected category will be presented to the users. More relevant search results are thus expected.

The developed system consists of four main parts as shown in Figure 3-1, namely, *Web search, the ODP data extraction, text categorization*, and the *user interface*. The *Web search* component retrieves the Web pages directly from the Yahoo! indexed text database by employing *Yahoo! Search Web Services API*. The *ODP semantic data extraction* part analyzes and extracts the ODP data. The third part, the *text categorization* component of the special search-browser indexes the extracted semantic ODP data produced by the *ODP semantic data extraction* component, classifies and then filters search results. Lucene (http://lucene.apache.org) is a platform to implement these functions of the third part. The *user interface* component accepts users' input and presents retrieval results to the users; this part allows the interaction between users and the developed special search-browser. The ODP categories represented by a tree are presented on the left of the user interface.

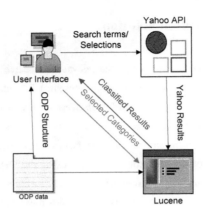

Figure 3-1 Main components of the system

3.2 An Interactive Information Retrieval Model

As pointed out by Baeza-Yates and Ribeiro-Neto (1999, pp. 9-10), a user generally employs two approaches to acquire information from an IR system. The first approach is *browsing,* which implies that users do not have definite information needs at the very beginning. They may randomly walk from one subject to another, or from one Web page to another page until an interesting subject or Web page is found. Another method is information *retrieving.* In this scenario, users have clear information needs that are usually translated into queries, or search-terms which convey the semantics of the information needs and can be processed by an IR system. In both cases, the users are searching for information needed and executing *retrieval* tasks. Of course, users may first do a browse, and then retrieve when definite information needs are formed during the browsing procedure, or vice versa.

However, computers at present still have problems understanding human languages (Chowdhury 2003, Chowdhury 2004, pp. 396-397), and because of the polysemy and synonymy problems of the natural languages, IR systems are far from perfect. A lot of users' efforts interacting with the IR system are required before an IR system can present the relevant information in front of the users to satisfy their information needs. Therefore, the interactive process is a remarkable feature of IR. Following this section, an interactive IR model is proposed, and the interactive process between users and the IR system is described.

3.2.1 Interactive Character of Information Retrieval

Web IR is inherently an iterative process (Robins 2000, p. 58, Xie 2003, p. 900). The purpose of interaction for an IR system is to provide more effective and efficient services to its consumers. Information consumers (information seekers or searchers) may have clear information needs in their minds when an IR session starts, or there are only obscure information needs and the obscure information needs may be changed with the information searching processes (Chowdhury 2004, p. 194). On the other hand, users may not have any clear information needs at the very beginning, and they are just browsing an IR system, and some information needs are developed with the browsing procedures (Baeza-Yates and Ribeiro-Neto 1999, pp. 9-10). To satisfy the information needs of users (Chapter 2, section 2.1.1), an IR system is, in fact, an information retrieval service provider, and IR system users are consumers of this kind of service. Without interactions between the service providers and the service consumers, the information retrieval services can not happen. Figure 2-1 and Figure 2-3 in Chapter 2 clearly demonstrate that IR is essentially an interactive process. Hearst (1999), from the perspective of user interface design in IR system, presents a simplified standard model of the information access process as shown in Figure 3-2.

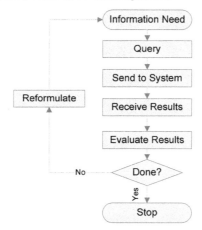

Figure 3-2 A simplified standard model of the information access process
Adaption of: Hearst 1999, p. 263

In the real world environment, users may combine both browsing and searching approaches in an information retrieval session. Users learn during the search process (Hearst 1999,   p. 264). The simplified standard IR model downplays the interaction between users and an IR system. Bates (1989) argues that users' information needs do not remain the same throughout the search session as suggested by the standard model of the information access process. Search queries are not static but rather evolve. Furthermore, users' information needs are not satisfied by "one grand best retrieved set"; they instead "gather information in bits and pieces" (Bates 1989, p. 18), thus named the berry-picking model. Hearst (1999,   p. 264) points out that the berry-picking model is widely supported by many other observational studies.

In the spirit of iterative refinement, Dreher (1997) proposed a "Generative Conceptualisation"
model as illustrated in Figure 3-3, which

> *depicts the operations involved in working with vast quantities of sense-data derived from
> what can be termed a researcher's information space and with the goal of generating new
> concepts and knowledge. Such information spaces are filled with, Internet Newsgroup
> postings, results of wide-ranging bibliographic searches, full-text versions of journal articles,
> special purpose collections of textual material on CD-ROMs (quality assurance
> documentation, legal statutes and cases, transcripts of proceedings, catalogues, procedures
> manuals, and so on), education material, and other eclectic data repositories.*

Generative Conceptualisation

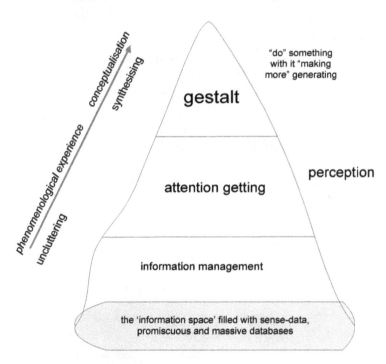

Figure 3-3 Generative Conceptualisation
Adaption of: Dreher 1997, p. 31

An exploration of the newly developed NWT technology (Williams, 2006), which is capable of
dynamically analyzing natural language text for conceptual content, can be seen in the "Assisted
Query Formulation" process as proposed by Dreher and Williams (2006, p. 283). The Query-
formulation → Find → Re-formulation process proposed by Dreher and Williams (2006) is
demonstrated in Table 3-1 .

Table 3-1 Query-formulation → Find → Re-formulation (QFR)

Step 1)	Person P has idea → constructs keywords or some text to explain the concept → call it Q.
Step 2)	Via a special browser, Q is 'acquired' by the NWV technology which makes computations based on some 'reference data' set. This is typically a thesaurus or alternative corpus obtained by some search-categorization process or by reference to a seed ontology – the Open Directory Project (www.dmoz.com) would be a suitable starting point.
Step 3)	A set of Normalised Concepts are returned in the context of the 'reference data' set and categorized by the reference to the current ontological view.
Step 4)	The special browser facilitates P to adjust (augment, amend, re-arrange, re-categorized, delete) Q, we now have Qi (i range from 1 for the first iteration to integer values such as 3 or 4, perhaps 7 at most).
Step 5)	Re-iterate through Steps 2)3) and 4) until P is satisfied that Qn represents the true idea P had in mind for the search.
Step 6)	Submit Qn into ontological filter/disambiguation system to match the query/ontology/target data repository for the search.
Step 7)	Present results to P with options of re-iterating Step 6) after P refines/adjusts and/or repeats Step 5).

Adaption of: Dreher and Williams 2006, p. 284

With the dramatic increase of information on the Internet, the interactive characteristic of IR is becoming more and more prominent and important. A well designed Web IR system will aim at facilitating the interactive process between user and the IR system; and thus lead users to acquire relevant information effectively and efficiently.

To capture the iterative nature of the user-IR system, a gyroidal pyramid Web information retrieval model is proposed.

3.2.2 A Proposed Gyroidal Iterative Information Retrieval Model

As mentioned at the beginning of section 3.2, to satisfy users' information needs, two approaches are available now: *browsing* and *search-term searching*. For search-term searching, search engines today usually return millions of search results, and approximately half of them are irrelevant (Chapter 1, section 1.3). For browsing, although the *precision* of the search results is very high, the *recall* is extremely low. Therefore, categorizing the returned results into a socially constructed hierarchical knowledge structure, such as the ODP, is a possible and promising approach to organize the huge returned search results. The user can then choose an interesting category and according to this selection, an IR system can thus ontologically filter the search results.

With this intuition (that is, combining the advantages of browsing and retrieving, from a user's perspective), a gyroidal pyramid interactive Web information retrieval model is proposed, as shown by Figure 3-4.

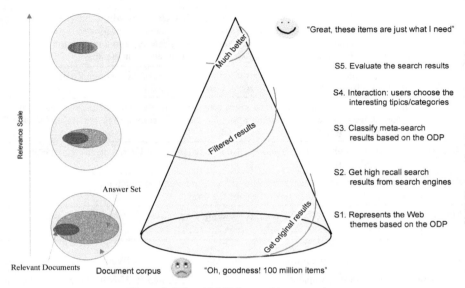

Figure 3-4 Gyroidal Web searching procedure

From the perspective of an IR system, the architecture to implement the above information retrieval model is given in Figure 3-5.

The information retrieval process illustrated in Figure 3-5 corresponds to the gyroidal IR model of Figure 3-4. The eight steps, s1 through s8, described above are marked by corresponding labels beside the arrows. There are two iterative processes in this model. The first circle, marked by blue lines (solid), provides users with original Web search results; furthermore, it also categorizes these original Web results under the categories of the ODP. The second iterative process is marked by red lines (dashed), and provides users with refined search results by presenting only ontologically categorized results, to echo users' selection of a specific ODP category. The processes in the bottom right of Figure 3-5 without marked numbers are retrieving and classifying processes. The implementation details of components in Figure 3-4 are to be explained in Chapter 4.

Based on this interactive searching model, a proposed gyroidal Web searching procedure consists of the eight steps (Table 3-2).

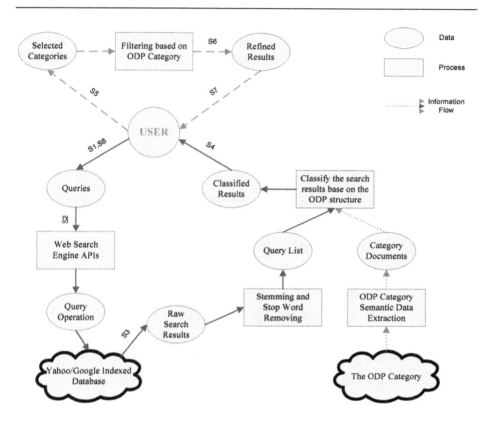

Figure 3-5 An interactive information retrieval and categorization system architecture

3.2.3 Improving the Quality of Search Results

In the gyroidal model, filtered search results are based on user interaction, especially when a search-term has more than one meaning, such as the term "jaguar" and "ups". When using jaguar as a search-term, Google returns 63,500,000 search results (Chapter 1, section 1.2, Figure 1-1). The first page of the search results includes the jaguar car, an operating system named jaguar, a Formula One racing team, the animal jaguar and so on. Figure 3-6 is the screenshot of the first page of the search results of Google when search for "ups". As can be seen from the screenshot, the search results include information about the United Parcel Service, Uninterrupted Power Supply, University of Puget Sound, and so on. If a user wants to find some information about the animal jaguar, the *precision* of the search results returned is very low because, among the ten search results, only one of them is relevant; that is, the *precision* is as low as ten per cent.

Table 3-2 A gyroidal Web searching procedure

Step	Process	Procedure in Figure 3-4
s1	A user first has a general information need in mind, for example, try to find some information about the animal jaguar.	
s2	The user selects a search engine - for example, Google (http://www.google.com) - and uses jaguar as a search-term to perform a search.	
s3	The search engine returns millions of search items. Of the top ten ranked search results presented in the first page, perhaps only one or two are relevant to the animal jaguar; most of the search results are irrelevant.	p1, p2
s4	At the same time, the proposed IR system categorizes all the search results based on a hierarchical structure of a predefined ontology (such as the ODP), and manifests this classification by utilizing a tree view.	p1, p2
s5	The user selects one interesting category which indicates the search results categorized under this category that may be relevant to his or her information needs.	p3
s6	The IR system filters the search results according to the user's selection, and presents only the filtered results to the user. The filtered search results are further categorized into the next level of hierarchical structure of the predefined ontology, supposing it has not reached the last level of the hierarchical structure.	p3
s7	The user browses the ontologically filtered results. If the results are still too broad (still containing many irrelevant search items), the procedure goes back to step 5. If the filtered search results can satisfy the user's information need, this search session will finish.	p4, p5
s8	The user may start another search session, or go back to step 5 to find information under other categories (maybe, "jaguar car").	

When an IR system categorizes the search results into an ontology, such as the ODP, the different search items will be categorized into different categories. For example, returned items about the animal jaguar may be classified under the category *Science: Biology: Flora and Fauna*. Other returned items may be categorized under categories like "*Shopping*" and "*Recreation*". When a user searches for information about the animal jaguar, he or she most likely selects the category *Science: Biology: Flora and Fauna*. The gyroidal IR system then presents the user only search results categorized under this category. Among these filtered search results, most of them are about the animal jaguar; the *precision* is thus expected to be improved. If there are still many irrelevant returned items under the selected category, selecting a more specific category will further limit the returned search results to be presented to the user according to the selected subcategory. The quality of search results is therefore expected to be improved by using this gyroidal pyramid interactive Web information retrieval model.

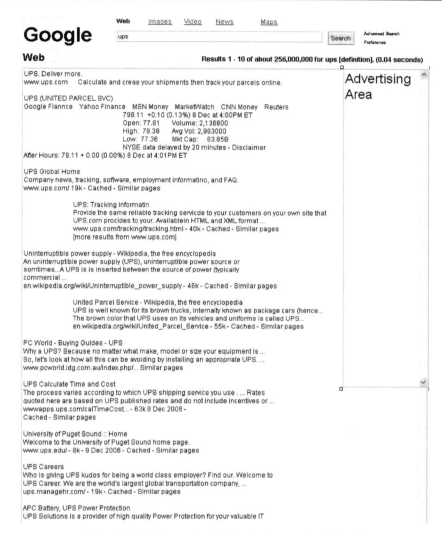

Figure 3-6 The first page returned by Google when searching for "ups"
Adaption of: *www.google.com*, retrieved on November 9, 2006

3.3 Using Web Services APIs to Retrieve Information from the Web

3.3.1 Web Service

"Web services provide a standard means of interoperating between different software applications, running on a variety of platform and/or frameworks" (Booth et al. 2004, p. 5). *Yahoo! Search Web Services* allow accessing Yahoo! content and services. *Yahoo! Search Web Services* are one of a list of Web Services provided by Yahoo! Using *Yahoo! Search Web Services APIs* allows a user application to retrieve *Yahoo! Web Search Systems* without leaving the user website or interface, and incorporates the results in a user application (Yahoo! Developers Network).

3.3.2 Yahoo! Search Web Services APIs

Yahoo! Search Web Services API allows searching the Internet for Web pages by submitting queries via Representational State Transfer (REST) (Fielding 2000), "a software architectural style for distributed hypermedia systems like the world wide web"(Wikipedia   http://en.wikipedia.org). Yahoo! has bundled together libraries and "example code" which illustrate how to access *Yahoo! Search Web Services* as a *Software Development Kit* (SDK). The SDK now supports many programming languages, such as Perl, PHP, Java, Python, JavaScript, and Flash. Some third-party SDKs include C sharp.net and Visual Basic.net. These SDKs are available to download from http://developer.yahoo.com/download/.

To use *Yahoo! Search Web Services APIs*, an application ID is needed. The ID can be applied for from http://developer.yahoo.com/search/index.html. For applications of non-commercial purpose, Yahoo! allows 100 queries for each application ID per day. For each query, the limits are usually 50 search results. Because users tend to view very few pages of search results (Chapter 2, section 2.3.1), 50 search results will not have too many negative effects on this study. Google also provides Web Services API; however, the limitation is ten search results per query. This limitation is the main reason *Google Web Services* is not used in this study.

The following simple example demonstrates how to use Java to access *Yahoo! Search Web Services API*.

```
import com.yahoo.search.*;
import java.io.IOException;
/** Code for using the Yahoo! Java API to perform a web search.
 * Adapted from Ryan Kennedy
 */
public class WebSearch {
    public static void main(String [] args) {

        // Create the search client. Pass in an application ID.
        SearchClient client = new SearchClient("application-ID");

        // Create the web search request. In this case using searching term "jaguar".
        WebSearchRequest request = new WebSearchRequest("jaguar");

        try {
            // Submit the search request to Yahoo! to execute the search.
            WebSearchResults results = client.webSearch(request);
            // Print out how many hits were found.
            System.out.println("Found " + results.getTotalResultsAvailable() +
                " hits for jaguar! Displaying the first " +
```

```
                results.getTotalResultsReturned() + ".");
        // Iterate over the results.
        for (int i = 0; i < results.listResults().length; i++) {
                WebSearchResult result = results.listResults()[i];
                // Print out the document title and URL.
                System.out.println("      " + (i + 1) + ": " + result.getTitle() + " - " +
                result.getUrl());
        }
    }
    catch (IOException e) {
        // Most likely a network exception of some sort.
        System.err.println("Error calling Yahoo! Search Service: " + e.toString());
        e.printStackTrace(System.err);
    }
    catch (SearchException e) {
        // An issue with the XML or with the service.
        System.err.println("Error calling Yahoo! Search Service: " + e.toString());
        e.printStackTrace(System.err);
    }
  }
}
```

3.4 Semantic Characteristics Extraction from the ODP

The Open Directory Project (ODP) was set up by Rich Skreta and Bob Truel in June 1998 in response to the shortcomings of *Yahoo! Web Directory* (Sherman 2000). Maintained by a small group of editors, the growth of *Yahoo! Web Directory* could not keep pace with the explosive growth of the Web. Spurred by the success of Open Source movement, the ODP originators reasoned that a Web directory could keep up with the growth and decay speed of the Internet, if there were enough volunteer editors to index the Internet. Practice has proven they are correct. Since creation of the ODP, the number of volunteers, the indexed Web pages, and the categories are all growing rapidly (Sherman 2000). Today, the ODP is the largest, most comprehensive human-edited directory of the Web (http://www.dmoz.com/about.html). It now contains over 4 million submitted Web sites, 74,719 editors and 590,000 categories (on 25 January 2007), and these numbers are increasing continuously. The size of the RDF/XML format content file of the ODP is now 311MB (http://rdf.dmoz.org/rdf/ on 25 January 2007). Under each category, there are several subcategories, a *description* of the category, and a list of submitted Web pages, each with a concise and accurate *description* of the submitted page. All the data included in a category is actually a further explanation of the category; this data therefore represents the semantic characteristics of the category. For a given document, if it has the most similarity with the semantic characteristics of a category, the document can be assigned to that category. This intuition is the foundation of the study. This section will address how to extract the semantic characteristics of each category in the ODP[19].

3.4.1 The ODP

The ODP is a Web directory of Internet resources and it is the most widely distributed data base of Web content classified by humans (http://www.dmoz.org/about.html). A Web directory is somewhat like a huge reference library. The directory is arranged in a hierarchical structure, the broader topic is on the higher level of the structure, the more specific subject is placed in the lower level of the structure. All the Web pages submitted to the ODP are subject to human editor evaluation (The Open Directory Project).

Each of the categories in the ODP contains the *title* and the *topic* of the category, a number of *subcategories,* a *description* of the category, and a list of *submitted Web pages.* The *topic* of the category is a full path from the root of the ODP to the specific category; for example, "Top: Science: Biology: Flora and Fauna" is the *topic* of the category "Flora and Fauna". The *title* of a category does not include its super-categories, for example, "Flora and Fauna" is the *title* of category with the *topic* "Top: Science: Biology: Flora and Fauna". The *description* of the category is usually a further explanation of the meaning of the category, and some informative and subjective matters about the category. It may also contain some editorial information to emphasise what kind of Web sites should not be submitted under this category. This editorial information is not semantically related to the category, and will not be extracted as the semantic characteristics of the category. For each submitted Web page, beside the *title* to identify the site, there is also a concise and accurate *description* of the Web page which tells the end users what they will find when the site is visited.

3.4.2 The Hierarchical Structure of the ODP

Categories in the ODP are hierarchically structured as shown in Figure 3-7. From the Root category, the ODP (or TOP), there are 15 first level categories. In addition to the 15 categories, category "World" supports the ODP in different languages. Figure 3-8 is a screenshot of the 15 + 1 categories; it is also the home page of the ODP.

Each of the fifteen first level ODP categories has its own subcategories. For example, under category "Society", the level two subcategories are: Activism; Advice; Crime; Death ... and so on. Figure 3-9 is a screenshot of the subcategories of the category "Society". Subcategories under the category "Society" may have their own sub-subcategories, and these sub-subcategories may in turn each have their own subcategories, until a category reaches the end (leaf node) of the tree structure.

---

[19] Issues of using the ODP are discussed in Chapter 4, section 4.3.4

Each category in the ODP can be identified by the *topic* of the category. For example, "Top: Society: Future: Utopias" is the *topic* of the category titled "Utopias"; its direct supercategory is "Future"; its first level supercategory (immediately after "Top") is "Society".

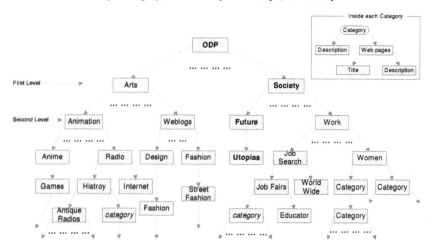

Figure 3-7 The hierarchical structure of the ODP

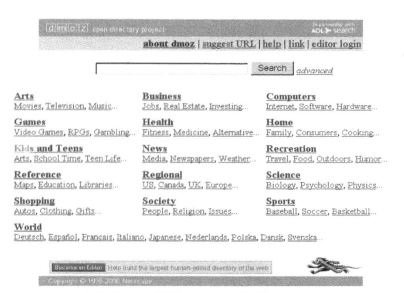

Figure 3-8 The 15 + 1 first level categories of the ODP
Source: *www.dmoz.com*, retrieved on September 9, 2006

One subcategory may be arranged under more than one category in the ODP. If an @ character (symbolic link) runs after the name of a subcategory, it indicates that although this subcategory is arranged under this category, it is originally categorized at another category. For example, in Figure 3-9, there is an @ character running after the category "Economics". When "Economics" is clicked, it reaches "Top: Science: Social Sciences: Economics". This indicates that the category "Economics" is originally categorized under the category "Top: Science: Social Sciences: Economics"; nevertheless, it can also be classified under "Top: Society".

In this research, each returned search result is categorized into only one category to avoid confusion; that is, subcategories are only arranged under their original supercategory. A category with an @ character is not considered as a subcategory of the category in which it appears.

3.4.3 Semantic Characteristics of the ODP

Most categories in the ODP contain four parts, the *topic* of the category, *subcategories*, the *description of the category,* and a *list of submitted Web pages,* each with the *title* of the Web page, and a concise and accurate *description* of the submitted page. The information included in the category can be used to represent the *semantic characteristics* of the category, and the semantic characteristics can then be utilized to categorize and filter search results.

The *topic* of the category is actually the path from the root of the ODP hierarchy to the given category. It shows how to gradually narrow down from the most general concepts (the whole Web) to the more specific concepts represented by the category. Each category lower down the hierarchical structure represents a more specific concept. The concepts represented by supercategories are relevant to the given category.

Most categories have a *"Description"* link. The *description* of a category gives further explanation of the meaning of *topic*, what subcategories are included in this category, some informative and subject matters about the category, and sometimes editorial information to guide the Web submitters as to what kind of Web sites should not be submitted under this category. For example, the editorial information about "Recreation: Autos: Makes_and_Models" is:

> *Please try and find the most specific subcategory that your site would be suited to.*
> *Auto dealership sites should be submitted to the proper location in Regional. Dealership links will NOT be listed anywhere in Recreation/Autos.*
>
> *If your site is selling products online, please submit your site to the proper subcategory of Shopping/Vehicles. Such sites will NOT be listed anywhere in Recreation/Autos.*

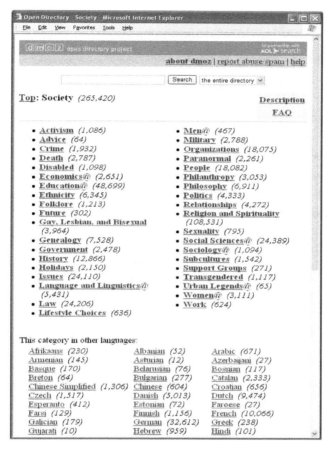

Figure 3-9 Subcategories of the category "Society" in the ODP
Source: www.dmoz.com, retrieved on November 12, 2006

As can be seen from the above citation, editorial information is not semantically related to the category because it only instructs how to find a proper category and not to include a category or to submit a Web page, and is thus not be used to represent the semantic characteristics of the category.

For each submitted Web page under a category, in addition to a *title* to identify the site, there is also a concise and accurate informative *description* of the Web page which informs the end users what they will find when the site is visited. The *title* and the brief *description* are semantic characteristics of the Web page submitted under the category. The submitted Web pages under a category are actually a cluster of semantically related Web pages which are considered suitable to be classified under the category. They can therefore be used to represent the semantic characteristics of the category. Figure 3-11 shows a list of the submitted Web pages with their brief *description*s under the category "Science: Biology: Flora and Fauna".

Two kinds of information in a category are not used to represent the semantic characteristics of the category. The first type is the name of the subcategories under the category. Each subcategory has its own semantic characteristics, its own *description*, and submitted Web pages. Therefore, using subcategories to represent the semantic characteristics introduces noise to both the category and its subcategories. Another type of information comes from the "FAQ" part of some categories. FAQ contains some useful information about where is the best place to submit a Web page. Some information contained in the FAQ may semantically relate to the category. However, most of the information in the FAQ relates to other categories. This can be seen from Figure 3-10 where most of the information is irrelevant to the category.

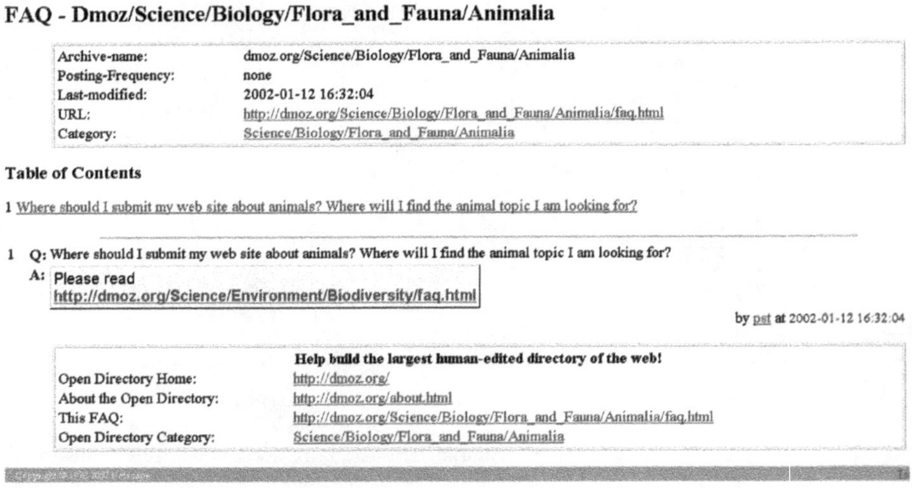

FAQ - Dmoz/Science/Biology/Flora_and_Fauna/Animalia

Archive-name:	dmoz.org/Science/Biology/Flora_and_Fauna/Animalia
Posting-Frequency:	none
Last-modified:	2002-01-12 16:32:04
URL:	http://dmoz.org/Science/Biology/Flora_and_Fauna/Animalia/faq.html
Category:	Science/Biology/Flora_and_Fauna/Animalia

Table of Contents

1 Where should I submit my web site about animals? Where will I find the animal topic I am looking for?

1   Q: Where should I submit my web site about animals? Where will I find the animal topic I am looking for?
   A: Please read
      http://dmoz.org/Science/Environment/Biodiversity/faq.html

by pst at 2002-01-12 16:32:04

	Help build the largest human-edited directory of the web!
Open Directory Home:	http://dmoz.org/
About the Open Directory:	http://dmoz.org/about.html
This FAQ:	http://dmoz.org/Science/Biology/Flora_and_Fauna/Animalia/faq.html
Open Directory Category:	Science/Biology/Flora_and_Fauna/Animalia

Figure 3-10 FAQ screenshot of "Science: Biology: Flora_and_Fauna: Animalia"
Source: www.dmoz.com, retrieved on November 12, 2006

Combining the *topic* of the category, the *description* of the category, and the submitted Web pages under this category (*title* and brief *description* of each page) can form a *category-document* which represents the semantic characteristics of the category. The following example demonstrates how to form a *category-document*.

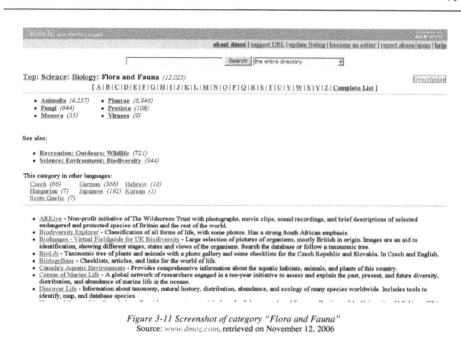

Figure 3-11 Screenshot of category "Flora and Fauna"
Source: *www.dmoz.com*, retrieved on November 12, 2006

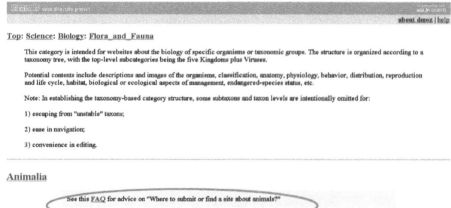

Figure 3-12 Screenshot of "Description" of category "Flora and Fauna"
Source: *www.dmoz.com*, retrieved on November 12, 2006

Figure 3-11 is the screen of the category "Flora and Fauna". Figure 3-12 is the screenshot of the *description* of the category "Flora and Fauna". The *category-document* of the category "Flora and Fauna" is composed of the following elements:

1) The *topic* of the category: "Science: Biology: Flora and Fauna".
2) The *description* of the category as demonstrated in Figure 3-12.
3) The submitted Web pages with a brief *description* (Figure 3-11).

3.5 Indexing the ODP Data

With all the formed *category-documents*, a document set, or a document collection D, is consequently constructed. However, before indexing the documents, some pre-processing, such as stop word removing, stemming, and feature selection/extraction (Chapter 2, section 2.5.3) is needed. Appendix 2 is an English stop word list given by Wikipedia. Port and Port2 (Porter 2006) stemming algorithms are presented by Snowball[20]. In this study, feature space is not further reduced because the calculation cost is not so high at present; on the other hand, effectiveness of categorization is essential for this study.

To weight the terms in each of the *category-documents*, let T be a term set, and for any given term t_i in document $d_j \in D$, $t_i \in T$, and for any $t_i \in T$, there always exists at least one $d_j \in D$ and $t_i \in d_j$. Further, let N be the total number of documents in D, R is total number of terms in T. Term frequency $tf_{i,j}$ can be calculated by (refer to Chapter 2, section 2.2.3)

$tf_{i,j} = freq_{i,j} / max_l \, freq_{l,j}$

$freq_{i,j}$ is the raw frequency of term t_i in document d_j, and $max_l \, freq_{l,j}$ is the maximum term frequency in document d_j.

Inverse Document Frequency (idf) for term t_i can be calculated by the following formula:

$idf_i = \log_2(N / n_i)$

where n_i is the documents number where term t_i appears.

Then, the tf-idf term weighting scheme can be given by

$w_{i,j} = tf_i \times idf_i = (freq_{i,j} / max_l \, freq_{l,j}) \times \log_2 (N / n_i)$

For the query (information request), the weight can be computed by

$w_{i,q} = t_q \times idf_q = (0.5 + 0.5 \times freq_{i,q} / max_l \, freq_{l,q}) \times \log_2 (N / n_i)$

Here, $freq_{i,q}$ is the raw frequency of the term k_i in the text of the query q.

3.6 Using Vector Space Model as a Classifier to Categorize Search Results

So far, search results are returned by utilizing *Yahoo! Search Web Services API*; the semantic characteristics of each category in the ODP are represented by a constructed *category-document*. To arrange each of the search items returned from *Yahoo! Search Web Services API* to an appropriate category, or to categorize the search items into the ODP categories, many categorization algorithms

---

[20] "*Snowball* is a small string processing language designed for creating stemming algorithms for use in Information Retrieval." http://snowball.tartarus.org

are available. For simplicity and effectiveness reasons (Chapter 2, section 2.4), cosine similarities between each returned items and *category-documents* are calculated, and each of the returned items is consequently classified based on the calculated similarities. VSM is selected for its proven effectiveness and simplicity (Chapter 2, section 2.1).

3.6.1 VSM as a Classifier

Each *category-document* in the document collection D is actually a high dimensional vector which can be denoted as vector $\vec{d}_j$. The search results returned by the *Yahoo! Search Web Services API* are taken as query vectors, therefore, the similarity between query vector $\vec{v}_q$ (returned item from the *Yahoo! Search Web Services API*) and $\vec{d}_j$ (j = 1, 2, ... N) can be measured as:

$$sim(\vec{v}_q,\vec{d}_j) = \frac{\vec{v}_q \bullet \vec{d}_j}{|\vec{v}_q| \times |\vec{d}_j|} = \frac{\sum\limits_{i=1...N} W_{i,j} \times W_{i,q}}{\sqrt{\sum\limits_{i=1...N} W_{i,j}^2 \times \sum\limits_{i=1...N} W_{i,q}^2}}$$

For each query vector $\vec{v}_q$, the similarity between this query vector and the *category-document* vector $\vec{d}_j$ (j = 1, 2, ..., N) will be ranked decreasingly by the calculated similarity. The search result item represented by $\vec{v}_q$ can thus be classified to the category represented by the *category-document* $\vec{d}_j$ if $\vec{d}_j$ is the top ranked document in the similarity list of vector $\vec{v}_q$ and $\vec{d}_j$ (j = 1, 2, ..., N). In this research, a modified *Majority Voting* scheme (Sebastiani 1999) is employed to arrange $\vec{v}_q$ based on the ranked similarity list.

3.6.2 Utilizing TreeView to Represent the ODP Hierarchical Structure

The *TreeView*[21] scheme is adopted to represent the ODP hierarchical structure, because it is one of the most convenient tools to represent a structured hierarchy. Users can browse the ODP Web knowledge structure by traversing the *TreeView*. However, the ODP now has established more then 590,000 categories and the hierarchical structure is more than nine levels deep. If all of the categories are represented by a *TreeView*, the *TreeView* will become very hard to browse; users will easily get lost among the very complex hierarchy. On the other hand, for the purpose of disambiguating search-terms, in most cases, the categories in the first two levels of the ODP are sufficient, because there are 573 categories contained in these two levels of the ODP. **The** *TreeView*

---

[21] The TreeView component is a user interface control that can be used to create a variety of hierarchical dynamic tree structures. http://developer.yahoo.com/yui/treeview/

in this study is composed of the 15 first-level categories of the ODP and their direct subcategories. All the rest of the categories are represented by their supercategories within the *TreeView*. Dumais and Chen (2000) also utilize a two level hierarchical structure to classify Web content.

3.6.3 Assign a Search Item into an Appropriate Category in the ODP

Considering only the top ranked documents in the ranked list may sometimes assign search items inappropriately (Frommholz 2001). The scenario is demonstrated in Figure 3-13. Suppose that for a query q, there are five *category-documents* selected, *category-document* numbered 1-3 has the highest similarity score followed by the *category-document* numbered 2-2, 2-3, 2-5, and lastly *category-document* 15-1. Categorizing q to category 1-3 is not appropriate, because category 2-2 is arguably more proper. To counter the possibly negative effect of *ad arbitrium* consideration of only the top document, *Majority Voting* (MV) strategy (Sebastiani 1999) is employed and adapted in this study. For the first k *category-documents* in the ranked list of the VSM classifier, the majority *category-document* of $(k+1)/2$ voting, if it exists, is taken as the category to assign the query. If no such majority vote exists, then the first ranked *category-document* is simply selected as the category.

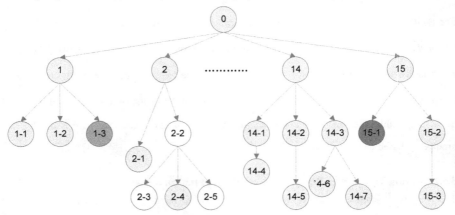

Figure 3-13 Demonstration of Majority Voting

3.7 Filtering Search Results Based on the ODP Lightweight Ontology

With the search results classified based on the ODP as a Web content directory, search results are now "clustered" according to the topics/categories in the ODP, and users can now select the interesting topics. Once a topic/category is selected, the search results will be filtered, and only the documents related (categorized) to the selected topic are presented to the user. This is an interactive process. The users can select different categories at their will until their information needs are satisfied. With the assistance of the categorized Web search results, it is expected the user can find the relevant documents effectively and efficiently.

3.8 An Example to Illustrate VSM as a Classifier

To illustrate how VSM can be used as a classifier, an example which uses real data from the ODP is presented in Appendix 15. In the example, four *category-documents* are formed, the number of indexed terms is 72, and the search-terms are "jaguar" and "jaguar vehicle".

3.9 Design Principle and Alternatives

The main concern of this research is to design a special search-browser which 1) allows a user to choose an interesting topic from a tree like human-edited Web knowledge structure manifested by the ODP; 2) disambiguates search-terams based on the selection of the user by filtering out irrelevant search results and presenting with users only results categorized under the topic chosen. The search-browser is then evaluated by the measures of *precison* and *recall* to examine the improvement of relevant of the search strategy proposed. At this research stage, the design rationale of usuability engineering (Nielsen 1993, pp.115-155) and software engineering (Sommerville 2004) are less concerned. However, the following principles are followed when designing the special search-browser. The design alternatives are also discussed.

Effectivity

The algorithm selected to categorize the returned Web search results should work effectively. In this research, categorization process is actually to compare the similarities between each returned search results with the category-documents. VSM (Chapter 2, section 2.2.2) and the probability model (Crestani et al. 1998) are the two most effective IR models at present (Chapter 2, section 2.2.1) and both are satisfied effectivity requirement.

Web search results can be obtained by developing a search engine, or utilizing Web search service APIs provided by Google or Yahoo!. Building a search engine requires a lot of resources[22] and obvious not satisfy the effciency criterion as discussed below. Google limits the returned search results for each query to ten for non-commercial license. This small number of returned item is hard to test the effective of categorization algorithm and thus not acceptable. Yahoo! provides 50 search items for each query and this is much better than that of Google's ten results limitation for this research, although a bigger figure is more appropriate for the categorization purpose.

Efficiency

The search results returned from search engines should be categorized on-the-fly; therefore, efficiency is very important. Probability model, according to Baeza-Yates and Ribeiro-Neto (1999, p. 30), is not as efficiency as VSM and thus not accepted in this research.

---

[22] refer to http://en.wikipedia.org/wiki/Search_engines (Retrieved on 26th May, 2007)

Using build-in tree component to represent the Web knowledge structure is also for the efficiency purpose because it works faster than other information visualization metaphor like the one employed by Kartoo (www.kartoo.com)

3.10 Summary

An approach aimed at improving the search result's quality was presented in this chapter. An interactive information retrieval model was first introduced which categorizes search results ontologically. Web search results are obtained by *Yahoo! Search Web Services API*, and the hierarchical structure of the ODP is serviced as an ontology. Each category in the ODP is represented by a *category-document* which is composed of the extracted semantic characteristics of the ODP category. The semantic characteristics of each ODP category is extracted from the *topic* of the category, the *description* of the category, and a list of submitted Web pages – each has a *title* and a brief *description* – under the category. VSM is employed as a classifier to categorize the Web search results into the ODP category. An example is presented to illustrate how to use the VSM to categorize the Web search results. In next chapter, implementation details of the proposed conceptual solution is presented, a special search-browser is developed.

Chapter 4.   Implementation

This chapter describes the implementation details of the special search-browser, based on the design presented in Chapter 3. It also presents how the first three objectives proposed in Chapter 1, section 1.8 are accomplished as the implementation of each designed outcomes. An overview of the special search-browser is first introduced in section 4.1. In section 4.2, the system structure diagram is discussed in detail. Section 4.3 addresses how to extract semantic characteristics from the ODP by utilizing JAXP. Section 4.4 discusses how to use Lucene to index the semantic ODP data. Section 4.5 presents the approach of using the Tree component of Java to represent the ODP ontology and thus to achieve objective one. Using *Lucene Searcher* – a modified VSM model – to classify search results is discussed in section 4.6. Ontologically filtering search results is presented in section 4.7. With all of the above have been implemented, the objective two and three are also achieved consequently. Finally, the summary of this chapter is provided in section 4.8.

4.1 Introduction

The aim of this study is to develop a special search-browser which combines search engine results, the ODP-based ontology as a navigator, and search results categorization to improve the quality of Web search results. The developed special search-browser is in fact a Web-oriented application. As discussed in Chapter 3, section 3.1, the special search-browser consists of four parts: the *Web search* engine component to obtain search results from Yahoo! by utilizing *Yahoo! Search Web Service API*; the *ODP semantic data extraction* component analyzes and extracts semantic characteristics of the ODP data; the *text categorization* part categorizes search results from Yahoo!, and then ontologically filters the search results based on user interaction; the last part is the *user interface* which focuses on input / output and interaction with users. Java is selected as the programming language because it is suitable for network environment programming, and the interfaces between Java and meta-search engines are widely supported. Java Studio Creator (http://developers.sun.com) is selected as the development platform. It is an easy-to-use Integrated Development Environment (IDE) for Web development based on the Java programming language. It allows building Web application visually, with minimal code creation. Its drag-and-drop (including Web services) components, automatic page navigation, and tree component supports are all attractive features to this application.

4.2 System Structure

The four parts of the special search-browser are illustrated in Figure 4-1.

Part A is a *Web search* engine interface. *Yahoo! Search Web Service API* is utilized to implement the search-term-based Web searching. The input of this part is users' search-terms (query), using

WebSearchRequest (String query) and *SearchClient. WebSearch (WebSearchRequest request)* of the *Yahoo! Search Web Service API*, Yahoo! returns a search result for the given query and stores the result in an instance of class *WebSearchResults*. This search result is the output of Part A, and it is also the input of Part C. *Google Web Services* also supports the same function, but for each query, only ten search results are available for a non-commercial licence. Therefore, in this research, *Yahoo! Search Web Services APIs* are employed.

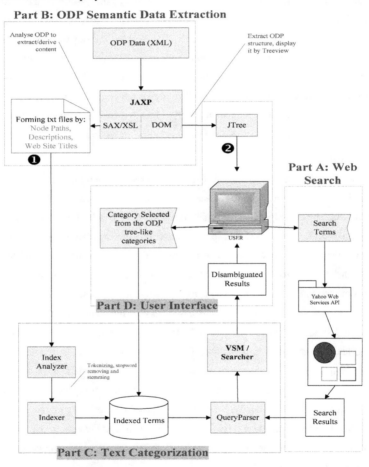

Figure 4-1 System structure of the special search-browser

The functions of Part B, the *ODP semantic data extraction* part, are to analyze the ODP data, and to extract the semantic characteristics of each category in the ODP by utilizing Java API for XML Processing (JAXP). The ODP data can be downloaded directly from the Web site of the ODP;

another approach is to crawl the home page of the ODP. In this research, the ODP data is downloaded from http://rdf.dmoz.org/rdf/.

Part B is further divided into two parts, B1 and B2, as shown in Figure 4-2. The goal of the first part of Part B (B1) is to produce a set of *category-documents* in text file format that can then be used by the Lucene search engine. Simple API for XML (SAX) and the eXtensible Stylesheet Language Transforms (XSLT) are both supported by JAXP and are employed to analyze the content and the structure of the ODP data. The ODP provides two separate RDF files: content.rdf, which contains all the related information of each category and links with each category; and structure.rdf which includes the category hierarchy information. The constructional elements of these text files include the *topic* of each category, the *description* of each category, and the *submitted Web sites* under this category with the brief *description* of these Web sites.

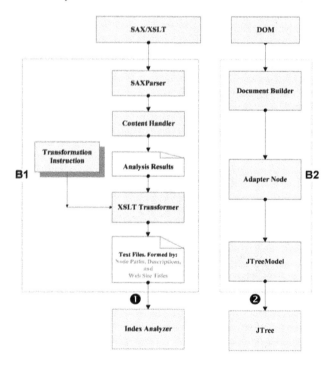

Figure 4-2 ODP semantic data extraction
(Part B of Fig 4-1)

The second part of Part B (B2) in Figure 4-2 extracts the hierarchy data of the ODP to be displayed by a *JTree* component of Java. In this part, the ODP hierarchical data is used to form an instance of the class Document Object Model (DOM). The node data of the DOM object is then adapted and taken as input by the object of the *JTreeModel* class. The *JTreeModel* object can then be used by the *JTree* object to display the hierarchical structure of the ODP data. An alternative to displaying the hierarchical structure data of the ODP is to create the JTree in design phase by adding the appropriate categories to the nodes of the JTree, or by utilizing items in a text file to form the nodes of the tree. This research uses the last scheme as described in section 4.5.

Part C of Figure 4-1 is the *text categorization* component which implements term indexing, searching, and search results categorization based on the hierarchical structured category of the ODP. Lucene is employed to achieve the objectives. The search engine takes the returned search results of Part A as queries. Each of the returned results is compared with the formed *category-documents* in Part B. MV (*Majority Voting*) strategy (Chapter 3, section 3.6.3, and section 4.6.3) is then used to pick up the most appropriate *category-document*. The category which is represented by the majority voted *category-document* will be marked in the corresponding position in the JTree to inform the user how the returned search results are classified according to the hierarchical structure of the ODP. The user then selects a category of interest which causes the results to be appropriately filtered and presented.

The *user interface* component is presented by Part D of Figure 4-1. The interaction between users and the special search-browser are implemented via this user interface. The Search-terms input area, search results display area, and *TreeView* are three main parts of the user interface as shown in Figure 4-12.

4.3 Extracting Semantic Characteristics from the ODP by JAXP

The ODP data is organized in two files, *structure.rdf* and *content.rdf*. The former contains category hierarchy information and the latter includes links within each category. To form the *category-document* (Chapter 3, section 3.4.3) which is composed of *topic* of the category, the *description* of the category, and a list of *submitted Web pages* (links) with their *descriptions*, data in both of the above two files needs to be analyzed and extracted. The first part (B1) in Figure 4-2 illustrates the techniques to form the *category-document* collection.

4.3.1 Data in structure.rdf file

The ODP is an open source project under the Open Directory Project Licence (http://www.dmoz.com/license.html), and all the ODP data is downloadable from http://rdf.dmoz.org/rdf. To illustrate the data structure of the ODP, *kt-structure.rdf.u8* (downloaded on 11 June 2006 at 10:05 a.m.) is used as an example because it gives a comprehensive structure of the subcategory of "Kids_and_Teens". Figure 4-3 is the corresponding screenshot of the category

"Kids_and_Teens"; Figure 4-4 is the screenshot of the *description* of the category
"Kids_and_Teens".

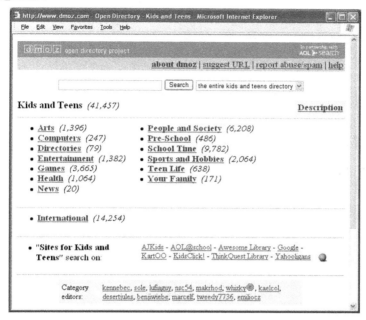

Figure 4-3 Screenshot of category "Kids and Teens"
Source: *www.dmoz.com*, retrieved on June 11, 2006

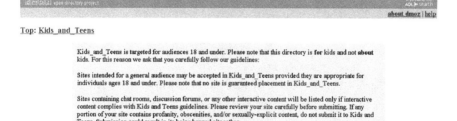

Figure 4-4 Screenshot of "Description" of category "Kids and Teens"
Source: *www.dmoz.com*, retrieved on June 11, 2006

The *kt-structure.rdf* file has the following xml format (only a very small part of the file is presented here, and the lines are numbered for the purpose of explanation) as shown in Figure 4-5:

```
1)    <?xml version='1.0' encoding='UTF-8' ?>
2)    <RDF xmlns:r="http://www.w3.org/TR/RDF/"
      xmlns:d="http://purl.org/dc/elements/1.0/"
      xmlns="http://dmoz.org/rdf">
3)    <!-- Generated at 2006-06-11 00:25:05 GMT on dust -->
4)    <Topic r:id="Top/Kids_and_Teens">
5)    <catid>471237</catid>
6)    <d:Title>Kids_and_Teens</d:Title>
7)    <d:Description>Kids and Teens is an Internet directory created especially for children and teenagers. It includes both
      sites designed specifically for children and/or .... </d:Description>
8)    <lastUpdate>2005-12-08 21:57:54</lastUpdate>
9)    <narrow1 r:resource="Top/Kids_and_Teens/Pre-School"/>
10)   <narrow1 r:resource="Top/Kids_and_Teens/Computers"/>
...
11)   </Topic>

12)   <Topic r:id="Top/Kids_and_Teens/Pre-School">
13)   <catid>468769</catid>
14)   <d:Title>Pre-School</d:Title>
15)   <d:Description>Sites in this category are aimed at children who cannot yet read. Subject matter ... with the 6-7 year age
      group. </d:Description>
...
16)   <narrow r:resource="Top/Kids_and_Teens/Pre-School/Animals"/>
17)   <narrow r:resource="Top/Kids_and_Teens/Pre-School/People"/>
...
18)   </Topic>
19)   <Topic r:id="Top/Kids_and_Teens/Pre-School/Animals">
20)   <catid>1379018</catid>
21)   <d:Title>Animals</d:Title>
22)   <d:Description>This category contains sites that ... games. </d:Description>
23)   <related r:resource="Top/Kids_and_Teens/School_Time/Science/Living_Things/Animals"/>
24)   <related r:resource="Top/Kids_and_Teens/Your_Family/Pets"/>
25)   <lastUpdate>2005-10-21 09:15:47</lastUpdate>
26)   <narrow2 r:resource="Top/Kids_and_Teens/Pre-School/Animals/Dinosaurs"/>
27)   <narrow2 r:resource="Top/Kids_and_Teens/Pre-School/Animals/Minibeasts"/>
28)   </Topic>
29)   <Topic r:id="Top/Kids_and_Teens/Pre-School/Animals/Dinosaurs">
30)   <catid>1379335</catid>
31)   <d:Title>Dinosaurs</d:Title>
32)   <d:Description>This category ... stories, songs and games. </d:Description>
33)   <related :resource="Top/Kids_and_Teens/School_Time/Science/The_Earth/Prehistoric_Times/Animals/Dinosaurs"/>
34)   <lastUpdate>2006-04-22 01:00:08</lastUpdate>
35)   </Topic>
...
```

Figure 4-5 Format of the ODP kt-structure.rdf

Lines 1 to 3 in Figure 4-5 are the head of the RDF file. Lines 4 to 11 are the XML description of the category "Kids and Teens" (note that category is called *"Topic"* in the RDF file) as shown in Figure 4-3. Elements of this category are enclosed between the <Topic> (line 4) and </Topic> tags (line 11). Each <Topic> tag has an r:id attribute (line 4) and encloses a <d:Description> tag (line 7), which encloses a topic description text. The <catid> (line 5) and <d:Title> (line 6) attributes stand for the *category identifier* and *category title* respectively. Text between <d:Description> and </d:Description> (line 7) is the description of the category. The content between lines 9 and 10 is the list of subcategories under the category "Kids and Teens", each of the subcategories is marked by a tag <narrow1 r:resource = "..." >.

Each of these subcategories under the category "Kids and Teens" has its own <Topic> and </Topic> pair which contains elements to describe these subcategories. Line 9 <narrow1 r:resource="Top/Kids_and_Teens/Pre-School"/> indicates that category "Pre-School" is a subcategory of "Kids and Teens". Data between lines 12 to 18 is the description of this subcategory, with a similar structure to the category "Kids and Teens". Figure 4-6 is the screenshot of the category "Pre-School". Information contained between lines 19 to 28 is the description of the category "Animals" which is a subcategory of "Kids and Teens/Pre-School". Furthermore, lines 29 to 35 describe the category "Dinosaurs", which is the subcategory of "Animals".

Figure 4-6 Screenshot of category "Pre-School"
Source: *www.dmoz.com*, retrieved on June 11, 2006

Based on the analysis above it can be seen that each category (topic) name is taken from the <Topic> tag's r:id attribute, that is, the path of the category follows directly after the tag "r:id=". Information between tags <d:Title> and </d:Title> only stands for the specific category (topic), and does not include it supercategories. The corresponding description information (if it has one) is enclosed within the tag pair <d:Description> and </d:Description>. Other elements, such as editorial information which contributes little to the semantics of the given category, are ignored in this research.

Because of the similarity of structure, the analysis process first identifies <Topic> and </Topic> pairs. Then, within each pair, extracting the topic name from the r:id tag, and the description text of this category, if there is a <d:Description> attribute. The category name and its corresponding description are organized into a java key-value hash data structure (java.util.HashMap) for later use.

4.3.2 Data in content.rdf file

The content.rdf file in Figure 4-7 contains all topics, their links (submitted Web pages, or resources) and resource descriptions. For example, kt-content.rdf is used to illustrate how to extract the data from the content.rdf file. Only part of the kt-content.rdf file is depicted in Figure 4-7. The corresponding screenshot is shown in Figure 4-8; the lines are numbered for the purpose of explanation. The kt-content.rdf file has the following xml format:

```
1)     <?xml version='1.0' encoding='UTF-8' ?>
2)     <RDF xmlns:r="http://www.w3.org/TR/RDF/"
       xmlns:d="http://purl.org/dc/elements/1.0/"
       xmlns="http://dmoz.org/rdf">
3)     <!-- Generated at 2006-06-11 00:25:05 GMT on dust -->
4)     <Topic r:id="Top/Kids_and_Teens">
5)     <catid>471237</catid>
6)     </Topic>
7)     <Topic r:id="Top/Kids_and_Teens/Pre-School">
8)     <catid>468769</catid>
9)     <link r:resource="http://www.enchantedlearning.com/rhymes/painting/"/>
10)    <link r:resource="http://www.megafile.com.br/"/>
...
11)    </Topic>

12)    <ExternalPage about="http://www.enchantedlearning.com/rhymes/painting/">
13)    <d:Title>Rebus Rhymes : EnchantedLearning.com</d:Title>
14)    <d:Description>Preschoolers paint ... they can read in their favorite rhymes.</d:Description>
15)    <ages></ages>
16)    <topic>Top/Kids_and_Teens/Pre-School</topic>
17)    </ExternalPage>
...
18)    <Topic r:id="Top/Kids_and_Teens/Pre-School/Animals">
19)    <catid>1379018</catid>
20)    <link r:resource="http://www.juliasrainbowcorner.com/html/animalsmain.html"/>
21)    <link r:resource="http://www.phonics.jazzles.com/html/freebie.html"/>
...
22)    </Topic>
23)    <ExternalPage about="http://www.juliasrainbowcorner.com/html/animalsmain.html">
24)    <d:Title>Julia's Rainbow Corner: Animals</d:Title>
25)    <d:Description>Play games ... and the noises they make.</d:Description>
26)    <ages>kids</ages>
27)    <topic>Top/Kids_and_Teens/Pre-School/Animals</topic>
28)    </ExternalPage>
....
```

Figure 4-7 Format of the ODP kt-content.rdf

- Activities in the Sunshine Room [Kids] - Online games, activities, and printable coloring pages to teach and reinforce basic skills.
- Ashley Marie's Playground for Kids [Kids] - Includes games, photos, songs, animations, and basic French.
- Bry-Back Manor [Kids] - Craft and activity ideas, and some Macintosh computer fun.
- ClassBrain [Kids] - Online games and educational activities for Pre-K and kindergarten children.
- Disney.com - Mouse House Jr. [Kids] - A place for preschoolers to play games, do online activities, read stories, and learn.
- Etch-a-Sketch [Kids] - Play with the online etch-a-sketch, color pages, read stories, play hidden shapes, numbers, and letters.
- Farm Service Agency for Kids [Kids] - Coloring, games, puzzles, agriculture trivia and cooking recipes. Parent's guide also provided.
- Fun with Spot [Kids] - Includes games, activities, and printable coloring pages featuring Spot and his friends. Requires Shockwave.
- Gamequarium [Kids] - Online learning games that teach numbers, alphabet, shapes and colors.
- Giraffism [Kids] - Offers educational online stories and teaches objects, letters, shapes and colours.
- Good Sports Gang [Kids/Teens] - Includes character profiles, games, coloring book, music, and an animated read along story.
- Identifying Time - The Hour [Kids] - Match the clock face to the time. Requires Flash plug-in.
- Interactica [Kids] - Animation and games for pre-readers. Following the metro to discover museum, park, music and English lessons.
- Jayzeebear [Kids] - Games and activities for children age 2 and up. Includes coloring book fun, memory game, counting and letters.
- Jeb, The Giraffe [Kids] - Fun character that introduces his friends and offers coloring pages.
- KidsCom Jr. [Kids] - Features games, coloring pages, art projects, stories, and other interactive content.
- Kidzone [Kids] - Some original kids artwork, recipes, music and fingerpaint ideas.
- Kikki's Workshop [Kids] - Learn about construction machines such as bulldozers or dump trucks. In Japanese and English.
- KinderArt [Kids] - A wide variety of activities for preschoolers. Includes fun learning and play activities.
- Lalitha's Nursery Rhymes [Kids] - Flash animations of traditional nursery rhymes and some pre-school oriented games and activities.
- Literacy Center [Kids] - Games with sound that teach shapes, colors, letters, numbers and keyboarding. Requires Flash plug-in.
- MegaFile [Kids] - Educational freeware and shareware games for children who do not read.
- Mimi Ella Morley Izzatt [Kids] - Introduces colors, shapes, alphabet, numbers and nursery rhymes.
- Nicky's Nursery Rhymes [Kids] - A collection of nursery rhymes and songs to share and enjoy, with pictures to print off and color in.
- Noggin [Kids/Teens] - Play games, check show times, and check in on Bert and Ernie, Franklin, Miffy and the gang.
- Nursery Rhymes and Silly Stuff [Kids] - Rhymes, pictures and music.
- Nursery Tutor [Kids] - Test number, letter, colors, and shapes knowledge with this tool.
- Oliver Morley's Play Site [Kids] - Playing, painting, sounds, pictures, animals, letters, numbers and story are all included.
- Peep and the Big Wide World [Kids] - Play science games and activities with Peep. Television show on IVO, TLC and Discovery Kids.
- Peter Rabbit Fun and Games [Kids] - With coloring pages, e-cards, games, activities, stories, and a description of the characters.
- Quaker Toddler Fun and Games [Kids] - Find activities organized by age, category, and season.
- Rebus Rhymes : EnchantedLearning.com [Kids] - Preschoolers paint online while picking out the words they can read in their favorite rhymes.
- Ronald.com [Kids] - Make magic, color, and play games like McNugget Moonbounce and Sauce Splat with all your McDonaldland friends!
- Theodore and Tilly-Bear's Funsite [Kids] - Stories and things to do introduced by two teddy bears.
- This is Daniel Cook. [Kids] - Explore, learn and create with Daniel Cook. Includes painting, write a song, create a story, and puzzles.

- **"Pre-School"** search on: AJKids - AOL@school - Awesome Library - Google - KartOO - KidsClick! - ThinkQuest Library - Yahooligans

Figure 4-8 Links (resources) under category "Kids and Teens/Pre-School"
Source: www.dmoz.com, retrieved on June 11, 2006

In Figure 4-7, lines 1 to 3 contain the RDF file head information. Data between lines 4 to 6 show that under the category "Kids and Teens", there are no external links. However, an empty template is provided. Information between lines 7 to 11 is an overview description of the links under category "Kids and Teens/Pre-School". Line 7 and 8 give the name of the category and the category identifier respectively. From line 9 to 11 is the list of Web addresses of the external links under this category. Each of the elements has a format <link r:resource="…">. The *title* of each of these external links and their brief *description* are followed immediately after each <Topic> and </Topic> pair. For example, content included between lines 12 to 17 provide the descriptive information of the Web site http://www.enchantedlearning.com/rhymes/painting, that is, the *title* of the Web site (line 13), the brief description of the Web site (line 14), and which category the Web site is submitted to (line 16). Information between line 18 to line 28 are similar to that of line 7 to line 17, which provide descriptive information of the external links under category "Kids and Teens/Pre-School/Animals", a subcategory of the category "Kids and Teens/Pre-School". The whole structure of the content.rdf file is similar to the structure described above.

According to the above analysis, all the categories in the ODP with their *descriptions* (if the *descriptions* exist) are extracted from the structure.rdf file. The name of submitted Web pages and their brief *descriptions* are extracted from the content.rdf file. By matching the topic in the two files, a text file, named as category-document for each category, is constructed for our purpose with the following three elements:

1) the *topic* of the category
2) the *description* of the category
3) a list of submitted Web pages with their brief *descriptions*

The full name of each topic (such as "Top/Kids_and_Teens/Pre-School/Animals") identifies different categories in the ODP. This is used to form the name for the textual *category-document*. Two minimal changes are made before using the topic name for naming the text file: first, note that the word "Top" is the same for all topics and contributes nothing for identifying the differences among categories and is therefore removed from the corresponding text file name. Second, the underscore character "_" is used as the separator between supercategory and subcategory instead of the slash ("/") character. To eliminate the confusion between the separator "_" with the underline used in some of the ODP categories, such as "Kids_and_Teens", a pre-process is performed to change the underscore in the topic to a dash "-", that is , "Kids_and_Teens" should be changed to "Kids-and-Teens". After the two processes, the corresponding text file name for the topic "Top/Kids_and_Teens/Pre-School/Animals" is changed to "Kids-and-Teens_Pre-School_Animals". From the name of the category, it is clear that the first level category is "Kids_and_Teens", the second level category is "Pre-School", and the third level category is "Animals".

Furthermore, the constructed textual *category-document* can be easily organized into a tree-like file directory structure, just as the files organized in Microsoft Windows. In fact, in this research, all the text files are stored in a directory tree structure which is the same as the directory tree structure of the ODP.

This design is acceptable for this prototype but in a future version the file structure could be replaced with a database.

4.3.3 Data in Submitted Web Pages

One potential approach to obtain more semantic data of each category is to download all the Web pages submitted under this category and index the content of these pages. However, there are two reasons preventing this research exploring the Web page content data at present.

1) The ODP has more than five million submitted Web pages and it is still growing. If all the Web pages are downloaded, the huge amount of data will affect indexing and searching effectiveness.
2) Many submitted Web pages include many multimedia components which not only contribute nothing to the semantic characteristics of the corresponding category, but also introduce noise to the category. Some Web pages are general purpose Web pages and thus have many irrelevant material and links in them.

4.3.4 Improperly Submitted Web Pages and Criticism on the ODP

Some Web pages are not submitted to the appropriate categories in the ODP. This may happen when the submitter of the Web pages notices only the meaning expressed by the *title* of the subcategory, but fails to notice the meaning expressed by the "topic" of the category (see section 3.4.1 about the difference between "*title*" and "*topic*" in the ODP). For example, a Web page with the *title* of "Y-Vote Mock Elections" was submitted to the category "Society/History/Education". However, the page aims to activate students by giving them the opportunity to stand as party candidates, or as speech writers in a mock election. Obviously, this page is education-related, but not really relevant much to the category "History". This kind of problem is out of the range of this research and is thus not addressed.

According to Open Directory Project (2007), there are allegations that volunteer ODP editors treat their own Web pages on high priority and concomitantly thwart the efforts of their competition. In this research, the main concern is if the submitted Web pages under a category are relevant to the category, and gives less attention to anything that is irrelevant to the process of semantic characteristics extraction. Therefore, this criticism has little impact on the semantic characteristics extraction process of each category of this research if only the submitted pages to the category are relevant to the category.

This section describes how to use JAXP to analyze and extract the semantic characteristics of the ODP category contained in two rdf file: content.rdf and structure.rdf. The *topic* of each category; the *description* of each category; and the submitted Web pages with the *titles* and the brief *descriptions* of the Web pages are used to form a *category-document* which is used as the input data of the *text categorization* part in Figure 4-1.

4.4 Using Lucene to Index the Semantic ODP Data

Lucene is a free text-indexing and searching API written in Java. It is a member of the Apache Jakarta family of projects, licensed under the liberal Apache Software License (http://www.apache.org/foundation/licence-FAQ.html). Lucene is composed of two main relatively independent parts, text indexing (Section 4.4.1) and text searching (Section 4.6), although indexing inherently affects searching (Gospodnetić & Hatcher 2005, pp. 10-11). This section discusses the Lucene indexing process and how to use Lucene to index the semantic data of the ODP. Index Analyzer and Indexer components of Part C in Figure 4-1 are two main components of Lucene to index text files.

4.4.1 Indexing with Lucene

The Lucene indexing process is composed of three major steps: converting data into text; analyzing the text; and writing the index; as shown in Figure 4-9. Lucene digests always plain text format data. Therefore, before passing on data to Lucene to analyze, the data in other formats, such as HTML, XML, RDF, or MS WORD needs first be converted into plain text (Gospodnetić & Hatcher 2005, p. 19 & p. 29). In this study, JAXP is employed to extract data (semantic characteristics of each category) from the ODP and to convert this data into plain text (see section 4.3).

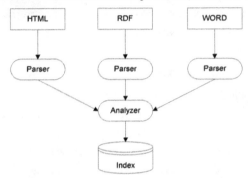

Figure 4-9 Lucene indexing
Adaption of: Gospodnetić & Hatcher 2005, p. 30

The Analyzer in Figure 4-9 converts plain text into the fundamental indexed representation - *terms*. The analysis process removes stop words, splits the textual data into chunks, or *tokens*, discards punctuation, removes accents from characters, lowercases the tokens, and so on. There are some different built-in *Analyzers* in Lucene. *WhitespaceAnalyzer* is the simplest one which only splits tokens at white space; *SimpleAnalyzer* divides text at non-letter characters and lowercases; *StopAnalyzer* in addition removes stop word. *StandardAnalyzer* is the most generally useful built-in analyzer which tokenizes terms on top of *StopAnalyzer* (Gospodnetić 2003a, 2003b, Gospodnetić & Hatcher 2005, pp. 109-121).

SnowballAnalyzer, supporting multi-language stemming algorithm, was created by Dr. Martin Porter who also developed the Porter stemming algorithm (Porter 2006). Snowball is a small language which processes strings. It is designed for creating stemming algorithms for use in IR. The *SnowballAnalyzer*, along with other language specific analyzers, is available in the Sandbox of Lucene.

The last step of Lucene indexing is the *writing index* which adds terms to the index. Lucene also uses an *inverted index* data structure to store the index terms (Chapter 2, section 2.2.4). "Inverted index" means that instead of attempting to search each document by checking if the document contains a given query Q, the inverted index structure is optimized for quick answering to the question of which documents contain the query Q. This structure is adapted by all the search engines today for its proven efficiency and effectiveness (Gospodnetić & Hatcher 2005, p. 31).

The Lucene *indexes* are organized as *segments, documents, fields,* and *terms.* One *index* consists of one or more *segments,* one *segment* has one or more *documents,* one *document* has one or more *fields,* one *field* contains one or more *terms.* Each term is a pair of *Strings* representing a field name and a textual value (Gospodnetić 2003a, 2003b, Gospodnetić & Hatcher 2005, pp. 395-399, see also Appendix 5). Figure 4-10 is the index structure of Lucene.

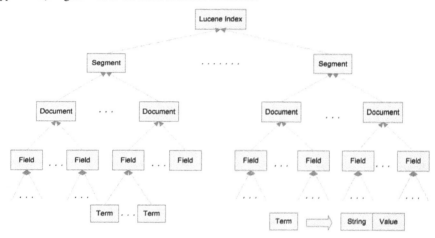

Figure 4-10 Lucene index structure

Lucene provides four fundamental classes for indexing text. They are *IndexWriter, Analyzer, Document,* and *Field. IndexWriter* is used to create a new index and to add *Documents* to an existing index. *Analyzer* takes plain text as input to extract indexable tokens out of the text and eliminates the rest (stop words, punctuation, accents). *Documents* are primary retrievable units in Lucene. *Documents* consist of a sequence of *fields.* Each *field* has a name, such as filename, author, year of publication, content of document, and so on. *Field* textual values are a sequence of terms; terms are the smallest units of the Lucene index (Gospodnetić 2003b).

The basic indexing operation code is relatively simple in Lucene. To index a text collection, Lucene prefers that plain text documents be organized in a file directory tree. The created index by Lucene can be assigned to another file directory. The following four steps illustrate how to utilize the above four Lucene classes, *IndexWriter, Analyzer, Document,* and *Field* to index a plain text document collection in a file directory and to store the built index in another file directory.

Step 1: Create an IndexWriter

An *IndexWriter* creates and maintains an index. Three parameters are needed to initialize an *IndexWriter* class: the *directory* where the index is to be stored; an *Analyzer* which analyzes the text; and a *Boolean variable* which indicates whether a new index is created, or whether an existing index is opened for the addition of new documents. Documents are added with the *addDocument()* method. The *close()* method should be called when documents adding process finished. In the case of no more documents being added, the call *optimize()* method can optimize search performance, as shown below (Apache Software Foundation 2006, Hatcher 2004).

```
public static void index (File indexDir, File dataDir) throws IOException {
    if (!dataDir.exist () || !dataDir.isDirectory ()) {
        throw new IOException (dataDir + "does not exist or is not a directory");
    }
    IndexWriter writer = new IndexWriter (indexDir, new StandardAnalyzer (), true);
    indexDirectory (writer, dataDir);
    writer.optimize ();
    writer.close ();
}
```

An instance of the class *IndexWriter*, *writer*, is created by the sentence *"IndexWriter writer = new IndexWriter(indexDir, new StandardAnalyzer(), true);"* – the last parameter is *"true"* which indicate a new index is to be created. To add documents into the index, *indexDirectory()* function is called which combines the created *writer* and *dataDir*, a directory instance where raw text document is stored.

The second parameter specifies that one of the Lucene built-in *Analyzers*, the *StandardAnalyzer()* is used to analyze the text documents. When using *SnowballAnalyzer()*, another two parameters are needed; one indicates the language of the text documents; and the other one indicates the corresponding stop words list. For example, when indexing English language documents, the following statement allows *SnowballAnlayzer()* be utilized to replace the standard Lucene built-in *StandardAnalyzer*.

```
Analyzer anlz = new SnowballAnalyzer ("English",
StopAnalyzer.ENGLISH_STOP_WORDS);
IndexWriter writer = new IndexWriter (indexDir, anlz, true);
```

Step 2: Locate Text Documents in a File Directory Tree

The next step is to locate each of the plain text documents to be indexed by *IndexWriter()*. The following code illustrates how to recursively call *indexDirectory()* which traverses the whole file directory tree indicated by an instance of File class.

```
private static void indexDirectory(IndexWriter writer, File dir) throws IOException {
    File [] files = dir.listFiles();
    for(int i=0; i<files.length; i++) {
    File f = files[i];
```

```
    if (f.isDirectory())
        indexDirectory (writer, f); //call recursively
    else if (f.getName().endsWith (".txt"))
        indexFile (writer, f);
    }
}
```

The *if* statement "*if(f.isDirectory()) indexDirectory(writer, f);*" recursively call *indexDirectory()* method when the currently processing file is still a directory but not a text document. Otherwise, if the "file" is a plain text file which ends with suffix ".txt", *indexFile()* method is called which indexes the plain text file with the created instance of *IndexWriter* class, *writer*.

Step 3: Create a Document for Each Text File with Proper Fields

The *indexFile()* method accepts two parameters; one is the text file to be indexed, and another is the *IndexWriter*. Note that *indexFile()* indexes one text file each time. Therefore, different fields can be created for different text files. However, if all the text files have an identical structure, the code will be very simple, as shown below:

```
private static void indexFile (IndexWriter writer, File f) throws IOException {
    Document doc = new Document (); //Document class of Lucene.
    doc.add (Field.Text("contents", new FileReader (f)));
    doc.add (Field.Keyword("filename", f.getCanonicalPath ()));
    writer.addDocument (doc);
}
```

An instance of class *Document* is created by the statement "*Document doc = new Document();*" *doc* is an empty *Document* without any fields. Suppose that the given text file has two interesting fields: filename and contents. Call *add()* method adds these two fields to the *doc*. *Field.Text()* method of *Field* class indexes and tokenizes the plain text specified by the second parameter. The filename is indicated by the first parameter. The *Field.Keyword()* method indexes and stores, but does not tokenize the plain text indicated by the second parameter. *Keyword* fields are useful for data which needs to stay unchanged like filenames, part numbers, primary keys, and so on.

In this research, the content of each *category-document* is added to a *field* of Lucene *Document* class named "contents", and the corresponding text file name is added to a field of Lucene *Document* class named "filename", as shown in the code in Figure 4-11.

Step 4: Add the Document to the IndexWriter Instance-writer

The last step is to add the indexed document to the *IndexWriter*. This can be simply implemented by coding as (the last code line in Step 3):

```
    writer.addDocument (doc);
```

in case all the proper fields of text have been added to the instance of Document class - *doc*.

4.4.2 Implementation of Indexing the ODP Data

Up to now, the semantic characteristics of each category in the ODP have been extracted and organized in a text file collection (section 4.3), and all the essential elements necessary to index the textual *category-document* with Lucene have also been discussed. The following source code assembles these elements to create an indexer class which indexes the created *category-documents*.

```java
/* indexer.java */
import java.io.File;
import java.io.IOException;
import java.io.FileReader;

...
/** @author Dengya Zhu **/
public class indexer {
    public static void index(File indexDir, File dataDir) throws IOException {
        if (!dataDir.exists () || !dataDir.isDirectory ()) {
            throw new IOException(dataDir + " does not exist or is not a directory");
        }
        SnowballAnalyzer analyzer = new SnowballAnalyzer ("English",
        StopAnalyzer.ENGLISH_STOP_WORDS);
        IndexWriter writer = new IndexWriter (indexDir, analyzer, true);
        indexDirectory (writer, dataDir);
        writer.optimize ();
        writer.close ();
    }
    private static void indexDirectory (IndexWriter writer, File dir) throws IOException {
        File[] files = dir.listFiles ();
        for (int i=0; i < files.length; i++) {
            File f = files[i];
            if (f.isDirectory()) {
                indexDirectory (writer, f);
            } else if (f.getName().endsWith(".txt")) {
                indexFile (writer, f);
            }
        }
    }
    private static void indexFile (IndexWriter writer, File f) throws IOException {
        System.out.println ("Indexing " + f.getName());
        Document doc = new Document();
        doc.add (Field.Text("contents", new FileReader (f)));
        doc.add (Field.Keyword ("filename", f.getCanonicalPath ()));
        writer.addDocument (doc);
    }
    public static void main (String[] args) throws Exception {
        File indexDir = new File ("indexedFileDir");
        File dataDir = new File ("textfileDir");
        index (indexDir, dataDir);
    }
}
```

Figure 4-11 Source code for indexing the created category-document

So far, the category-documents have been indexed and an indexed term collection (Part C of Figure 4-1) has formed. The indexed terms are then used as basic unit when searching categorizing described in Section 4.6 is performed. The following section will discuss how the objective one in Section 1.8 is achieved with the implementation of above two sections.

4.5 Using a Tree to Represent the ODP Lightweight Ontology

The categories in the ODP are organized hierarchically. The first level categories of the ODP include fifteen categories, and an extra "World" category is also included to support multi-languages (Chapter 3, section 3.4.2). Under each of the first level categories, there are second level categories. Table 4-1 shows the fifteen first level categories and the number of subcategories under each of them.

Table 4-1 The 15 first level categories of the ODP and the number of their subcategories

Category Name	Number of Subcategories
Art	51
Business	53
Computers	50
Games	32
Health	45
Home	25
Kids and Teens	13
News	24
Recreation	42
Reference	27
Regional	10
Science	29
Shopping	44
Society	38
Sports	90
	Total: 573

Under each of these second level categories, there are third level categories; under each of the third level categories, there are fourth level categories, and so on. The total category number of the first and the second levels of the ODP are 588 (15 + 573). For the purpose of disambiguating and filtering Web search results, 588 categories are enough, because a deeper hierarchical structure with hundreds or thousands of categories is practically too complex and users easily get lost amongst the complex structure. The user's usual concern is only the first few pages of Web search results; they prefer simplicity (Jansen & Spink 2006, Spink et al. 2002). Therefore, in this research, only the first two levels of categories are presented in the developed special Web search-browser.

The two levels of the ODP categories can be constructed and represented by the *Tree Node component* of Sun Java Studio Creator 2. The Tree Node component allows creating a node in a hierarchical tree structure. Tree node is used to represent the categories in the ODP, and the two-level structure of the ODP can be represented by the hierarchical tree structure of these Tree Node components. Figure 4-12 is a screenshot of the interface of the special search-browser. The left part of the interface is the ODP category tree. Each of the nodes in the ODP tree represents a category in the ODP directory, and can be expanded and collapsed based on users' selection.

This section introduced how to use a JTree to represent the hierarchical structure of the ODP. The left part of Figure 4-12 is the concrete representation of the JTree component in Figure 4-1 and Figure 4-2.

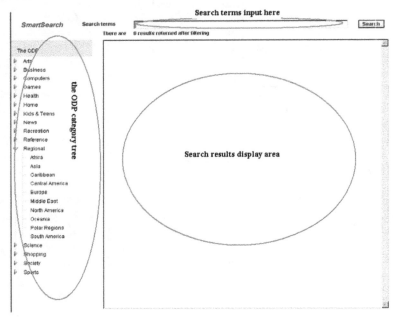

Figure 4-12 An interface screenshot of the special search-browser

The semantic characteristics of each category in the ODP have been represented by the *category-document*, and the Web directory is also represented hierarchically by a tree like structure, **the objective one of this research (Chapter 1,** section 1.8) **is now achieved.** The problems of poorly organized search results (Chapter 1, section 1.5) and mismatching human mental model of clustering engines (Chapter 1, section 1.6) are improved because the search reslts are now hierarchically organized based on the widely used human edited Web directory – the ODP.

4.6 Using Lucene Searcher to Classify Search Results

Lucene utilizes a modified and extended VSM (to be discussed in section 4.6.3) to calculate the similarities between a query and the indexed *category-documents* described in section 4.4. Each of the indexed documents represents the semantic characteristics of the corresponding category in the ODP. Given a search result Q returned by *Yahoo! Search Web Service API*, the similarities between Q and each of these indexed documents are calculated by Lucene. Based on the calculated similarities, Q is to be classified to the ODP category that has the similar score to Q. That is, the search result will be categorized to the ODP category when its semantic characteristics representation, a *category-document*, is assigned to the highest cosine similarity score with Q, or decided by MV strategy (Chapter 3, section 3.6.3). This section first discusses how the cosine similarity formula introduced in Chapter 2 section 2.2.2 are adapted in Lucene, then discusses how to search an index and, finally, provides the implementation details of search results classification.

4.6.1 Cosine Similarity Calculation in Lucene

Lucene provides a powerful similarity score calculation schema (*Formula 4-1*) with considerably many boosting factors that allow complex and flexible searching. Nevertheless, its default scoring strategy is actually a modified VSM. The details of Lucene's similarity score calculation formula is discussed below.

The similarity score between a query **q** and a document **d** is defined in terms of these methods as (Apache Software Foundation 2006, Gospodnetić & Hatcher 2005, pp. 78-80):

score (**q, d**) =

$$\sum_{t \, in \, q} (tf \times (idf)^2 \times boost(t,q) \times boost(t.field,d) \times LN(t.field,d)) \times coord(q,d) \times QN(ssw)$$

.... *Formula 4-1*

Table 4-2 is the description of these factors. Note that boost factors provide a flexible way to affect a query or field's influence on a similarity score.

The above factors are encapsulated by Lucene in a class called *Similarity*, with other methods which are related to the calculation of cosine score. The *Similarity* class is an abstract class; the default implementation of this class in Lucene is class *DefaultSimilarity*. This structure allows a specific application to overload these methods to provide its own cosine similarity calculation method. This research employs directly the *DefaultSimilarity* class to calculate the similarity between search results returned from Yahoo! and the *category-documents* that represent the semantic characteristics of categories in the ODP.

By default, the cosine similarity calculation formula is simplified to:

$$score(\vec{q},\vec{d}) = \sum_{t \in q}(tf \times (idf)^2 \times \frac{1}{\sqrt{numTerms}}) \times \frac{1}{\sqrt{\sum_{t \in q}(idf)^2}}$$

$$= \sum_{t \in q}(\sqrt{\frac{freq}{numTerms}} \times (idf)^2) \times \frac{1}{\sqrt{\sum_{t \in q}(idf)^2}}$$

$$= \sum_{t \in q}(\sqrt{\frac{freq}{numTerms}} \times (\log\frac{numDocs}{docFreq+1}+1)^2) \times \frac{1}{\sqrt{\sum_{t \in q}(\log\frac{numDocs}{docFreq+1}+1)^2}}$$

where $\dfrac{1}{\sqrt{\sum_{t \in q}(\log\frac{numDocs}{docFreq+1}+1)^2}}$ = QN(ssw) is a normalization factor of query q.

4.6.2 Searching in Lucene

The core classes to perform the basic search operations are *IndexSearcher, Term, Query, TermQuery* and *Hits*. Searching in Lucene without considering boosting factors is very simple; only a few lines of code are needed. First, instances of class *IndexSearcher* and *FSDirectory* are constructed to create a Lucene searcher to search the directory indicated by *FSDirectory* where the created *index* is stored. *QueryParser* parses a human-readable *query* into *Query* class. *Search()* method of class *Hits* takes a *query* as parameter and searches against the created index. The *Hits* object contains references to the underlying documents which are obtained when call *Hits' doc* method () in a "lazy fashion" – only when requested with the *hits.doc(int)* call. The following code snippet illustrates how to use Lucene to perform a searching (Gospodnetić & Hatcher 2005, pp. 69-78).

```
{
    File indexDir = File new ("index dir"); //the directory path where index is stored
    ...
    String q = "java"; //obtain search-terms, here the search-term is "java"
    search(indexDir, q); //call search to perform searching
}
public static void search (File indexDir, String q) throws Exception
{
    Directory fsDir = FSDirectory.getDirectory(indexDir, false); //create a directory
    //create an IndexSearcher object and open index
    IndexSearcher is = new IndexSearcher(fsDir);
    Query query = QueryParser.parse(q, "content", new StandardAnalyzer()): //parse query
    Hits hits = is.search(query);  //searching index with given query
    for (int k = 0; k < hits.length(); k++ ) {
        Document doc = hits.doc(k); //retrieve matching document
        //process the retrieved document: display filename here
        System.out.println (doc.get("filename");
```

}
}

Table 4-2 Factors in cosine similarity score calculation

Factors	Meaning	Lucene's Default Implementation
tf	Term frequency.	$\sqrt{freq}$, freq – the frequency of a term within a document.
idf	A score factor based on the term's document frequency (the number of documents which contain the term).	idf = log (*numDocs* / (*docFreq*+1)) + 1, *numDocs* – the total number of documents in the collection *docFreq* – the number of documents which contain the term
boost (t, q)	Documents matching this q will (in addition to the normal weightings) have their score multiplied by boost.	boost(t,q) = 1.0
Boost (t.field, d)	Documents field matching this q will (in addition to the normal weightings) have their score multiplied by boost.	boost (t, q) = 1.0
LN (t.field, d)	The normalization value for a field given the total number of terms contained in a field	$LN = \dfrac{1}{\sqrt{numTerms}}$ *numTerms* – the total number of tokens contained in the field
coord (q, d)	A score factor based on the fraction of all query terms that a document contains.	$coord\ (q, d) = \dfrac{overlap}{\max Overlap}$ *overlap* – the number of query terms matched in the document *maxOverlap* – the total number of terms in the query
ssw	Sum of square weights	$\displaystyle\sum_{t\ in\ q}(idf \times boost(t,q))^2$
QN(ssw)	The normalization value for a query given the sum of the squared weights of each of the query terms. This does not affect ranking, but rather just attempts to make scores from different queries comparable.	$QN = \dfrac{1}{\sqrt{ssw}}$

IndexSearcher class includes several *search()* methods that are used to search what *IndexWriter* has indexed. A simple, typically used *search()* method takes only one *Directory* parameter which indicates where the index is located. For example, the following statement creates an IndexSearcher object:

IndexSearcher is = new IndexSearcher (FSDirectory.getDirectory ("/temp/index", false));

A *term* is the basic unit for indexing and searching; it contains the name of a field and the value of the field. Used with *TermQuery* object, a *Query* object can be created and passed to an *IndexSearcher* object for searching. The following code searches documents contain the search-term "java" in a field named "content".

Query q = new TermQuery (new Term ("content", "java"));

Hits hits = is.search(q);

Query is an abstract base class with many implemented subclasses such as *TermQuery, BooleanQuery, PhraseQuery, PrefixQuery, RangeQuery, FuzzyQuery,* and so on. Table 4-3 is a brief description of these classes (Gospodnetić & Hatcher 2005, pp. 81-100, Apache Software Foundation 2006).

A user's search needs vary dramatically; *QueryParser* uses human-readable textual query representation to construct one of the *Query* subclasses in Table 4-3. With the parsed query, searching is performed as if the query had been created directly by the subclasses of *Query*. *QueryParser* takes three parameters: a *search expression*; the *default field name*; and an *analyzer*. For example, "*Query query = QueryParser.parse (q, "content", new StandardAnalyzer ());*" uses *QueryParser's parse ()* method returns a *Query* object, q is the expression of user input query which is analyzed by *StandardAnalyzer ()* method. This statement also indicates the search is performed against the "content" field.

4.6.3 Implementation of Search Results Classification

In section 4.4.2, the *category-documents* have been indexed and stored in a directory "*indexedFileDir*" with two *fields*: contents and filename. Using *Yahoo! Search Web Service API*, 50 search results are returned for each query, and all the search results are stored in an instance of class *WebSearchResults* (Chapter 3, section 3.3.2). To categorize the returned search results to the hierarchical structure of the ODP, each of the search results is taken as a query, and searched against the indexed *category-documents* with Lucene *IndexSearcher*. For the top k *category-documents* in the ranked list of Lucene *IndexSearcher*, the majority *category-document* of $(k+1)/2$ voting, if exist, is chosen as the category to assign the query – search result from Yahoo!. As discussed in Chapter 3, section 3.6.3, if no such MV exists, then the first ranked *category-document* is simply selected as the category. Figure 4-13 is the flowchart of categorization processing. Figure 4-14 is the detailed categorizing process. Figure 4-15 is the MV processing flowchart, and Figure 4-16 is the implementation of the MV class. Note that in Figure 4-14, the vote number is assigned as three. In practice, K can be any odd natural number.

Table 4-3 Brief description of Query and its subclasses

Queries	Description
TermQuery	An elementary class matches documents containing a term.
BooleanQuery	A Query that matches documents matching Boolean combinations (AND, OR and NOT) of other queries such as TermQuery, PhraseQuery.
PhraseQuery	PhraseQuery matches documents containing a particular sequence of search-terms such as "New York". A PhraseQuery is built by QueryParser for input.
PrefixQuery	PrefixQuery matches documents containing terms beginning with a specified string. A PrefixQuery is built by QueryParser for input.
RangeQuery	RangeQuery retrieves documents within an exclusive range, e.g. (100 to 200). A RangeQuery is built by QueryParser for input.
FuzzyQuery	A Query retrieves documents containing similar terms. The similarity of a term is determined by Levenshtein distance algorithm[23] (Gilleland). QueryParser creates a FuzzyQuery by suffixing a term with a tilde (~).

This section introduced how the developed search-browser categorizes the returned search results from Yahoo!. The implementation details demonstrated how QueryParser and VSM searcher components of Figure 4-1, and *Majority Voting* strategy (Section 4.6.3, Figure 4-15, Figure 4-16) are used to achieve the categorization purpose.

4.7 Ontologically Filtering Search Results

With the classified search results, the corresponding categories in the ODP are marked. The user can then choose an interesting topic/category. To response the selection, the selected ODP category Tree node is expanded; at the same time, the search results are filtered based on the selection; that is, only the search results categorized under the selected category are presented to the user. If one of the subcategories is selected consequently, the search results are further filtered and only the search results categorized under the selected subcategory are presented to the user.

To implement the above process, three classes are designed to store the classified search results under each category. The filtering operation is achieved by calling the methods of the three classes. This section first describes the three classes, namely, *RetResults*, *ExTreeNode*, and *FirstLevelNode*. The relationship between these classes is then presented, and finally is the introduction of how to use the classes to filter the search results.

4.7.1 Using Classes to Re-organize and Store the Categorized Web Search Results

The following code shows some of the functions of class RetResults

---

[23] Levenshtein distance is also referred to as edit distance which measures the similarity between two strings. The distance is the number of deletions, insertions, or substitutions required to transform one string s to another string t. e.g. LD("test", "tent") =1, LD("tree", "three") = 1, and LD("distance", "distance") = 0.

```
public class RetResults {
     private static String title; //the title of the Web page
     private static String URL; //the URL for the Web page
     private static String summary; //summary text with the Web page
     ...
     public RetResults (); //constructor
     public RetResults (RetResults rr);
     public RetResults (String title, String url, String summary);

     public void setTitle ();
     public void setURL ();
     public void setSummary();
     ...
     public String getTitle ();
     public String getURL ();
     public String getSummary();
     public RetResults getRetResults ();

...

}
```

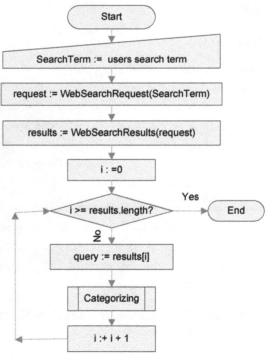

Figure 4-13 Categorization processing flowchart

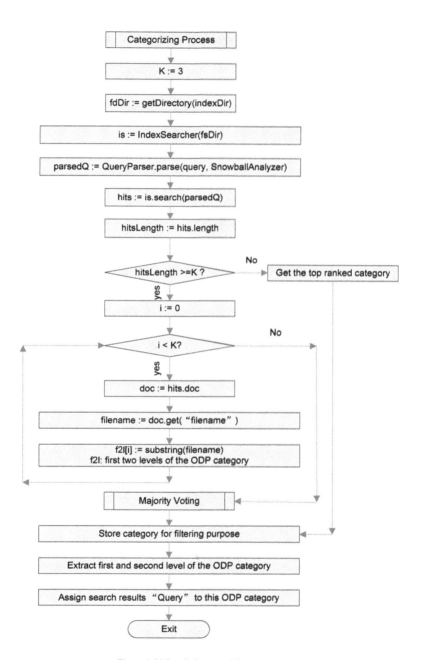

Figure 4-14 Detailed categorizing process.

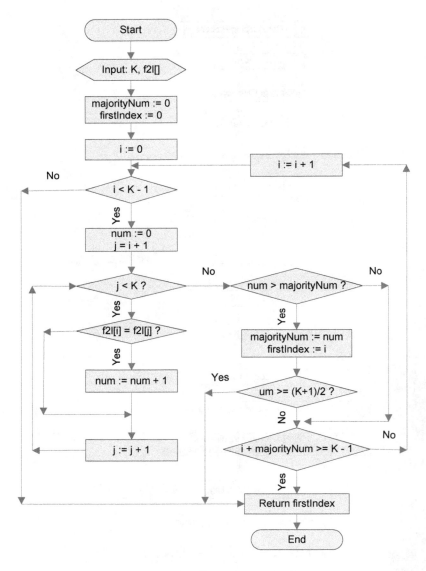

Figure 4-15 Majority Voting processing flowchart

```
/** @author Dengya Zhu */
public class MajorityVoting {
    private int K; //number of voters, should be odds, but not checked here
    private String [] content; //list of voters
    private int majorityNum; //if exist majority, the number of majority voter
    private int firstIndex; //if exist majority, the first index of majority voter

    public MajorityVoting(int K_in, String [] content_in) {
        this.K = K_in;
        this.content = content_in;
        this.majorityNum = 0;
        this.firstIndex = -1;
    }

    public int voting() {
        majorityNum = 1; //in case of all the K elements differ from each other,
        firstIndex = 0;      //majorityNum = 1, firstIndex = 0;
        for(int i = 0; i < K - 1; i++) {
            int num = 0;
            for(int j = i + 1; j < K; j++) {
                if(content[i] == content[j])
                    num++;
            }
            if(num > majorityNum) {
                majorityNum = num;
                firstIndex = i;
                if(majorityNum >= (K + 1) / 2 )
                    break;
            }
            //if the rest unchecked elements less then the majorityNum, stop this process
            if(i + majorityNum >= K - 1)
                break;
        }
        return firstIndex;
    }

    public boolean hasMajority() {
        if(majorityNum == 0)
            voting();
        if(majorityNum > (K + 1) / 2) return true;
        else return false;
    }

    public int getMajorityNum() {
        if(majorityNum == 0) voting();
        return majorityNum;
    }

    public int getMajority() {
        if (firstIndex < 0) return voting();
        else return firstIndex;
    }
}
```

Figure 4-16 Implementation of Majority Voting class

Class *RetResults* is designed to store the returned search results of *Yahoo! Search Web Service API*. Each of the returned Web search results includes the title of the Web page, the URL for the Web page, the summary text of the Web page, and so on. In this research, for the purpose of categorizing and filtering search results, only the title of the Web page, the URL for the Web page, and the summary text of the Web page are considered; although other kinds of information are also included in the class for further development. Methods of class *RetResults* mainly deal with setting and retrieving the above information.

After the search results are categorized based on the category of the ODP, some categories may have a number of Web pages categorized under it. Therefore, class *ExTreeNode* is designed which includes the name of the category represented by the ODP-Tree, and a *linked list* of *RetResults* composed by a sequence of Web pages categorized under this category. Because the ODP-Tree only have two levels (see section 4.5), therefore, class *ExTreeNode* represents only the leaf nodes of the ODP-Tree. The methods of the class, similar to that of class *RetResults*, are mainly designed for accessing data in this class. The corresponding Tree Node in this class is identified by the name of the Tree Node – *secondLevel.NodeName*, not the node object. Several lines of code of this class are shown as following.

```
public class ExTreeNode
{
        List results; //a list to store the search results under this category
        private String secondLevelNodeName; // a category-node under which some Web //pages are categorized
        public ExTreeNode ();
        public ExTreeNode (RetResults rrs, String sln);
        public ExTreeNode (ExTreeNode etn);

        ...
        public RetResults getRetResults ();
        public RetResults getRetResults (int i);
        public String getTreeNodeName();
        public void setRetResults (int i, RetResults rrs);
        public int appendResult (RetResults rrs);
        boolean contains (String sln);

        ...
}
```

The *FirstLevelNode* class has two data elements; one is the name of the first level node which represents the first level category in the ODP, and another is a *linked list* consisting of objects of class *ExTreeNode*. Similar to class *ExTreeNode*, methods in class *FirstLevelNode* are also built for the purpose of providing access to the two data elements. The *contains (String categoryName)* method allows for judgment of whether the given category (represented by *categoryName*) is represented by the instance of this class. The *containsSubNode (String subCategoryName)* method judges whether a subcategory of the ODP is contained in the list of the second level category represented by *ExTreeNode*. The following code shows the data elements of the class *FirstLevelNode* and some of the methods of this class.

```
public class FirstLevelNode {
```

```
private String nodeName;
private List exTreeNode;
   public FirstLevelNode ();
public FirstLevelNode (ExTreeNode etn, String nn);
public FirstLevelNode (FirstLevelNode fln);
...
public String getNodeName ();
public ExTreeNode getExTreeNode (int x);
public String getExTreeNodeName (int x);
public int appendResult (int exTreeNodeIndex, RetResults rrs);
public boolean isExTreeNodeEmpty ();
public boolean containsSubNode (String nn);
public boolean contains (String st)
...
}
```

The search results returned from *Yahoo! Search Web Service API* for a search-term may be categorized into more than one first level category in the ODP. Therefore, the objects of *FirstLevelNode* are organized as an array list.

Figure 4-17 illustrates how the categorized search results are organized and stored under the hierarchical structure of objects of these three classes, namely, *FirstLevelNode*, *ExTreeNode*, and *RetResults*.

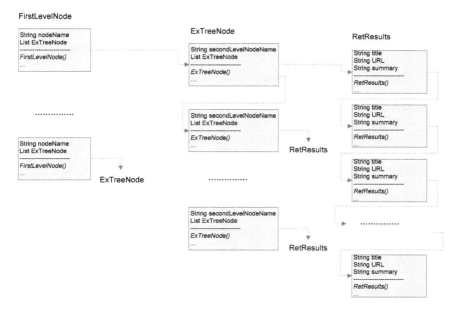

Figure 4-17 Relationship among classes FirstLevelNode, ExTreeNode and RetResults

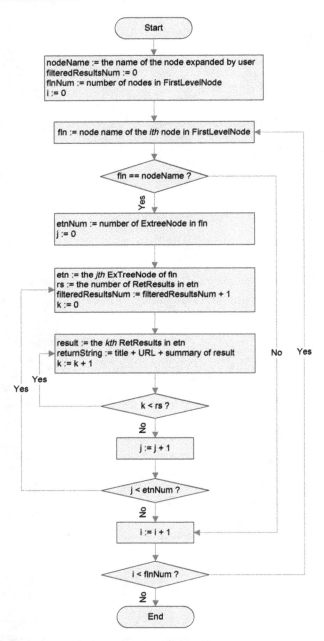

Figure 4-18 Flowchart of search results filtering

4.7.2 Filtering Search Results

Filtering search results is to select the search results categorized under an ODP category which is selected by a user. The categorization process described in section 4.6 has classified Web search results into proper categories. Using classes designed in section 4.7.1 can store these categorized results easily, because the three classes are specially designed for storing the results. The *setTitle()*, *setURL()* and *setSummary()* methods of class *RetResults* store the title, URL and the summary of a search result; search results categorized under the same category are stored in class *ExTreeNode*, and all the search results are stored and organized by class *FirstLevelNode*.

With the entire search results organized and stored in the three classes, the first step of the filtering process is to select the object in the list of *FirstLevelNode* whose name is the same as the category name selected by the user. The second step is to traverse all the *ExTreeNode* objects in the selected *FirstLevelNode* object. The last step is retrieving all the *RetResults* objects when traversing the *ExTreeNode*. Figure 4-18 is the flowchart of the process of filtering search results.

So far, a special search-browser which integrates search results of search engine and the ODP-based ontology has been developed, and thus **achieved the objective two** proposed in Chapter 1, section 1.8. Because the search-browser integrated a Web search services to retrieve search results, but not let users to navigate a Web directory to search information, it therefore overcomes the problem of low recall of Web Navigation discussed in Chapter 1, section 1.7. Further, search results from Yahoo! have been categorized under the categories of the ODP, and filtered when a user select a category of interest. The functions of the "Disambiguated Results" and the "Category Selected from the ODP tree-like categories" components of Figure 4-1 have been implemented, and this is also **accomplished the objective three** of this research. With the achievement of this objective, returned search results are well organized, and when an interesting topic is chosen, only relevant results are presented. The problems of information overload (Chapter 1, section 1.2) and mismatch of search results (Chpater 1, section 1.3) are improved. The measurement of the improvement is discussed in next chapter with the implementation of objective four of this research.

4.8 Summary

This chapter introduced the implementation details of the special search-browser and the achievement of the first three objectives proposed in Chapter 1, section 1.8. Semantic characteristics of the ODP categories are extracted from two RDF files, structure.rdf and content.rdf. The extracted data from each category is used to build text format *category-documents* that are then indexed by Lucene *Indexer*. Lucene *Searcher* is employed to compare the Web search results returned from *Yahoo! Search Web Services API* with the category-documents. Each returned search result will be assigned to one of the ODP categories based on the *Majority Voting* algorithm. The categorized search results are organized by using three classes which record the results categorized under the corresponding category. The ODP categories are presented to users by a Java Tree structure which services as an interactive instrument between the developed special search-browser and the users (objective one). Search-term disambiguation is achieved when the user selects an interesting category of the ODP and, as a response, the special search-browser filters and presents only results categorized under the selected category. The quality of search results is expected to be improved when only filtered results are provided (objective two and objective three).

Chapter 3 section 3.3 described the implementation details of Part A in Figure 4-1; this chapter presented how the functions of other components in Figure 4-1 are implemented. An alternative to implement the similar function of Part B2 of Figure 4-2 is simply create a JTree component of Java at interface design phase, therefore the implementation details are not presented here. Next Chapter will concentrate on the evaluation of the special search-browser – the evaluation part of design research methodology.

Chapter 5.   Special Search-browser Performance Evaluation

This chapter presents IR evaluation measurements, relevance judgment, experimental results of the special search-browser and consequently achieves the research objective four. Section 5.1 presents the objectives of the evaluation. Section 5.2 discusses the testing strategy with the description of search-term selection criteria. Section 5.3 introduces measurements utilized in this experiment. Evaluation procedure is presented in section 5.4, and relevance judgment results are analyzed in section 5.5. Performance comparison between the special search-browser and the *Yahoo! Search Web Service API* is provided in section 5.6; limitation, special cases are discussed in section 5.7. Finally, section 5.8 summarizes this chapter.

5.1 The Objectives of the Evaluation

The focus of this research is to improve the relevance of search results via search-term disambiguation and ontological filtering of search results. The ODP hierarchical structure is taken as the pre-defined knowledge structure upon which basis the search results are categorized. *Yahoo! Search Web Service API* is employed to search the Web and 50 search results can be returned from Yahoo! for each query. All the search results are categorized into the ODP knowledge structure by using Lucene as a classifier which adopts VSM to calculate similarity scores between queries and documents. With the categorized search results, when an interesting category is selected, most of the search results under this category are expected to be relevant to the user's information need, not like the 50 search results of Yahoo! which include many irrelevant information items.

Precision (Chapter 2, section 2.2.5) is a principal measurement of a retrieval strategy to retrieve only relevant documents within a retrieved answer set, and is an appropriate and important measurement for this study. *Recall* (Chapter 2, section 2.2.5) indicates how well an IR system retrieves more relevant documents within the system. Some Web search performance researchers (Hawking et al. 2001, Leighton & Srivastava 1999) do not measure *recall*. However, when a study involves categorizing and clustering, *recall* may be affected, if some relevant results are categorized into another category[24]. Therefore, *recall* is an important measurement for us, especially when each search result is only categorized into one unique category. The objectives of the evaluation are:

1) to compare the *precision* of the categorized search results with the 50 search results output of *Yahoo! Search Web Service API*;

2) to calculate the *recall* of the categorized search results, and to examine the reduction in *recall*;

---

[24] There is usually only partial agreement on whether or not a document is properly categorized, because relevance judgment is inherently subjective (Mizzaro 1997, Saracevic 1996, Voorhees 2005b, also refer to Chapter 5, section 5.2).

3) to analyze the experimental results for further research.

5.2 The Testing Strategy

5.2.1 Search Queries

In this experiment, five queries are selected as shown in Table 5-1 which is constructed based on Zeng et al. (2004) study on clustering Web search results.

Table 5-1 Search-terms used in the experiment

Query type (Zeng et al. 2004)	Query	Information need
Ambiguous query	jaguar	Information about the animal jaguar
	UPS	Information about how UPS (Uninterruptible Power Supply) works; key specification of UPS
Entity name	Clinton	The American president William J. Clinton
	Ford	Henry Ford, the founder of the Ford Motor Company
General term	health	How can one keep healthy

One principle to select queries is that search-terms should not only be motivated by genuine user information need (Gordon & Pathak 1999, Hawking et al. 2001), but should also directly come from users. When evaluating Web search services, queries (search-terms) play an essential role, because they represent users' information needs that an IR system attempts to satisfy (Mizzaro 1997, 1998). Leighton and Srivastava (1999) indicate that deciding information needs and choosing exact search-terms submitted to search services are two steps to develop test suites. In the experiment of Gordon and Pathak (1999), users submitted their information needs to a group of well trained searchers; the well trained searchers tried to find the best search-terms to express users' information need, and the best search-terms decided by the trained searcher were then submitted to Web services. Nowadays, with the wide spread of the Internet, more and more people use the Internet to search for information everyday and everywhere. However, users are not good at expressing their information needs (Chapter 2, section 2.3.1). They prefer very short queries—30 per cent are one-word queries; 66 per cent one or two-word queries—and seldom use Boolean operators (Jansen et al. 2000, 2005). Therefore, in this research, search queries are selected as a subset of Zeng et al.'s (2004) search query suite based on actual searches conducted with the MSN search engine.

The second consideration in selecting queries is that the selected queries should cover a wide range. Zeng et al. (2004) categorize their 30 queries into three types, namely, *Ambiguous queries, Entity names, and General terms.* Jansen et al. (2005) indicate that in 2002, nearly half (49.27 per cent) of Web searching is about "people", "places" or "things", 12.52 per cent is about "commerce", "travel", "employment" or "economy", 12.40 per cent is about "computers" or "Internet" or "technology" items, and 7.49 per cent of searching is about "education" or "humanities". For the five selected queries used in this experiment, two of them are about "people" (Clinton and Ford), one is about a "thing" (jaguar), one is about "computer" or "technology" items (UPS[25]), and one is about "health" (health). These five queries are therefore representing a typical and wide range (49.27 + 12.4 + 7.49 = 69.16 per cent) of Web search topics based on the survey data presented by Jansen et al. (2005).

Lastly, recall that the purpose of this study is to disambiguate search-terms. The selected search-terms should have more than one meaning, and should easily cause search engines to retrieve different categories of information. From this point of view, queries employed by Zeng et al. (2004) are also appropriate for this research.

5.2.2 Search Results

Both *Yahoo! Search Web Services API* (http://developer.yahoo.com/search) and Google Search API (http://www.google.com/apis) can be used to access the database of Yahoo! and Google respectively for study purposes. One must first obtain a user *Application ID* before using the Web services APIs. For a non-commercial licence, both services limit the search results to 1,000 per day. In addition, Google returns only 10 search results for each query, whereas Yahoo allows 50 search results for a single query.

Users can easily pick up which returned results are relevant to their information needs within ten search results. Furthermore, categorizing 10 search results into 15 categories is less value for categorizing purposes, because classifying/categorizing/clustering techniques are mainly developed for organizing a large amount of data items when the number of data items is much larger than the number of categories. Taking this into account, *Yahoo! Search Web Service* is selected as an approach to retrieve Web information, although 50 search results is the maximum number obtainable for categorizing purposes in non-commercial work such as this. Appendix 3 is a list of search results of the five queries of *Yahoo! Search Web Service API*.

5.2.3 Hierarchical Structure Data – the ODP Category

Chapter 3, section 3.4.2 describes the hierarchical structure of the ODP. Figure 3-8 is the screenshot of the home page and the 15 categories of the ODP. Although the top 15 categories are seldom changed, the subcategories of each of the top categories are changed occasionally. Appendix 4 is a list of the 15 first level categories of the ODP and their subcategories respectively (based on the

---

[25] UPS: Uninterruptible Power Supply.

downloaded ODP data on Aug 16, 2006). The following list is an example of the category "Computers" and its subcategories.

> *Computers*
> *Algorithms, Artificial Intelligence, Artificial Life, Bulletin Board Systems, CAD and CAM, Chats and Forums, Companies, Computer Science, Consultants, Data , Communications, Data Formats, Desktop Publishing, Directories, E-Books, Education, Emulators, Ethics, Graphics, Hacking, Hardware, History, Home, ,Automation, Human-Computer Interaction, Internet, Intranet, Mailing Lists, Mobile Computing, Multimedia, News and Media, Open Source, Organizations, Parallel Computing, Performance and Capacity, Programming, Robotics, Security,*
> *Shopping, Software, Speech Technology, Supercomputing, Systems, Usenet, Virtual , Reality*

5. 3 Measuring Search Effectiveness

5.3.1 TREC Style *Precision* and *Recall*

TREC (Text REtrieval Conference), started in 1992, is purposed to support and encourage research within the IR society by providing the infrastructure necessary for large-scale evaluation of text retrieval methodologies; and to increase the speed of lab-to-product transfer of technology (http://trec.nist.gov/overview.html). TREC claims that within the first six years of the workshops, the effectiveness of retrieval systems approximately doubled. It was also the first to hold large-scale evaluations of non-English documents, speech, video and retrieval across languages. Additionally, the challenges have inspired a large body of publications. Technology first developed in TREC is now included in many of the world's commercial search engines (http://en.wikipedia.org/wiki/Text_Retrieval_Conference).

Precision and *recall*, introduced in Chapter 2, section 2.2.5, are two important factors to evaluate the effectiveness of Web IR also (Gordon & Pathak 1999, Hawking et al. 1999). However, as the document collection is getting larger, and the search engines return more search results (Chapter 1, section 1.1 and section 1.2), calculating *precision* and *recall* becomes more difficult, or even impractical (Hawking et al. 2001, Leighton & Srivastava 1999). Therefore, TREC uses *recall* and *precision* at various *cut-off levels* to compare the performance of an IR system (Hawking et al. 1999, Voorhees 2005b). A *cut-off level* is a rank that defines the retrieved set. For example, a *cut-off level* of 10 defines the top ten retrieved documents in the ranked list. If seven out of the ten returned documents are relevant, the *precision* at *cut-off level* ten (P@10) is then $7/10 = 0.7 = 70$ per cent.

To evaluate *recall*, TREC uses a "pooling" technology which combines submitted search results of participants (Hawking et al. 1999, Voorhees 2005b). Because this research only addresses how search performance is improved after the search results are categorized, TREC's approach to calculate *recall* is not proper to this study. A method to calculate *recall* suitable for this research will be introduced in the following section. Recently, some researchers (Hawking et al. 2001, Leighton & Srivastava 1999) expressed belief that people are not interested in *recall* in the Web context; they use only *precision* as the measurement to evaluate the performance of Web search results.

5.3.2 Evaluating *Precision* and *Recall* of the Special Search-browser

Precision is a measurement of purity of search results, that is, the proportion of relevant documents among the total search results returned (Voorhees 2005b). Let N be the total number of search results returned, Ra be the relevant document within N, and P denote *precision*, then

$P = Ra/N$.

Confined by the non-commercial license of *Yahoo! Search Web Service API*, only 50 search results can be obtained for each query; the *precision* is thus calculated by:

$P = Ra/50$

After ontological categorizing (Chapter 3, section 3.7), the 50 documents are classified into categories of the ODP. Suppose that within the user selected category, there are S (S <= 50) documents; among S documents, Rc documents are relevant. The *precision* of the selected category is Ps:

$$Ps = Rc/S$$

Now, the improvement of *precision* can be expressed as:

$$Ps - P = Rc/S - Ra/50$$

Recall is the proportion of relevant documents that are retrieved (Voorhees 2005b).To simplify calculation, suppose that for the given query, there are all Ra relevant documents; therefore, the *recall* R of the search results returned by *Yahoo! Search Web Service API* equals Ra/Ra = 1. The *recall* of categorized results in the selected category Rs is

$$Rs = Rc/Ra$$

Obviously, Rc <= Ra, and for a selected category, in case of Rc < Ra, it is impossible for *recall* Rs to reach 1; therefore, the *precision-recall* curve as discussed below may be cut off at *recall* level Rs.

Based on the calculation of Ps, the TREC style *precision* at different cut-off levels, such as P@5, P@10, P@15, and P@20 will be calculated in this research if the data is available (e.g. if there are less than 20 results classified into a category, it is impossible to calculate P@20). *Recall* is calculated by Rs. In next section, an intensively used *precision-recall* curve which allows "to evaluate quantitatively both the quality of the overall answer set and the breadth of the retrieval algorithm" (Baeza-Yates & Ribeiro-Neto 1999, p. 79) is introduced

5.3.3 *Precision-Recall* Curve

Search engines present retrieved documents in a ranked list according to the degree of relevance of the document to a given query. Users then examine the ranked list starting from the top of this list. Thus, the *recall* and *precision* measures vary as the users proceed with their examination of the retrieved answer set. To evaluate the ranked lists, *precision* is plotted against *recall* after each retrieved document – astandard 11 points *precision versus recall* is usually employed as an overall evaluation of search results (Baeza-Yates & Ribeiro-Neto 1999, pp. 75-76, Voorhees 2005a).

Suppose there is a document collection which contains 20 documents; four of the documents are relevant to a query q. Assume an IR system retrieves three of the four relevant documents and ranks the relevant documents at the position of one, four and fifteen. The *recall* points of the three relevant documents are 1/4 = 25 per cent, 2/4 = 50 per cent, 3/4 = 75 per cent, at the ranked document position one, four and fifteen. The first ranked document is relevant, the *precision* thus equals 1/1 = 100 per cent, and the *recall* level is now 25 per cent; at the *recall* level of 50 per cent, four out of two documents are relevant and, therefore, the *precision* is 2/4 = 50 per cent. The *recall* point 75 per cent happens at the fifteenth document which is the third relevant document. Therefore, the *precision* at this *recall* point is 3/15 = 20 per cent. For the *recall* point bigger than 75 per cent, the *precision* is zero, because no further relevant documents are retrieved by this IR system.

Precision versus *recall* curve is usually based on eleven *standard recall* levels which are 0 per cent, 10 per cent, 20 per cent, ..., 100 per cent (Baeza-Yates & Ribeiro-Neto 1999, p. 76, Voorhees 2005a). Figure 5-1 is the *precision-recall* curve of the above example.

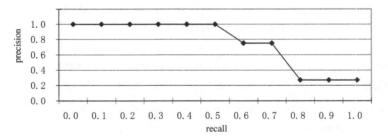

Figure 5-1 An example of precision-recall curve

Adaption of: Voorhees 2005a, p. 1

When drawing *precision-recall* curve, a particular interpolation rule is employed. The rule used to interpolate *precision* at standard *recall* level i is to use the maximum *precision* obtained for the query for any actual *recall* level greater than or equal to i. For the above example, now assume that all four relevant documents are retrieved and ranked at position one, two, four and fifteen. The interpolated *precision* for all standard *recall* levels up to 50 per cent (0.5) is 100 per cent, the interpolated *precision* for *recall* levels 60 per cent and 70 per cent is 75 per cent, and the interpolated *precision* for *recall* level 80 per cent or greater is 4/15 = 26.7 per cent (Voorhees 2005a).

In this research, *precision-recall* curve will be treated as the major measure of the performance of the Yahoo! search engine and the special search-browser. Comparison is made based on the *precisions* at the 11 standard *recall* levels between Yahoo! and the proposed approach.

5.4 Evaluation Procedure

Evaluation procedure in this research includes the following steps. First, we select five queries and defines the corresponding information needs as shown in Table 5-1 (Section 5.2.1).

The second step is to search the Web through the developed special search-browser for the search-term "Clinton". The special search-browser searches the Web and categorizes the returned search results. Figure 5-2 is the screenshot of the categorized search results of the query "Clinton".

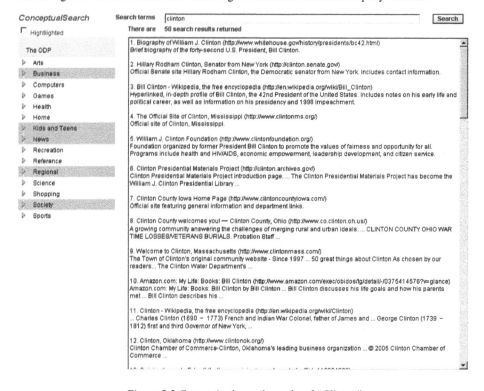

Figure 5-2 Categorized search results of "Clinton"

The next step is expanding the marked categories alphabetically to view the categorized results under each marked category. Figure 5-3 is the screenshot when the last marked category "Society" is expanded. Note that when "Highlighted" is ticked, the special search-browser shows only the marked categories. Under the category "Society", there are 15 search results, and these 15 search results are further categorized under the subcategory "History".

The fourth step is to store the retrieved and categorized results of a given query. The search results of the second step and categorized results of step three will be recorded in a log file named SearchLog.txt. After the last marked category is expanded (viewed), a directory with query name ("Clinton") is created, and the SearchLog.txt log file is then saved under this directory.

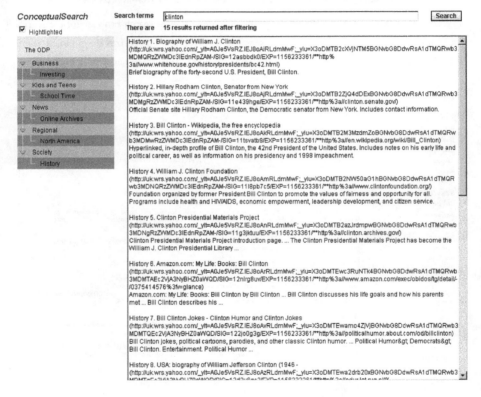

Figure 5-3 Categorized search results of "Clinton" under category "Society"

Repeat steps two to four for the queries "Ford", "health", "jaguar", and "UPS", store the corresponding log files under each directory.

Step five obtains relevance judgments from the judges (see section 5.5). A relevance judgment document based on the 50 Yahoo! search results of the five queries is created and presented to the five judges. There are 5*50 = 250 search results to be judged. Appendix 8 is the relevance judgment document. This document with the consent form (see Appendix 6) and information form (see Appendix 7) will be distributed to the judges. After the judgment is finished, the relevance judgment documents are collected.

As can be seen from the relevance judgment documents, there is no information about categorization revealed to the judges. They are presented with only the uncategorized 50 Yahoo! search results and asked to judge whether the returned search results are relevant to the given information needs. The judges are not aware of the categorization process.

Step six is to process and analyze the relevance judgment results obtained in step five, and classify the relevance judgment into three groups for the purpose of Average Judgment, Strict Judgment and Enlarged Judgment as described in section 5.5.2.

Step seven calculates *precision* and *recall*, and compares the search results returned by *Yahoo! Search Web Service API* and the categorized search results of the special search-browser based on the ODP category. For the 50 uncategorized search results of Yahoo!, for each query, P@5, P@10, P@15, P@20, P@30, P@50, and the average of the above six *precisions* are calculated if available. *Recall* and *precision* curve is drawn with an assumption that all the relevant documents are contained in the 50 search results of Yahoo!. For each marked category, *precision* at the same cut-off level as the 50 search results of Yahoo! is calculated, and *precision* and *recall* curve is presented as well.

The reason for calculating *precision* for each marked category is that sometimes it is hard to decide which category contains relevant information. For example, when searching for "Clinton" to find information about "the American president, William J. Clinton", category "Society" and "Regional" may both include relevant information. Browsing one category may satisfy a user's information, or may not. Due to the difficulty to decide a definite category, the *precision* and *recall* are therefore calculated for each marked category, as well as for the combined results of both.

5.5 Relevance Judgment of Search Results

To calculate *precision* and *recall*, first of all, relevant documents must be picked up from the answer set (retrieved results), or from the set of all documents. Relevance judgment has been central to IR from the beginning of IR research (Harter 1992, Saracevic 1996). However, relevance judgment is inherently subjective (Mizzaro 1997, Saracevic 1996, Voorhees 2005b) and based on psychological factors (Harter 1992). This means that it is very hard to define what relevance is and how to judge the relevance. Comprehensive reviews of research on relevance and relevance judgment are given by Mizzaro (1997, 1998), Saracevic (1996), and Greisdorf (2000). In this research, to make the relevance judgment more objective, or in other words, to reduce the subjective effect of relevance judgments which are further utilized to calculate *precision* and *recall*, relevance judgments are performed by five experts, as elaborated in section 5.5.2.

5.5.1 Relevance

Mizzaro (1997, 1998) proposes a framework to describe various kinds of relevance. There are four sets related to the framework. **Problem set** (PS) include four elements: a *problem* which is to be solved by an IR system; an *information need* built by the user to represent the problem when it is perceived; a *request* usually expressed in natural language to explicate the information need; and a *query* which is a translated form understandable by the IR system. **Information set** (IS) contains three elements: *surrogate* (S) is the document representation stored in an IR system; *document* (D) is the physical entity that the user of an IR system will obtain; and *information* (I) is the entity that the user receives/creates when reading a document. The **Components set** (Co) also includes three components: *topic* refers to the user interested subject area; *task* refers to the user executed activities with the retrieved documents; *context* refers to all other thing not included in topic and task. **Time set** (T) contains components when elements (not including the problem) in the problem set are changed. For example, a request may change at time t_r from r_i to r_j. The relevance set *Rel* of all the kinds of relevance is thus defined as

$$Rel = PS \times IS \times Co \times T$$

Partial order[26] can be defined on any of the four sets, for example, on IS, S < D < I. The partial order represents how much a relevance document is near to the user interested relevance.

Mizzaro (1997) further provides seven aspects of relevance for research purposes. The seven aspects are: *Foundations* (definition of relevance from different standpoints using different mathematical instruments and conceptual approaches); *Kinds* (as defined by *Rel*); *Surrogates* (the type of surrogate used can affect relevance judgment and relevance *per se*); *Criteria* (used by users to express their relevance judgment); *Dynamics* (relevance judgment at a certain point of time may change at another point of time, presentation ordering, the first seen document can affect the relevance of the next one); *Expression* (a way for judges to express in a consistent manner their relevance judgment); and *Subjectiveness* (different judges may express different relevance judgments).

---

[26] A partial order ≤ on a set S is a binary relation that is reflexive, antisymmetric and transitive, i.e., it holds for all a, b and c in S that: a ≤ a (reflexivity); if a ≤ b and b ≤ a, then a = b (antisymmetry); if a ≤ b and b ≤ c, then a ≤ c (transitivity). (Webster's online dictionary, http://www.websters-online-dictionary.org/definition/partial+order)

Saracevic (1996) points out that *Nature* (an appropriate framework within which relevance may be considered and defined), *Manifestation* (ways and contexts in which relevance manifests itself), *Behaviour* (variability in observable behaviour of relevance for given contexts and variables), and *Effects* (utilization of relevance in development of IR system, processes, algorithms, and evaluation of these) are four issues repeatedly addressed in explications of relevance. He believes that relation, intention, context, inference, and interaction are five general features of relevance. That is, "as a cognitive notion relevance involves an interactive, dynamic establishment of a relation by inference, with intentions toward a context." (Saracevic 1996, p. 205) This definition of relevance expanded the simple topical relevance and derived from the intuitive understanding of relevance.

5.5.2 Relevance judgment Scale

According to Mizzaro (1997, 1998), *relevance judgment* is an assignment of a value of relevance by a judge at a certain point of time. It can be represented as: $RJ = Rel \times J \times T$, where $J = \{user, nonuser\}$ is the set of judges. No matter if it is the user or nonuser, *Rel* is the relevance, and T is the time set as defined in the previous section. Obviously, relevance is different from relevance judgment within this framework.

Relevance judgment in TREC is simple and binary characterized. Voorhees (2005b) suggests that relevance assessors are told they are writing a report about a topic; if the information contained in a document is useful in the report, the document should be marked relevant.

Leighton and Srivastava (1999), Shafi and Rather (2005) use graded relevance judgment criteria. The following relevance categories are defined by Leighton and Srivastava (1999, pp. 874-875).

> *Duplicate links:...*
> *Inactive links:...*
> **Category zero**: *The page is irrelevant because it does not satisfy an important aspect of the search expression.*
> **Category one**: *The page technically satisfies the search expression (structured) or contains all of the search terms or synonyms of them (unstructured), but it is not relevant to the user's query, either because is not related to the topic indicated or because it was too brief to be useful.*
> **Category two**: *Relevant to the request and relevant to at least some narrow range of information needs described by the request. These pages are at least potentially relevant to some users. Also pages that have links to category three pages.*
> **Category three**: *Relevant to a wide range of possible information needs described by the request, such as a clearinghouse of links, or a particularly thorough treatment of the subject.*

Search results are assigned one of the above categories. The categories defined by Shafi and Rather (2005) are similar to the above categories.

When evaluating performance of different Web search services, as the approach of TREC (Voorhees 2005b), Leighton and Srivastava (1999), Shafi and Rather (2005), it is proper to have one judge to conduct judgment of the search results of the same search-term over the different Web search services. This strategy can avoid inconsistency introduced by different judges on the same topic due to the subjective character of relevance judgments.

In this research, to avoid bias introduced by the subjectiveness of individuals, five judges are employed. Furthermore, graded relevance categories are utilized. Judges are presented with a query and the supposed information need, as shown in Table 5-1 (Section 5.2.1). They are then asked to judge whether each of the listed information snippets (returned search results) is relevant, partially relevant, irrelevant to the information need, or not sufficient information provided to make a decision.

Judges' judgments are quantified to facilitate making a final binary decision on whether a returned search result is relevant or not. To quantify the relevance judgments, a "reward positive, punish negative" strategy is proposed in this research. An information snippet is assigned three (positive three) points if it is judged as relevant; one (positive one) point if it is partially relevant; minus three (negative three) points if the item is judged as irrelevant; and zero point if the information is insufficient to make a relevance judgment, as shown in Table 5-2.

Table 5-2 Relevance judgment score

Relevance Judgment	Relevant (R)	Partially relevant (P)	Irrelevant (I)	Not sufficient information (N)
Scores	3	1	-3	0

In this research, the following three situations are analyzed and the corresponding judgment approaches are proposed. Strict Judgment and Enlarged Judgment are two novel strategy proposed in this research when a final binary relevance judgment is made.

1) Average Judgment (AJ): For a given information snippet, the points of the five experts will be added together, according to the summed scores (SS), if SS is bigger than zero, the returned item will be treated as relevant; if less then zero, the item will be treated as irrelevant; if SS equals zero, the search result is judged as neutral (in the special scenario, this search result will be specially marked, because the final relevant decision is binary). AJ is the case in a sense that judges' judgment is smoothed or averaged.

2) Strict Judgment (SJ): If no judge considers the search results as irrelevant, and at least one of them considers it is relevant, the search result is judged as relevant; otherwise, if any of the five judges makes an irrelevance judgment on the research result, the search result is regarded as irrelevant. This case is considered because it reveals the strict relevance judgment of the group of judges.

3) Enlarged Judgment (EJ): If any judge's judgment is "relevant" or "partially relevant", this returned search result is considered as relevant; otherwise, the search result is regarded as irrelevant. In this situation, there is the least loss of relevance judgment. Relevance judgment is subjective; if any one judge finds this information snippet is relevant, it is reasonable for an IR system also considering it as relevant, no matter how others make their relevance judgment decision. If a categorizing algorithm ignores this

kind of search result, some Web information searchers will miss this useful information when they select the corresponding category.

A returned survey result of one judge is presented in Appendix 16.

5.5.3 Relevance Judgment Analysis

Table 5-3 summarizes the relevance judgments of the five judges for the five queries. R, P, I, N represent *Relevant, Partially relevant, Irrelevant,* and *Not sufficient information* to make a relevance judgment. For example, when judging the relevance of search results of the query "Ford", Judge4 (J4) indicates there are six relevant search results, five of them are partially relevant; 38 search results are irrelevant; and one search result can not be judged because the information delivered by the search result is not sufficient.

The row labelled *Intersection* gives the number of items out of the 50 returned by *Yahoo! Search Web Service API,* for which the relevance judgment (R, P, I or N) is the same for all five judges. For example, in Table 5-3 it can be seen that there are only two relevant items (the first item of row *Intersection*) which all five judges agree are R (Relevant) to the query "Clinton"; no one items (the second item of row *Intersection*) which all judges agree are P (Partially relevant); and all five judges agree that there are 25 items (the third item of row *Intersection*) which are I (Irrelevant).

Table 5-3 Summary of relevance judgments of the five judges (50 results for each query)

Queries	Judge	J1	J2	J3	J4	J5	Interaction	Union
Clinton	R	7	13	18	15	9	2	22
	P	7	4	3	3	4	0	15
	I	31	33	29	30	35	25	38
	N	5	0	0	1	2	0	7
Ford	R	2	2	4	6	3	2	7
	P	6	2	1	5	7	0	11
	I	38	46	43	38	40	32	46
	N	4	0	2	1	0	0	7
health	R	22	33	7	11	32	1	43
	P	23	16	25	21	14	0	44
	I	4	1	18	18	3	0	26
	N	1	0	0	0	1	0	1
jaguar	R	14	13	11	4	13	2	14
	P	0	0	3	10	0	0	11
	I	36	35	35	36	35	35	38
	N	0	2	1	0	2	0	3
UPS	R	8	5	7	4	8	1	11
	P	6	7	3	6	1	1	13
	I	33	38	38	40	36	33	40
	N	3	0	2	0	5	0	7

The row labelled *Union* in Table 5-3 presents the numbers of returned search items (out of the 50) of Yahoo! where at least one judge has given that column the corresponding rating. For example, the first item of row *Union* indicates that there are 22 items which are judged R (relevant) by at least one of the five judges; the second item of the row indicates 15 returned search results are judged P (partially relevant) by at least one judges; and third item of row *Union* reveals that there are 38 returned items which are judged I (irrelevant) by at least one of the five judges.

As can be seen from Table 5-3, the judges are not quite agreeing with each other on the relevance judgments. For the five queries, two out of 50 search results are judged relevant by all the five judges for the query "Clinton", "Ford" and "jaguar", whereas only one out of 50 search results are judged relevant by all of the five judges for the search-term "health" and "UPS". On the other hand, judges easily reach agreement on what is irrelevant, except for the query "health". Twenty-five out of the 50 search results for the search-term "Clinton" are judged irrelevant by all five judges. The numbers of agreement on irrelevant for search-term "Ford", "jaguar" and "UPS" are 32, 35 and 33 out 50 respectively. These figures verify that most Web search results of search engines are irrelevant (section 1.3).

Figure 5-4 illustrates the average percentage of R, P, I, N for each of the five queries, and the overall average percentage of R, P, I, N.

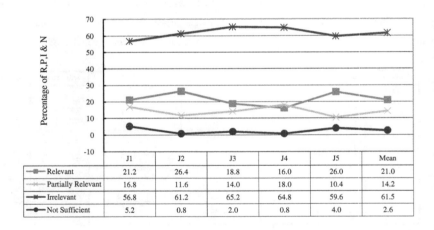

	J1	J2	J3	J4	J5	Mean
Relevant	21.2	26.4	18.8	16.0	26.0	21.0
Partially Relevant	16.8	11.6	14.0	18.0	10.4	14.2
Irrelevant	56.8	61.2	65.2	64.8	59.6	61.5
Not Sufficient	5.2	0.8	2.0	0.8	4.0	2.6

Figure 5-4 Average percentage of relevance judgment of the five judges[27]

A pairwise comparison similar to the one conducted by Voorhees (1998) is presented in
Table 5-4. The data in the table reveals how well each pair of judges agrees with each other on relevance judgments. For example, in the 50 returned search results of Yahoo!, seven out of 50 items are judged relevant by both J1 (Judge1) and J3 (Judge3); one item is judged partially relevant by both J1 and J3; 29 out of 50 items are judged irrelevant by the two judges.

---

[27] The fourth judge missed one judgment; therefore, the sum of the four types of judgment is 99.6 per cent (249/250)

Table 5-4 Judgment overlap of judge pairs (number of agreement)

Judge Pairs		J1,J2	J1,J3	J1,J4	J1,J5	J2,J3	J2,J4	J2,J5	J3,J4	J3,J5	J4,J5
Clinton	R	6	7	5	5	12	8	7	11	8	7
	P	2	1	0	2	0	0	0	1	0	0
	I	31	29	26	30	29	27	30	26	28	28
	N	0	0	1	0	0	0	0	0	0	0
Ford	R	2	2	2	2	2	2	2	3	3	2
	P	2	1	1	3	0	1	1	0	1	2
	I	38	36	33	35	43	38	40	36	38	38
	N	0	0	0	0	0	0	0	0	0	0
health	R	18	5	8	16	5	8	25	2	6	11
	P	9	16	10	8	7	5	8	13	7	5
	I	0	2	2	1	1	1	1	11	2	2
	N	0	0	0	0	0	0	0	0	0	0
jaguar	R	13	11	4	13	11	3	12	3	10	3
	P	0	0	0	0	0	0	2	0	0	0
	I	35	35	36	34	35	35	34	35	35	34
	N	0	0	0	0	1	0	1	0	1	0
UPS	R	4	5	3	6	4	2	4	2	7	2
	P	3	1	4	1	2	3	1	1	1	1
	I	33	33	33	33	38	38	36	38	36	36
	N	0	0	0	0	0	0	0	0	2	0

The summary of these pairwise relevance judgments is presented in Table 5-5, which indicates the overlap of relevance judgments between pairs in this research. Data in row labelled "No." indicates out of the 250 returned search items (5 queries, each has 50 retrieved items), the number of items for which two judges make the same relevance judgment decision. For instance, out of the 250 returned items, J1 (Judge1) and J3 (Judge3) have 185 common relevance judgments. The overlap percentage is thus 185/250 = 74.0%. The last column labelled "Average" is the overall pairwise relevance judgment overlap among the five judges, the average percentage is as high as 73.5. One possible reason for this high pairwise relevance judgment overlap is that the judges of this experiment are all from the same knowledge domain background; another reason is maybe the total number of documents to be judged is relatively small - 250 information items to be judged.

Table 5-5 Summary of pairwise agreement comparison

	J1, J2	J1, J3	J1, J4	J1, J5	J2, J3	J2, J4	J2, J5	J3, J4	J3, J5	J4, J5	Average
No	196	185	168	187	190	171	204	182	183	171	183.7
%	78.4	74.0	67.2	74.8	76.0	68.4	81.6	72.8	73.2	68.4	73.5

Aggregation of pairwise judgments by judge is demonstrated in Table 5-6. As can be seen from this table, J1 (Judge1) has an overall 73.6 [(78.4 + 74.0 + 67.2 + 74.8) / 4] per cent pairwise relevance judgment overlap. J2 (Judge2) has the highest, 76.1 per cent, pairwise relevance judgment overlap, and J4 (Judge4) has the lowest relevance judgment overlap. While the average pairwise relevance judgment overlap is 73.5 per cent, the sample standard deviation[28] S.D. is only 2.6, this figure further demonstrates that the relevance judgments of the five judges are reliable.

Table 5-6 Aggregation of pairwise judgments by judge

Judge	J1	J2	J3	J4	J5	Average	S.D.
%	73.6	76.1	74.0	69.2	74.5	73.5	2.6

So far, the five judges have finished their relevance judgment, and the relevance judgment results have also been analyzed. In next section, the performance of the special search-browser is evaluated.

5.6 Special Search-browser Evaluation

Using the results obtained in the previous section, this section first calculates *precision* at different cut-off levels of the 50 returned search results from Yahoo!; then calculates the *precisions* of the categorized search results of the special search-browser; a comparison is consequently made between these results. All of the results are shown by *recall-precision* curves at 11 standard *recall* levels.

5.6.1 *Precision* and *Recall* of the 50 Yahoo! Search Results

Based on data in Appendix 9 – "Statistical Results of the five Judges", *precision* at cut-off levels P@5, P@10, P@15, P@20, P@30, P@50, and the average of the above six *precisions* for AJ, SJ and EJ (section 5.5.2) are calculated and shown in Table 5-7.

Figure 5-5 illustrates the *precision-recall* curves of the 50 Yahoo! search results of the five search-terms respectively. The figure also includes the average standard 11 *recall-precision* curve (section 5.3.3) of the five search-terms. Calculation is based on Appendix 9 as well.

5.6.2 *Precision* and *Recall* of the Categorized Search Results

Relevant search results may be categorized into several different categories. The categorized search results are usually with a higher *precision* degree, but at a relatively lower *recall* level. Therefore, for each search-term, two categories with the most relevant search results are selected, and the categorized results of the two categories are compared with the 50 search results of Yahoo!. In addition, the combined categorized search results of the two selected categories are compared with the Yahoo! search results as well.

---

[28] standard deviation is calculated by $S.D. = \sqrt{\dfrac{\sum_{i=1}^{n}(x_i - \bar{x})^2}{n-1}}$, $where, \bar{x} = \dfrac{\sum_{i=1}^{n} x_i}{n}$, n is number of sample data and x_i is the sample data.

Table 5-7 **Precisions** *at different cut-off levels of the 50 search results of Yahoo! (%)*

		P@5	P@10	P@15	P@20	P@30	P@50	Average
Clinton	AJ	60.0	50.0	40.0	35.0	33.0	30.6	41.4
	SJ	40.0	40.0	33.0	30.0	26.0	24.5	32.3
	EJ	100.0	70.0	73.0	60.0	50.0	46.9	66.7
Ford	AJ	0.0	10.0	13.3	15.0	16.7	10.0	10.8
	SJ	0.0	10.0	7.0	10.0	13.3	8.0	8.1
	EJ	100.0	70.0	66.7	55.0	43.3	26.0	60.2
health	AJ	100.0	90.0	93.0	90.0	86.0	80.0	89.8
	SJ	80.0	70.0	80.0	80.0	60.0	48.0	69.7
	EJ	100.0	100.0	100.0	95.0	96.6	78.0	94.9
jaguar	AJ	40.0	20.0	26.7	20.0	26.7	28.0	26.9
	SJ	40.0	20.0	26.7	20.0	23.3	26.0	26.0
	EJ	40.0	20.0	26.7	20.0	26.7	28.0	26.9
UPS	AJ	0.0	20.0	13.3	10.0	16.7	24.0	14.0
	SJ	0.0	20.0	13.3	10.0	16.7	20.0	13.3
	EJ	0.0	20.0	13.3	10.0	20.0	30.0	15.6
Sub-Average	AJ	40.0	38.0	37.3	34.0	35.8	34.5	36.6
	SJ	32.0	32.0	32.0	30.0	27.9	25.3	29.9
	EJ	68.0	56.0	55.9	48.0	47.3	41.8	52.8
Average		46.7	42.0	41.7	37.3	37.0	33.8	39.8
Total Ave	39.8							

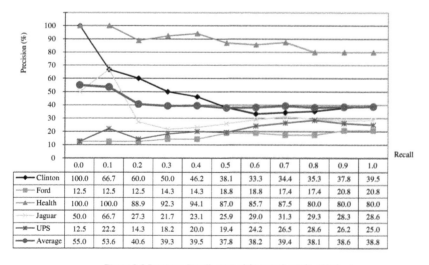

Recall	0.0	0.1	0.2	0.3	0.4	0.5	0.6	0.7	0.8	0.9	1.0
Clinton	100.0	66.7	60.0	50.0	46.2	38.1	33.3	34.4	35.3	37.8	39.5
Ford	12.5	12.5	12.5	14.3	14.3	18.8	18.8	17.4	17.4	20.8	20.8
Health	100.0	100.0	88.9	92.3	94.1	87.0	85.7	87.5	80.0	80.0	80.0
Jaguar	50.0	66.7	27.3	21.7	23.1	25.9	29.0	31.3	29.3	28.3	28.6
UPS	12.5	22.2	14.3	18.2	20.0	19.4	24.2	26.5	28.6	26.2	25.0
Average	55.0	53.6	40.6	39.3	39.5	37.8	38.2	39.4	38.1	38.6	38.8

Figure 5-5 Precision-Recall curve of the search results of Yahoo!

Comparison of search-term "Clinton"

There are 15 relevant search results which are categorized into three categories: Kids & Teens; News; and Society (see Appendix 10). Categories "Society" + "News" contain 14 out of 15 search results; the comparison among *recall-precision* curves is illustrated in

Figure 5-6. An average improvement on *precision* of the categorized results is:

(100.0-100.0 + 66.7-66.7 + 75.0-60.0 + 83.3-50 + 75.0-46.2 + 80.0-38.1 + 75.0-33.3 + 64.7-34.4 + 52.2-35.3 + 56.0-37.8 + 0-39.5) / 11 = (727.9 - 541.3) / 11

= 17.0 (%)

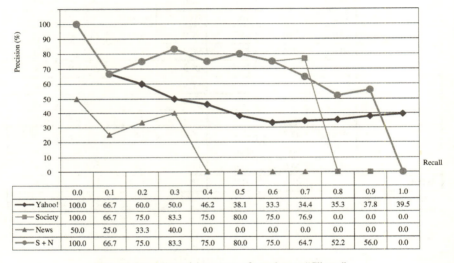

	0.0	0.1	0.2	0.3	0.4	0.5	0.6	0.7	0.8	0.9	1.0
Yahoo!	100.0	66.7	60.0	50.0	46.2	38.1	33.3	34.4	35.3	37.8	39.5
Society	100.0	66.7	75.0	83.3	75.0	80.0	75.0	76.9	0.0	0.0	0.0
News	50.0	25.0	33.3	40.0	0.0	0.0	0.0	0.0	0.0	0.0	0.0
S + N	100.0	66.7	75.0	83.3	75.0	80.0	75.0	64.7	52.2	56.0	0.0

Figure 5-6 Recall-precision curves of search-term "Clinton"

Comparison of search-term "Ford"

There are five relevant search results which are categorized into three categories: Reference; Society; and Recreation (see Appendix 11). Categories "Reference" + "Society" contain three out of five relevant results; comparison among *recall-precision* curves is illustrated in

Figure 5-7. An average improvement on *precision* of the categorized results is:

(100.0-12.5 + 100.0-12.5 + 100.0-12.5 + 100.0-14.3 + 100.0-14.3 + 100.0-18.8 + 0-18.8 + 0-17.4 + 0-17.4 + 0-20.8 + 0-20.8) / 110 = (600.0 – 180.1) /11

= 38.2 (%)

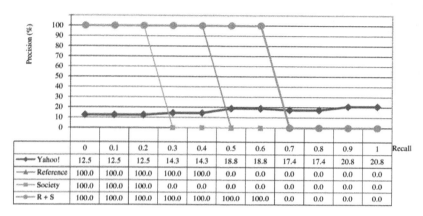

	0	0.1	0.2	0.3	0.4	0.5	0.6	0.7	0.8	0.9	1	Recall
Yahoo!	12.5	12.5	12.5	14.3	14.3	18.8	18.8	17.4	17.4	20.8	20.8	
Reference	100.0	100.0	100.0	100.0	100.0	0.0	0.0	0.0	0.0	0.0	0.0	
Society	100.0	100.0	100.0	0.0	0.0	0.0	0.0	0.0	0.0	0.0	0.0	
R + S	100.0	100.0	100.0	100.0	100.0	100.0	100.0	0.0	0.0	0.0	0.0	

Figure 5-7 Recall-precision curves of search-term "Ford"

Comparison of search-term "health"

There are 40 relevant search results which are categorized into nine categories: Arts; Business; Computers; Health; Kids & Teens; News; Regional; Science; and Society (see Appendix 12). Categories "Health" + "Regional" contain 29 out of the 40 relevant results; the comparison among *recall-precision* curves is illustrated in Figure 5-8. An average improvement on *precision* of the categorized results is:

(100.0-100.0 + 100.0-100.0 + 72.7-88.9 + 75.0-92.3 + 80.0-94.1 + 80.0-87.0 + 82.8-85.7 + 84.8-87.5 + 0-80.0 + 0-80.0 + 0-80.0) / 11 = (675.3 − 975.5) / 11

= **-27.3 (%)** (This negative figure indicates a worsening in the precision)

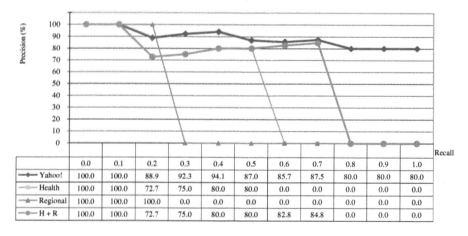

	0.0	0.1	0.2	0.3	0.4	0.5	0.6	0.7	0.8	0.9	1.0	Recall
Yahoo!	100.0	100.0	88.9	92.3	94.1	87.0	85.7	87.5	80.0	80.0	80.0	
Health	100.0	100.0	72.7	75.0	80.0	80.0	0.0	0.0	0.0	0.0	0.0	
Regional	100.0	100.0	100.0	0.0	0.0	0.0	0.0	0.0	0.0	0.0	0.0	
H + R	100.0	100.0	72.7	75.0	80.0	80.0	82.8	84.8	0.0	0.0	0.0	

Figure 5-8 Recall-precision curves of search-term "health"

Note that this is the unique exceptional circumstance in which categorized search results do not outperform the Yahoo! search results.

Comparison of search-term "jaguar"

The 12 relevant search results are categorized into three categories: Game; Kids & Teens; and Science (see Appendix 13). Categories "Science" + "Kids & Teens" contain eleven out of the 14 relevant search results; the comparison among *recall-precision* curves is illustrated in Figure 5-9. An average improvement on *precision* of the categorized results is:

(100-50 + 100-66.7 + 100-27.3 + 100-21.7 + 100-23.1 + 100-25.9 + 100-29 + 100-31.3 + 100-29.3 + 0-28.3 + 0-28.6) / 11 = (900 – 361.2) / 11

= 50.0 (%)

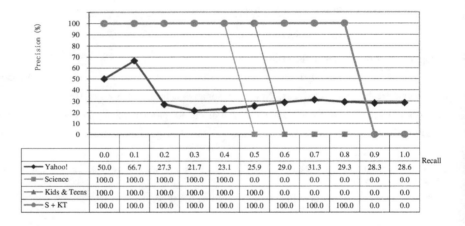

	0.0	0.1	0.2	0.3	0.4	0.5	0.6	0.7	0.8	0.9	1.0
Yahoo!	50.0	66.7	27.3	21.7	23.1	25.9	29.0	31.3	29.3	28.3	28.6
Science	100.0	100.0	100.0	100.0	100.0	0.0	0.0	0.0	0.0	0.0	0.0
Kids & Teens	100.0	100.0	100.0	100.0	100.0	100.0	0.0	0.0	0.0	0.0	0.0
S + KT	100.0	100.0	100.0	100.0	100.0	100.0	100.0	100.0	100.0	0.0	0.0

Figure 5-9 Recall-precision *curves of search-term "jaguar"*

Comparison of search-term "UPS"

The 12 relevant search results are categorized into two categories: Computers; and Business (see Appendix 14). Categories "Computers" + "Business" contain all of the 12 relevant search results; the comparison among *recall-precision* curves is illustrated in Figure 5-10. An average improvement on *precision* of the categorized results is:

(50-12.5 + 50-22.2 + 60-14.3 + 57.1-18.2 + 26.3-20 + 30-19.4 + 36.4-24.2 + 39.1-26.5 + 41.7-28.6 + 44-26.2 + 46.2-25) / 11 = (480.8 – 237.1) / 11

= 22.2 (%)

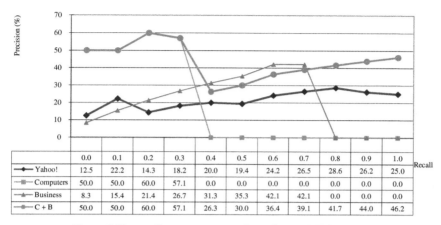

	0.0	0.1	0.2	0.3	0.4	0.5	0.6	0.7	0.8	0.9	1.0
Yahoo!	12.5	22.2	14.3	18.2	20.0	19.4	24.2	26.5	28.6	26.2	25.0
Computers	50.0	50.0	60.0	57.1	0.0	0.0	0.0	0.0	0.0	0.0	0.0
Business	8.3	15.4	21.4	26.7	31.3	35.3	42.1	42.1	0.0	0.0	0.0
C + B	50.0	50.0	60.0	57.1	26.3	30.0	36.4	39.1	41.7	44.0	46.2

Figure 5-10 *Recall-precision* curves of search-term "UPS" (1)

As can be seen from Appendix 9, all the eight relevant search results categorized under "Business" are further classified under the category "Electronics and Electrical". In this scenario, the comparison among *recall-precision* curves is illustrated in Figure 5-11.

An average improvement on *precision* of the categorized results is:

(50-12.5 + 50-22.2 + 60-14.3 + 57.1-18.2 + 62.5-20 + 66.7-19.4 + 72.7-24.2 + 75-26.5 + 76.9-28.6 + 78.6-26.2 + 80-25) / 11 = (729.5 - 237.1) /11

= **44.8 (%)**

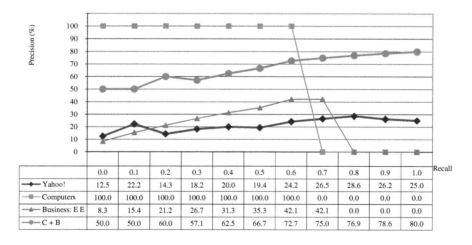

	0.0	0.1	0.2	0.3	0.4	0.5	0.6	0.7	0.8	0.9	1.0
Yahoo!	12.5	22.2	14.3	18.2	20.0	19.4	24.2	26.5	28.6	26.2	25.0
Computers	100.0	100.0	100.0	100.0	100.0	100.0	100.0	0.0	0.0	0.0	0.0
Business: E E	8.3	15.4	21.2	26.7	31.3	35.3	42.1	42.1	0.0	0.0	0.0
C + B	50.0	50.0	60.0	57.1	62.5	66.7	72.7	75.0	76.9	78.6	80.0

Figure 5-11 Recall-precision curves of search-term "UPS" (2)

Overall Average Comparison

The overall average *precisions* at the standard 11 *recall* level of Yahoo! search results and categorized results of the special search-browser are illustrated in Figure 5-12.

An average improvement on *precision* of the Categorized results is:

(90-55 + 83.3-53.6 + 81.5-40.6 + 83.1-39.3 + 76.3-39.5 + 78-37.8 + 78.8-38.2 + 57.7-39.4 + 38.8-38.1 + 40-38.6+ 9.24-38.8) / 11 = (716.74 – 458.9) / 11 = 65.2 – 41.7

= 23.5 (%)

The overall average *precision* of the 50 search results Yahoo! is:

(55+53.6+40.6+39.3+39.5+37.8+38.2+39.4+38.1+38.6+38.8) / 11 = 41.7%

The overall average *precision* of the categorized results is:

(90+83.3+81.5+83.1+76.3+78+78.8+57.7+38.8+40+9.24) / 11 = 65.2%

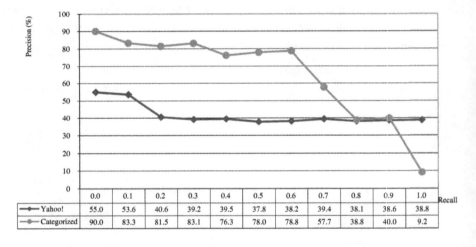

	0.0	0.1	0.2	0.3	0.4	0.5	0.6	0.7	0.8	0.9	1.0
Yahoo!	55.0	53.6	40.6	39.2	39.5	37.8	38.2	39.4	38.1	38.6	38.8
Categorized	90.0	83.3	81.5	83.1	76.3	78.0	78.8	57.7	38.8	40.0	9.2

Figure 5-12 Average recall-precision curves of Yahoo! search results and categorized search results over the five search-terms

5.6.3 *Precision* at different cut-off levels of the Categorized Search Results

Because only the search-term "Health" has more than 15 relevant search results, and search-term "Ford" has only five relevant search results, the search results of "Ford" will not be taken into account when comparing *precision* at different cut-off levels. *Precision* is compared at only two of the cut-off levels: P@5 and P@10. The comparison results are show in Table 5-8.

Table 5-8 P@5 and P@10 of Yahoo! and categorized search results (%)

	P@5	P@10	Average
Yahoo!	46.7	42.0	44.4
Categorized	85.0	70.0	77.5
Improvement	38.3	28.0	33.2

5.6.4 Comparison of Results

In the previous sections, the standard 11 *recall-precision* curve of Yahoo!'s 50 search results, and the *recall-precision* curves of the categorized search results are drawn. P@5, P@10 for categorized search results and the 50 Yahoo!'s returned results are also calculated. The following two main conclusions can be reached when the search results are compared.

1) The proposed approach can improve *precision* by 23.5 per cent when measured by the standard 11 point *recall-precision* interpolated curve. The average precision of Yahoo!'s 50 search results is 41.7 per cent, while categorized search results of the special search-browser is 65.2 per cent. (section 5.6.2, Overall Average Comparison)

2) The improvements of P@5 and P@10 are 38.3 per cent and 28.0 per cent respectively, the average improvement is 33.2 per cent. P@5 for Yahoo! and the categorized results are 46.7 per cent and 85.0 per cent; P@10 for Yahoo! is 42.0 per cent and 70.0 per cent for the categorized search results.

The results demonstrate that the special search-browser can improve the precision of Yahoo!'s search results as high as 23.5 per cent based on the standard 11 *recall-precision* curve; and average P@5 and P@10 improvement is reached 33.3 per cent.

5.7 Limitation and Discussion

While the proposed approach greatly improved *precision*, some issues need to be further dealt with, as discussed below.

5.7.1 Loss of *Recall*

For the five search-terms, no one category contains all the relevant search results. Most search results are categorized into more then two categories; only search results of "UPS" are classified into two categories. Table 5-9 illustrates the *recall* levels when one or two categories are selected.

Table 5-9 Recall of categories

	Clinton	Ford	health	jaguar	UPS	Average
One category	66.7	40.0	50.0	42.9	66.7	53.3
Two categories	93.3	80.0	72.5	78.6	100.0	86.0

When selecting two categories, the average *recall* is 86.0 per cent; that is, the *recall* loss is 14.0 per cent.

If all the relevant documents can be categorized into one category, there will be no *recall* loss. However, the following reasons result in relevant search results being categorized into more than one category:

1) How to build the Web category is *per se* ambiguous. For example, the ODP category is different from the *Yahoo! Web Directory*. Notice that even experts have no agreement on how to classify search results; it is therefore impossible for an algorithm to categorize all the relevant documents into only one category. Further, relevance judgment *per se* is subjective, and varies at different times as discussed in section 5.5.1 and section 5.5.2.

2) Search results are given in the form of information snippets; it does not purport to represent the semantic characteristics of the search results. Therefore, the information may not be fine grained enough to allow the proposed approach to classify the search results into a proper category.

3) The extracted semantic characteristics of the ODP category may be inaccurate, or insufficient to describe the concept represented by the category. In this circumstance, categorization may also be affected.

4) In this research, one search result is only categorized into one category. This also prevents relevant search results from clustering together.

Two approaches may alleviate the problems. The first one is to allow one search result to be categorized into more than one category. However, another problem arises when considering how many categories one result can be classified into. The second approach is to use ontologies instead of the ODP category, because well constructed ontologies can clearly represent the semantic characteristics of the concept in the ontologies.

5.7.2 Special Cases – Search-term "health"

When "health" is the query, Yahoo! outperforms the special search-browser. However, when analysing the five judges' judgments, it can be found that judges have the least agreement on this search-term. To facilitate discussion, the following four terms are introduced: *judgment number*; *agreement number*; *convergent degree* and *divergent degree*.

Judgment Number

Each search-term has 50 search results; each search result has four possible relevance judgments, namely *Relevant, Partially relevant, Irrelevant* and *Not sufficient information*. Therefore, each search-term has 200 (50 search results × 4 relevance judgment) possible (maximum) relevance judgments. For any of the 50 returned search items, it may be judged *relevant* by one judge, *partially relevant* by the rest judges; or it may be judged *irrelevant* by two out of the five judges and *partially relevant* by the other three judges. For a given search-term, one extreme situation is for each of the 50 search results, the five judges make four different relevance judgments, in which case the number of judgments made for the 50 search results is 200; another extreme case is for each of the 50 search results, the relevance judgment made by the five judges is same. For example, for the first returned item, all the five judges believe it is *partially relevant*; for the second returned item, all the judges believe it is *irrelevant*; for the third returned item, all the five judges think it is *relevant*, and the like. In this case, 50 out of 200 possible relevance judgments are made. *Judgment number* is defined as for the 50 returned search results of a given search-term, the number of relevance judgments made by the judges. *Judgment number* ranges from 50 to 200.

Agreement Number

For a given query, supposed out of 50 returned search items, n items obtained same relevance judgment (only if the relevance judgment is the same, no matter what the judgment, R, P, I or N, is) by all the five judges, the n is named *agreement number*. That is, for the 50 returned search results of a given search-term, the number of returned items that obtained the same relevance judgement by all the judges. The range of *agreement number* is from 0 to 50.

For a given query, if all the five judges agree with each other on all the 50 returned search items, the *judgment number* is 50, and the *agreement number* is 50 also. On the other extreme hand, for all the 50 returned items, each has four relevance judgments, in this circumstance the *agreement number* and *judgment number* are zero and 200 respectively. These two numbers, *judgment number* and *agreement number*, are suggested to describe how judges agree with each other on relevance judgments for a query. If they agree more with each other on one search-term, the *agreement number* is larger and the *judgment number* is smaller, and the overall judgment of human judges can be referred to as "convergent"; otherwise, the judgment is referred to as "divergent". The relevance judgment *convergent degree* can be measured by the ratio of *judgment number* to *agreement number*.

Convergent Degree = Agreement Number / Judgment Number

Table 5-10 shows the relevance judgment *convergent degrees* of the five search-terms.

Table 5-10 Relevance judgment convergent degrees of the five search-terms

	Clinton	Ford	health	jaguar	UPS
Agreement Number	27	34	1	37	35
Judgment Number	82	71	114	63	71
Convergent Degree	0.3	0.5	0.0^{29}	0.6	0.5
***Precision* Improvement**	18.7	42.0	-30.2	53.9	24.4/49.2

---

[29] The actual number is 0.009.

To evaluate a categorization algorithm, an intuition is that if the judgment of human judges is convergent, or the convergent degree is higher, the algorithm should perform better as well; on the other hand, if the judgment of human judges is divergent, that is, the convergent degree is lower, it is arguable to use the data to evaluate a categorization (or IR) algorithm.

Based on this intuition, Figure 5-13 demonstrates the relationship between the *relevant convergent degree* and the *precision* improvement of this research. As illustrated by this figure, there is a linear relationship (roughly) between the *precision* improvement and the *relevance judgment convergent degree.*

The *relevance judgment convergent degree* of the search-term "Health" is the smallest among the five *convergent degrees.* Among the 200 possible relevance judgments, there is only one agreement of all the five judges; on the other hand, the five judges give 114 different judgments for the 50 search results. These figures reveal that the human judges are disagreeing with each other on this search-term. **Therefore, this negative precision improvement should not be regarded as a fault of the proposed approach.**

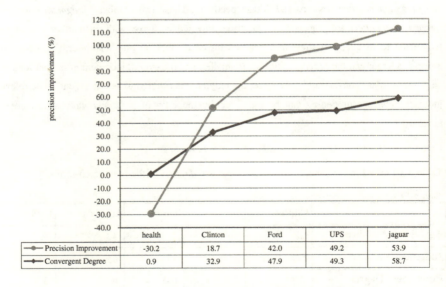

	health	Clinton	Ford	UPS	jaguar
Precision Improvement	-30.2	18.7	42.0	49.2	53.9
Convergent Degree	0.9	32.9	47.9	49.3	58.7

Figure 5-13 Relationship between precision *improvement and relevance judgment convergent degree*

5.7.3 Category Selection

How to choose the correct categories which contain more relevant search results than others is another issue to be considered. Search results are usually categorized into more than one category, and the categories will be highlighted if there are search results categorized under it (refer to Figure 5-2). For the categorized search results of the search-term "UPS", if a user selects "Computers" first, and "Business" second, the categorized results will be better than when other categories are selected, even when category "Computers" is selected first.

One approach to address this issue is to combine text clustering techniques. Before search results are classified into the ODP categories, search results are first clustered into several groups, and features of these clusters are extracted subsequently. The extracted feature(s) can than combine with the ODP categories to manifest the semantic characteristics of the cluster and the ODP categories.

5.8 Summary

This chapter discussed how objective four is achieved. Experiment data reveals that the proposed categorization approach can improve the average *precision* at the 11 standard *recall* levels of Yahoo! Web search results by 23.5 per cent, from Yahoo!'s average *precision* of 41.7 per cent to 65.2 per cent of this research. The improvement of P@5 and P@10 is 38.3 per cent (85.0 - 46.7) and 28.0 per cent (70.0 – 42.0) respectively. Because search results are categorized into different categories, it is very hard to obtain a high *precision* while keeping the *recall* high. The *recall* may be improved by classifying one search result into more than one category. If the *relevance judgment convergent degree* is very low, it is arguable to employ the data to evaluate the performance of an IR algorithm, because human judges at this circumstance tend to disagree with each other. This scenario happens when search results of "health" are categorized. However, the proposed approach of this research revealed a linear relationship between *precision* improvement and the *relevance judgment convergent degree*. If human judges tend to agree with each other, the special search-browser also tends to perform well. Further research which combines clustering techniques is needed to improve the *recall* level while keeping high *precision*, and to facilitate users to select appropriate categories effectively. In next chapter, several text categorization techniques which can be utilized in the next stage of this research and the conclusion of this research are presented.

Chapter 6.   Conclusion and Future Work

Lucene (Gospodnetić & Hatcher 2005) uses a modified Vector Space Model (Arasu et al. 2001, Baeza-Yates & Ribeiro-Neto 1999, pp. 27-30, MOLE 2005, Salton & Buckley 1988, Salton et al. 1996) when calculating the similarities between search-terms and the document collection. The Probabilistic Model (Crestani et al. 1998, Jones et al. 2000, Jones 2003, Rijsbergen 1979, pp. 87-110) can also be used as a classifier based on the ODP to disambiguate search-terms. Mladenic (1998) uses machine learning approach to classify Web pages based on the *Yahoo! Web Directory*; for the 14 Yahoo! categories, a separate classifier is built. Labrou and Finin (1999) utilize n-gram algorithm to automatically classify Web pages. Frommholz (2001) uses the knowledge about the hierarchy (such as *Yahoo! Web Directory*) to achieve a better categorization result.

The data of the ODP is dynamic and increasing because new Web sites are going to be submitted, and existing Web sites may also change their contents. To reduce the high dimensionality of the vector space, Latent Semantic Indexing algorithm (Deerwester et al. 1990, Sebastiani 1999) is widely used. A recent and computationally more efficient technology named Normalised Word Vector (Williams 2006) is also proposed, and applied to reduce the high dimension of term vectors. Machine learning (Sebastiani 1999, 2006) is becoming the dominant approach applied in text categorization and text clustering. Research communities of ontology and IR are now seeking to cooperate also (Ding et al. 2003).

This chapter discusses some possible further research directions for this research in the future. Section 6.1 presents using the probability model to compare the similarities between *category-documents* and search-terms. Section 6.2 discusses the application of machine learning algorithms in IR and text categorization. Section 6.3 introduces ontology-based IR and text categorization, and section 6.4 is the summary of this chapter.

6.1 Probabilistic Model as a Classifier

Probabilistic models in IR have been intensively researched since it appeared around the decade of the 70s last century. The probabilistic models attempt to employ formal theories of probability and statistics in order to evaluate, or at least estimate, the probability that users will find the document relevant (interesting) to their information needs (Baeza-Yates & Ribeiro-Neto 1999, p. 30, Crestani et al. 1998). Probabilistic models are generally classified into *relevance models* and *inference models*, and seek to answer the basic question, "What is the probability that *this* document is relevant to *this* query?" (Jones et al. 2000, p. 783) To answer this question, a rule called *Probability Ranking Principle* is adhered to by all probability models. The principle asserts that "if retrieved documents are ordered by decreasing probability of relevance on the data available, then the system's effectiveness is the best to be gotten for the data." (Jones et al. 2000, p. 784)

VSM is by far the best-developed non-probabilistic model of IR, and its simplicity, effectiveness and efficiency is comparable to any other approaches; including the probabilistic model (Baeza-Yates & Ribeiro-Neto 1999, pp. 30, Crestani et al. 1998, Jones et al. 2000, pp. 829-830). As pointed out by Jones et al. (2000, pp. 829-830), the basic logic of the VSM is also common to the probabilistic model, and there are implementations of probabilistic ideas within the VSM. In practice, VSM and the probabilistic model borrow ideas from each other, and the original principle to some extent has been disguised by the implementation process. However, the fundamental difference is that VSM takes attributes as the axes of the space, and the similarity measure is based on distance of query and documents in this space; and the probabilistic model regards attributes as probability variables. It is therefore interesting to compare the results by using the probabilistic model as a classifier with the results when VSM is employed as a classifier.

6.2 Machine Learning

According to Lewis (1991, p. 235), the information retrieval process is divided into four main phases, namely, *indexing, query formulation, comparison*, and *relevance feedback*. As pointed out by Cunningham et al. (1999, p. 39), machine learning techniques are now widely used in all these four different phases of information retrieval, and the application is just beginning. On the other hand, Langley and Simon (1995) classify five major paradigms in machine learning research; they are *neural networks, instance-based methods, genetic learning, rule induction* and *analytic approaches*. Chen and Chau (2004, p. 293) identify a similar five major categories of paradigms, namely, *probabilistic models, symbolic learning* and *rule induction, neural networks, evolution-based models* and *analytic learning and fuzzy logic*. Cunningham et al. (1999, p. 7) indicate that all of the machine learning techniques have been successfully applied in the field of information retrieval, and the choice of these approaches seems to be based largely on the experience and preference of the researchers involved.

6.2.1 Machine Learning Paradigms

While some of the machine learning techniques are widely employed in IR, however, not all of these machine learning paradigms are suitable for the four different information retrieval phases. Cunningham et al.'s (1999, pp. 4-7) research indicates that *analytic learning algorithms* are in some way the antithesis of the usual information retrieval scenario, because these approaches need background knowledge and complex structure to store explanations of the knowledge. *Genetic algorithms* are also seldom adopted by information retrieval communities. Some possible reasons are the random nature of the genetic operators, the resulting non-deterministic behaviour, and the difficulty of setting control parameters to ensure good performance. *Decision tree and rule induction*, which create an explicit description of the concept represented by the input data, are the best-developed machine learning techniques, and the C4.5 algorithm[30] (Mitchell 1997, pp. 55-77) has become the benchmark for inductive machine learning techniques. *Instance-based methods* store training examples, and new examples are classified by comparing them with the stored examples. *Nearest-neighbour* is the simplest algorithm of this kind of learning approach. *Neural networks* try to model natural learning processes by representing knowledge as weighted links between nodes in a multilayer network, with activation spreading algorithms from input to output nodes during the classification process.

6.2.2 Machine Learning for IR

Chen (1995) presents an extensive review of machine learning techniques for IR, and his research mainly focuses on neural networks, symbolic learning and genetic algorithms. He discusses three popular machine learning algorithms: the *connectionist Hopfield network*; the *symbolic ID3/ID5R*; and the *evolution-based genetic algorithms*. He finds that "these techniques are robust in their ability to analyze user queries, identify users' information needs, and suggest alternatives for search" (p. 192). It is crucial for an IR system to select knowledge representation and the adaptation of machine learning algorithms. For example, an index term in the IR model should be represented by a *node* in the *Hopfield net* with the modified *parallel relaxation* search algorithm, or a *single bit* in a *genetic* evaluation with the modified *Darwinian selection algorithm*, or a *decision node* in the *symbolic learning* with the modified *entropy reduction scheme*. He also suggests that connectionist modelling and learning has attracted considerably more attention than symbolic machine learning and genetic algorithms, because connectionist modelling and learning has strong resemblance to some existing IR models and techniques, although all the new techniques have been found to exhibit promising inductive learning capabilities for selected IR applications.

Chen and Chau (2004, pp. 297-301) indicate machine learning techniques have been successfully used in the field of information extraction, relevance feedback, information filtering, text classification and text clustering, as summarized in Table 6-1.

As pointed out by Sebastiani (2006), *support vector machines* and *boosting* are now two dominant learning methods in text categorization. Therefore, using machine learning techniques, such as

---

[30] c4.5 is a decision tree generating algorithm based on the ID3 algorithm. It contains several improvements, especially needed for software implementation. Improvements include Choosing an appropriate attribute selection measure, Handling training data with missing attribute values, Handling attributes with differing costs, and Handling continuous attributes. (http://en.wikipedia.org/wiki/C4.5_algorithm)

neural networks, support vector machine and boosting, provides a space to improve the performance of the special search-browser in this research.

Table 6-1 Machine learning in IR

	Application	**Machine Learning Techniques**
Information Extraction	Identify useful information from text documents automatically, such as named-entity extraction	Neural networks, decision tree, hidden Markov model, entropy maximization, and combination of these techniques
Relevance Feedback	Help users conduct searches iteratively and reformulate search queries based on evaluation of previously retrieved documents to significantly improve search precision and recall	Genetic algorithms, ID3
Information Filtering	Apply user evaluation to improve performance of an IR system by learning users' interests from their evaluations and actions to alleviate the problem of information overload in IR system.	Decision tree
Text Classification	Classify textual documents into predefined categories (supervised learning)	Naive Bayesian method, k-nearest neighbour method, neural networks, support vector machine, boosting approach, self-organizing map (SOM)
Text Clustering	Group documents into categories defined dynamically, based on their similarities (unsupervised learning). Include hierarchical and non-hierarchical clustering.	Hierarchical clustering: k-nearest neighbour; Ward's algorithm. Non-hierarchical clustering: K-means algorithm; suffix tree; fuzzy clustering.

6.3 Ontology-Based Information Retrieval

Many research efforts have been contributed in IR to improve text indexing or query formulation with the help of ontologies; and IR is also considered as one of the favourite application field for ontologies (Aussenac-Gilles & Mothe 2004). In 2003, "ACM SIGIR Workshop on 'Semantic Web'" (Ding et al. 2003) first brought together IR community and the Semantic Web research groups. They agree with each other that ontologies that provide shared, common knowledge domain representations will play a key role in contributing to improved search outcomes.

Several prototypes of ontology-based information retrieval have been developed. Rocha et al. (2004) proposes a hybrid approach for searching in the Semantic Web. Each concepts relation instance in a given ontology is assigned a weight by similar *term-frequency/inverse document frequency* (tf-idf) strategy to measure the strength of the relation. Spread activation algorithm is employed to search the related concepts in the ontology with initial values derived from classic keyword retrieval technique. The approach of Vallet et al. (2005) is similar to Rocha's but focuses on ranking annotated documents than browsing-oriented searching. Paralic and Kostial (2003) compare traditional tf-idf and the *Latent Semantic Indexing* approach with the *ontology-based approach* and state that 20 per cent improvement in *precision* is gained. However, the main weakness of their approach is that users have to manually retrieve relevant concepts from the ontology to formulate their search query, and document collection is relatively small.

The relationship of concepts of an ontology can be used to navigate the Web sites (Antoniou & Harmelen 2004, p. 11). A new approach proposed by Aussenac-Gilles and Mothe (2004) is that information searching and exploring takes place in a domain-dependent semantic context. They suggest that index terms can be organized into a hierarchical structure to facilitate the query reformulation (relevance feedback), by providing more specific or more generic terms to guide the user to find a better query formulation. Instead of directly using ontologies as a querying language which may suffer from the complexity of the ontologies, ontologies are transformed into hierarchies that serve as representation for hierarchy definition and document classification, and thus make them more easily browsed and used. Users can browse the concept hierarchies, or select terms to add to their query.

6.4 Combining Categorization and Clustering to Improve Categorization Quality

Experimental data show that in this research, while the precision gains an overall 23.5% improvement, the precision of Yahoo! is no less than that of the special search-browser when the recall level is 80% or bigger. This is mainly because in this research, each search results only catgegorized under one category. Another reason is that no categorization algorithm is perfect. A third reson is the subjective property of the relevance judgment which plays a key role in measuring the precision and recall.

There are two possible approaches to improve the recall of a categorization result. The first approach is to assign a search results into more than one category; another method is to utilize the clustering results to improve the quality of categorization. In the future, both approaches will be tested and evaluated.

6.5 Larger Scale Experiment

At this research stage, only five queries are used in the experiment. This is obviously an limitation. An experiment with a large number of queries from real user is needed in the next research stage. Another work is to let the users who use the special search-browser to choose the interesting category themselves. A further experiment is to utilize users' search history to recommend which category to select and thus personalized search results.

6.6 Conclusion

Search engines are facing challenges of information overload, mismatch of search results and users' information needs, missing relevant documents, poorly organized search results, mismatching the human mental model of formed clusters, and lack of a commonly shared knowledge structure for search results classification. The main purpose of this research is thus to improve the relevance of search results via search-term disambiguation and ontologically filtering the search results. To achieve the purpose, four objectives are proposed and accomplished.

The first objective is to model the themantic content of the Web in a structured hierarchy by utilizing the categories of the ODP. This objective is obtained by extracting the semantic characteristics of each categories of the ODP to form a *category-document* set, and by using the Java Tree component to present the first two levels of the ODP Web directory (Chapter 3, section 3.4 and Chapter 4, section 4.3, section 4.4 and section 4.5).

The second objective is to develop a special search-browser which integrates search results of search engine and the ODP-based ontology using a navigation metaphor. *Yahoo! Search Web Services API* and Java Tree component are selected as the main components to implement the special search-browser (Chapter 3, section 3.3 and Chapter 4, section 4.2).

The third objective is to categorize the search results returned by Yahoo! according to the ontological filter based on the structure hierarchy of the ODP. Lucene, which utilizes a modified VSM, is selected to accomplish this objective. The functions of search results categorization and filtering are integrated into the special search-browser. Each search result is first categorized into one of the ODP category. When an interesting category is picked up, the irrelevant results will be filtered out and only results categorized under the selected category are presented (Chapter 3, section 3.2, section 3.6, section 3.7, Chapter 4, section 4.6, section 4.7).

The last objective is to evaluate the retrieval effectiveness of the developed search-browser by calculating the precision and recall of the search results. Chapter 5 presented the details of the evaluation experiment and the outcomes of the experiment.

To obtain the objectives, an interactive information retrieval model was first proposed which categorizes search results ontologically. A special search-browser is developed where semantic characteristics of the ODP categories are extracted to form text format *category-documents* that are then indexed by Lucene. Lucene is also employed to compare similarities between the search results from *Yahoo! Search Web Services API* and the category-documents. Each of the returned search result will be assigned to one of the ODP categories based on the similarities and the *Majority Voting* algorithm. Search-term disambiguation is achieved when the user selects an interesting category of the ODP and the special search-browser filters and presents only results categorized under the selected category.

Experiment demonstrates that categorization approach proposed in this research can improve the average *precision* at the 11 standard *recall* levels of Yahoo! Web search results from Yahoo!'s average *precision* of 41.7 per cent to 65.2 per cent of this research, 23.5 per cent precision improvement is achieved. The improvement of P@5 and P@10 is 38.3 per cent (85.0 - 46.7) and 28.0 per cent (70.0 – 42.0) respectively. This research also suggests that if the *relevance judgment convergent degree* is very low, it is arguable to employ the data to evaluate the performance of an IR algorithm. An intuition is further proposed that for an effective IR algorithm, a linear relationship should exist between *precision* improvement and the *relevance judgment convergent degree*. In this research, when the five human judges tend to agree with each other, the special search-browser also tends to perform well.

6.7 Summary

At the present stage, this research simply takes the ODP as an ontology and the VSM as a classifier for its proven effectiveness and efficiency. However, techniques introduced in this chapter, such as the probabilistic model, the inference network, different machine learning algorithms, and ontology-based text categorization are all potential research directions.

References

Allan, J & Raghavan, H 2002, 'Using Part-of-speech Patterns to Reduce Query Ambiguity', *Proceedings of the 25th ACM International Conference on Research and Development in Information Retrieval (SIGIR-02)*, ACM Press, New York, NY, pp. 307-314.

Almeida, RB & Almeida, VAF 2004, 'A Community-Aware Search Engine', *Proceedings of the thirteenth international conference on World Wide Web (WWW2004)*, ACM Press, New York, NY, pp. 413-421.

Antoniou, G & Harmelen, F 2004, *A Semantic Web Primer*, The MIT Press, Cambridge, Massachusetts, London.

Apache Jakarta Project, http://jakarta.apache.org/

Apache Lucene, http://lucene.apache.org/java/docs/index.html

Apache Software Foundation, 2006, *Lucene 1.9.1 API*. Retrieved March 15, 2006 from http://lucene.apache.org/java/docs/

Arasu, A, Cho, J, Garcia-Molina, H, Paepcke, A & Raghavan, S 2001, 'Searching the Web', *ACM Transactions on Internet Technology*, vol. 1, no. 1, pp. 2-43.

Aussenac-Gilles, N & Mothe, J 2004, 'Ontologies as Background Knowledge to Explore Document Collections', *Proceedings of the Recherche d'Information Assistee par Ordinateur (RIAO 2004)*, pp. 129-142. Retrieved on November 2, 2005 from http://www.irit.fr/recherches/IRI/SIG/personnes/mothe/pub/RIAO04a.pdf.

Baeza-Yates, R & Ribeiro-Neto, B 1999, *Modern Information Retrieval*, ACM Press, New York & Addison Wesley, Harlow.

Barker J 2006, *Meta-Search Engines: UC-Berkeley – Teaching Library Internet Workshops*. Retrieved March 5, 2007 from http://www.lib.berkeley.edu/TeachingLib/Guides/Internet/MetaSearch.html

Bates, MJ 1989, 'The Design of Browsing and Berrypicking Techniques for the On-line Search Interface', *Online Review*, vol. 13, no. 5, pp. 407-424.

Bergman, MK 2001, 'The Deep Web: Surface Hidden Value', *Journal of Electronic Publishing*, vol. 7, no. 1, August 2001. Retrieved March 13, 2005 from http://www.brightplanet.com/pdf/deepwebwhitepaper.pdf

Booth, D, Haas, H, McCabe, F, Newcomer, E, Champion, M, Ferris, C & Orchard, D 2004, Web Services Architecture: W3C Working Group Note 11 February 2004, *the World Wide Web Consortium*. Retrieved November 22, 2005 from http://www.w3.org/TR/ws-arch/

Brin, S & Page, L 1998, 'The anatomy of a large-scale hypertextual Web search engine', *Computer Networks and ISND Systems*, vol. 30, pp. 107-117.

Bruijn, J 2003, *Using Ontologies: Enabling Knowledge Sharing and Reuse on the Semantic Web*, DERI Technical Report DERI-2003-10-29, October, 2003. Retrieved May 8, 2005 from http://keom.khu.ac.kr/keomwiki/_bf_c2_c5_e7_b7_ce_c1_f6_20_b0_fc_b7_c3_20_c0_da_b7_e1_20_bc_f6_c1_fd

Caropreso, MF, Matwin, S & Sebastiani, F 2001, 'A Learner-independent Evaluation of the Usefulness of Statistical Phrases for Automated Text Categorization', in AG Chin (ed.), *Text Databases and Document Management: Theory and Practice*, Idea Group Publishing, Hershey, pp. 78-102.

Chen, H 1995, 'Machine Learning for Information Retrieval: Neural Networks, Symbolic Learning, and Genetic Algorithms', *Journal of the American Society for Information Science*, vol. 46, no. 3, pp. 194-216.

Chen, H & Chau, M 2004, 'Web Mining: Machine Learning for Web Applications', *Annual Review of Information Science and Technology*, vol. 38, pp. 289-329.

Chirita, P, Nejdl, W, Paiu, R & Kohlschütter, C 2005, 'Using ODP Metadata to Personalize Search', *Proceedings of the 28th annual international ACM SIGIR conference on Research and Development in Information Retrieval*, ACM Press, New York, NY, pp. 178-185.

Cho, J & Garcia-Molina, H 2002, 'Parallel Crawlers', *Proceedings of the eleventh international conference on World Wide Web (WWW'02)*, ACM Press, New York, NY, pp. 124-135.

Chowdhury, GG 2003, 'Natural Language Processing', *Annual Review of Information Science and Technology*, vol. 37, pp. 51-89.

Chowdhury, GG 2004, *Introduction to Modern Information Retrieval*, 2nd edn, Facet Publishing, London.

Cohn, M & Herring, R 2005, *Yahoo Claims Edge Over Google*. Retrieved July 7, 2006 from http://www.basex.com/press.nsf/0/E7D5C95F542F527F8525705900031804?OpenDocument

Cool, C & Spink, A 2002, 'Guest editorial: Issues of context in information retrieval (IR): an introduction to the special issue', *Information Processing and Management*, vol. 38, pp. 605-611.

Crestani, F, Lalmas, M, Rijsbergen, CJ & Campbell, I 1998, 'Is This Document Relevant? ... Probably: A Survey of Probabilistic Models in Information Retrieval', *ACM Computing Surveys*, vol. 30, no. 4, pp. 528-552.

Cunningham, SJ, Littin, J & Witten, IH 1999, 'Applications of Machine Learning in Information Retrieval', *Annual Review of Information Science and Technology*, vol. 34, pp. 341-384.

Deerwester, S, Dumais, ST, Furnas, GW, Landauer, TK & Harshman, R 1990, 'Indexing by Latent Semantic Analysis', *Journal of the American Society for Information Science,* vol. 41, no. 6, pp. 391-407.

Debole, F & Sebastiani, F 2003, 'Supervised Term Weighting for Automated Text Categorization', *Proceedings of 18th ACM Symposium on Applied Computing (SAC-03),* ACM Press, New York, NY, pp. 784-788.

Ding, Y, Rijsbergen, CJ, Ounis, I & Jose, J 2003, 'Report on ACM SIGIR Workshop on 'Semantic Web'', *ACM SIGIR Forum (SWIR 2003)*, vol. 37, no. 2, pp. 45-49.

Dreher, HV 1997, 'Empowerment of Human Cognitive Activity through Hypertext Technology', PhD thesis, Curtin University of Technology. Retrieved May 5, 2005, from Curtin University of Technology Digital Theses.

Dreher, H & Williams, R 2006, 'Assisted Query Formulation Using Normalised Word Vector and Dynamic Ontological Filtering', *Proceedings of the 7th International Conference on Flexible Query Answering Systems (FQAS 2006)*, Springer-Verlag, Berlin Heidelberg, pp. 282-294.

Dumais, S & Chen H 2000, 'Hierarchical Classification of Web Content', *Proceedings of the 23rd annual international ACM SIGIR conference on Research and development in information retrieval,* ACM Press, New York, NY, pp. 256-263.

Dumais, S, Cutrell, E & Chen, H 2001, 'Optimizing search by showing results in context', *Proceedings of the SIGCHI Conference on Human Factors in Computing Systems (SIGCHI'01)*, ACM Press, New York, NY, vol. 3, no. 1, pp. 277-284.

Fielding, RT 2000, 'Architectural Styles and the Design of Network-based Software Architectures', PhD Thesis, University of California, Irvine. Retrieved June 8, 2006 from http://www.ics.uci.edu/~fielding/pubs/dissertation/top.htm

Frommholz, I 2001, 'Categorizing Web Documents in Hierarchical Catalogues', *Proceedings of the 23rd European Colloquium on Information Retrieval Research (ECIR-01).* Retrieved July 7, 2005, from http://citeseer.ist.psu.edu/frommholz01categorizing.html

Gauch, S, Chaffee, J & Pretschner, A 2003, 'Ontology-based personalized search and browsing', *Web Intelligence and Agent System*, vol. 1, no. 3-4, pp. 219-234.

Gilleland, M n.d., *Levenshtein Distance*. Retrieved March 16, 2006 from http://www.merriampark.com/ld.htm

Glover, EJ, Lawrence, S, Gordon, MD, Birmingham, WP & Giles, CL 2001, 'Improving Web Search with user preference: Web Search—Your Way', *Communication of the ACM*, vol. 44, no. 12, pp. 97-102.

Gospodnetić, O 2003a, *Advanced Text Indexing with Lucene*. Retrieved March 15 2006 from http://www.onjava.com/lpt/a/3273

Gospodnetić, O 2003b, *Introduction to Text Indexing with Apache Jakarta Lucene*. Retrieved March 15 2006 from http://www.onjava.com/lpt/a/2944

Gospodnetić, O & Hatcher, E 2005, *Lucene IN ACTION: A guide to the Java search engine.* Manning Publications Co., Greenwich.

Google Search API, http://www.google.com/apis

Gordon M, & Pathak, P 1999, 'Finding information on the World Wide Web: the retrieval effectiveness of search engines', *Information Processing and Management*, Elsevier North-Holland Inc., New York, vol. 35, pp. 141-180.

Granitzer, M, Kienreich, W, Sabol, V & Dösinger, G 2003, 'WebRat: Supporting Agile Knowledge Retrieval through Dynamic, Incremental Clustering and Automatic Labelling of Web Search Result Sets', *Proceedings of the Twelfth IEEE International Workshops on Enabling Technologies: Infrastructure for Collaborative Enterprise (WETICE'03)*, IEEE Computer Society, Los Alamitos CA., pp. 296-301.

Greisdorf, H 2000, 'Relevance: An Interdisciplinary and Information Science Perspective', *Informing Science*, vol. 3, no. 2, pp. 67-71.

Gruber, TR 1993, 'Toward Principles for the Design of Ontologies Used for Knowledge Sharing', *International Journal of Human-Computer Studies*, vol. 43, no. 5-6, pp. 907-928.

Harter, SP 1992, "Psychological Relevance and Information Science", *Journal of the American Society for Information Science and Technology*, vol. 43, no. 9, pp. 602-615.

Hatcher, E 2003, *QueryParser Rules*. Retrieved March 15, 2006 from http://today.java.net/lpt/a/34

Hatcher, E 2004, *Lucene Intro*. Retrieved March 15, 2006 from http://www.darksleep.com/lucene

Hawking, D, Craswell, N, Thistlewaite, P & Harman, D 1999, 'Results and Challenges in Web Search Evaluation', *Computer Networks*, vol. 31, no. 11-16, pp. 1321-1330.

Hawking, D, Craswell, N, Bailey, P & Griffiths, K 2001, 'Measuring Search Engine Quality', *Journal of Information Retrieval*, Kluwer Academic Publishers, vol. 4, no. 1, pp. 33-59.

Hearst, MA 1999, 'User Interfaces and Visualization', in R Baeza-Yates & B Ribeiro-Neto (eds), *Modern Information Retrieval*, ACM Press, New York & Addison Wesley, Harlow, pp. 257-324.

Hearst, MA & Pedersen, JO 1996, 'Reexamining the Cluster Hypothesis: Scatter/Gather on Retrieval Results', *Proceedings of the 19th annual international ACM/SIGIR conference on Research and development in information retrieval*, ACM Press, New York, NY, pp. 76-84.

Hotho, A, Staab, S, & Maedche, A 2001, 'Ontology-based Text Clustering', *Proceedings of the IJCAI-2001 Workshop "Text Learning: Beyond Supervision"*, August 6, Seattle, USA. Retrieved on July 18, 2005, from http://www.aifb.uni-karlsruhe.de/WBS/Publ/2001/hothoetal.pdf

Jacobs, I & Walsh, N 2004, Architecture of the World Wide Web, Volume One: W3C Recommendation 15, December 2004, *the World Wide Web Consortium*. Retrieved on July 5, 2006 from http://www.w3.org/TR/webarch/#acks

Jansen, BJ & Spink, A 2006, 'How are we searching the World Wide Web? A Comparison of Nine Search Engine Transaction Logs', *Information Processing and Management*, vol. 42, pp. 248-263.

Jansen, BJ, Spink A, & Saracevic, T 2000, 'Real life, real users, and real needs: a study and analysis of user queries on the web', *Information Processing and Management*, vol. 36, no. 2, pp. 207-227.

Jansen, BJ, Spink, A, & Pedersen, J 2005, 'A Temporal Comparison of AltaVista Web Searching', *Journal of the American Society for Information Science and Technology*, vol. 56, no. 6, pp. 559-570.

Java Studio Creator, http://developers.sun.com

Joachims, T 1997, 'A Probabilistic Analysis of the Rocchio Algorithm with TFIDF for Text Categorization', *Proceedings of the 14th International Conference on Machine Learning (ICML-97)*, Morgan Kaufmann Publishers, San Francisco, CA, pp. 143-151.

Joachims, T 1998, 'Text Categorization with Support Vector Machines: Learning with Many Relevant Features', *Proceedings of the 10th European Conference on Machine Learning (ECML-98)*, Springer Verlag, Berlin, Heidelberg, pp. 137-142.

Jones, KS   2003, 'Document Retrieval: Shallow Data, Deep Theories; Historical Reflections, Potential Directions', in F. Sebastiani (ed.) *Advances in Information Retrieval, 25th European Conference on IR Research, ECIR 2003,* Springer-Verlag, Berlin Heidelberg, pp. 1-11.

Jones, KS, Walker, S & Robertson SE 2000, 'A probabilistic model of information retrieval: development and comparative experiments'. *Information Processing and Management*, vol. 36, no. 6, pp. 779-840.

Klas, C & Fuhr N 2000, 'A New Effective Approach for Categorizing Web Documents', *Proceedings of the 22nd Annual Colloquium of the British Computer Society Information Retrieval Specialist Group (BCSIGSG-00),* Cambridge, UK. Retrieved November 13, 2005, from http://citeseer.ist.psu.edu/klas00new.html

Kleinberg, JM 1999, 'Authoritative sources in a hyperlinked environment', *Journal of ACM,* vol. 46, no. 5, pp. 604-632.

Kobayashi, M & Takeda, K 2000, 'Information Retrieval on the Web', *ACM Computing Surveys,* vol. 32, no. 2, pp. 144-173.

Kunz, C 2003, 'SERGIO – An Interface for context driven Knowledge Retrieval', *Proceedings of eChallenges,* IOS Press, pp. 573-582.

Labrou, Y & Finin, T 1999, 'Yahoo! as an Ontology: Using Yahoo! Categories to Describe Documents', *Proceedings of the eighth international conference on Information and knowledge management*, ACM Press, New York, NY, pp. 180-187.

Langley, P & Simon, H 1995, 'Applications of Machine Learning and Rule Induction', *Communications of the ACM*, ACM Press, New York, NY, vol. 38, no. 11, pp. 55-64.

Leighton, HV & Srivastava, J 1999, 'First 20 *Precision* among World Wide Web Search Services (Search Engines)', *Journal of American Society for Information Science*, John Wiley & Sons, Inc. New York, vol. 50, no. 10, pp. 870-881.

Lewis, DD 1991, 'Learning in Intelligent Information Retrieval', *Proceedings of the 8th International Workshop on Machine Learning*, Morgan Kaufmann, San Mateo, CA, pp. 235-239.

Lewis, DD 1998, 'Naive (Bayes) at forty: The independence assumption in information retrieval', *Proceedings of the 10th European Conference on Machine Learning (ECML-98),* Springer Verlag, Berlin, Heidelberg, pp. 4-15.

Li, YH & Jain, AK 1998, 'Classification of Text Documents', *The Computer Journal,* vol. 41, no. 8, pp. 537-546.

Luca, EWD & Nürnberger, A 2004, 'Ontology-Based Semantic Online Classification of Documents: Supporting Users in Searching the Web', *Proceedings of the European Symposium on Intelligent Technologies (EUNITE 2004)*, June 10-12, Aachen, Germany. Retrieved June 21, 2005, from http://adiret.cs.uni-magdeburg.de/~deluca/eunite2004_deluca_nuernberger.pdf

Manning, CD, Raghavan, P & Schutze, H 2006, *An Introduction to Information Retrieval*, Cambridge University Press, Cambridge. Retrieved May 7, 2006 from http://nlp.stanford.edu/IR-book/pdf//1-intro.pdf

Mendenhall, W, Beaver, RJ & Beaver, BM 2006, *Probability and Statistics*, Thomson, Belmont.

Meng, W, Yu, C & Liu, K 2002, 'Building Efficient and Effective Metasearch Engines', *ACM Computing Surveys*, vol. 34, no. 1, pp. 48-89.

Mitchell, TM 1997, *Machine Learning*, The McGraw-Hill Companies, Inc., New York.

Mizzaro, S 1997, 'Relevance: The Whole History', *Journal of the American Society for Information Science*, vol. 48, no. 9, pp. 810-832.

Mizzaro, S 1998, 'How many relevances in information retrieval?', *Interacting with Computers*, vol. 10, no. 3, pp. 303-320.

Mladenic, D 1998, 'Turning Yahoo into an Automatic Web-Page Classifier', *Proceedings of the 13th European Conference on Artificial Intelligence Yong Research Paper*, John Wiley & Sons, Ltd, pp. 473-474.

MOLE – Text Analysis Group n.d., *Vector Space Model*. Retrieved November 4 2005 from http://isp.imm.dtu.dk/thor/projects/multimedia/textmining/index.html

Myers, MD 2005, 'Qualitative Research in Information Systems', *MIS Quarterly*, vol. 21, no. 2, pp. 241-242, last modified: April 14, 2005, www.qual.auckland.ac.nz

Nielsen, J 1993, *Usability Engineering*, Morgan Kaufmann, San Francisco.

Notes, G 1998, 'Northern Light: New Search Engine for the Web and Full-Text Articles', *Database Magazine*, vol. 21, no. 1, Feb-March, pp. 32-37.

Olson, GM & Olson, JS 2003, 'Human-Computer Interaction: Psychological Aspects of the Human Use of Computing', *Annual Review Psychology*, vol. 54, pp. 491-516.

Open Directory Project 2007. Retrieved May 29, 2007, from http://en.wikipedia.org/wiki/Open_Directory_Project

Osiński, S & Weiss, D 2005, 'A Concept-Driven Algorithm for Clustering Search Results', *IEEE Intelligent Systems*, May/June 2005, IEEE Computer Society, pp. 48-54.

Ozsoyoglu, G & Al-Hamdani, A 2003, 'Web Information Resource Discovery: Past, Present, and Future', in A Yazici, & C Sener (eds.) *Proceedings of the 18th International Symposium on Computer and Information Sciences (ISCIS 2003),* Springer-Verlag, Berlin Heidelberg, pp. 9-18.

Page, L, Brin, S, Motwani, R & Winograd, T 1998, 'The PageRank Citation Ranking: Bringing Order to the Web', *Stanford Digital Library working paper,* SIDL-WP-1999-0120 of 11/11/1999. Retrieved   March   13,   2005   from http://citeseer.ist.psu.edu/cache/papers/cs/7144/http:zSzzSzwww-db.stanford.eduzSz~backrubzSzpageranksub.pdf/page98pagerank.pdf

Paralic, J & Kostial, I 2003, 'Ontology-Based Information Retrieval', *Proceedings of the 14th International Conference on Information and Intelligent systems, IIS 2003,* Springer-Verlag, Berlin, pp. 23-28.

Picard, J. & Savoy, J 2003, 'Enhancing Retrieval with Hyperlinks: A General Model Based on Propositional Argumentation System', *Journal of the American Society for Information Science and Technology,* vol. 54, no. 4, pp. 347-355..

Pitkow, J, Schütze, H, Cass, T, Cooley, R, Turnbull, D, Edmonds, A, Adar, E & Breuel, T 2002, 'Personalized Search: A contextual computing approach may prove a breakthrough in personalized search efficiency', *Communications of the ACM,* vol. 45, no. 9, pp. 50-55.

Porter, M 2006, *The Porter Stemming Algorithm.* Retrieved June 10 2006 from http://tartarus.org/~martin/PorterStemmer/index.html

Ramakrishnanan, G & Bhattacharyya, P 2003, 'Text Representation with WordNet Synsets using Soft Sense Disambiguation', *Proceedings of the eighth International Conference on Application of Natural Language to Information Systems(NLDB 2003),* Springer-Verlag, Berlin Heidelberg, pp. 214-227.

Rasmussen, EM 2003, 'Indexing and Retrieval for the Web', *Annual Review of Information Science and Technology,* vol. 39, pp. 91-124.

Rijsbergen, CJ van 1979, *Information Retrieval,* 2nd edn, Butterworths, London. Online book, http://www.dcs.gla.ac.uk/Keith/Preface.html

Robertson, S 2004, 'Understanding Inverse Document Frequency: On theoretical arguments for IDF', *Journal of Documentation,* vol. 60, no. 5, pp. 503-520.

Robins, D 2000, 'Interactive Information Retrieval: Context and Basic Notions', *Informing Science,* vol. 3, no. 2 pp. 57-61.

Rocha, C, Schwabe, D & Aragão, MP 2004, 'A Hybrid Approach for Searching in the Semantic Web', *Proceedings of the thirteenth international conference on World Wide Web (WWW2004)*, ACM Press, New York, NY, pp. 374-383.

Sabol, V, Kienreich, W, Granitzer, M, Becker, J, Tochtermann, K & Andrews, K 2002, 'Applications of a lightweight, Web-Based Retrieval, Clustering, and Visualisation Framework', in D. Karagiannis & U. Reimer (eds.): *Practical Aspects of Knowledge Management : 4th International Conference, PAKM 2002 Proceedings*, Springer-Verlag, Berlin Heidelberg, pp. 359-368.

Salton, G & Buckley, C 1988, 'Term-Weighting Approaches in Automatic Text Retrieval', *Information Processing & Management*, vol. 24, no. 5, pp. 513-523.

Salton, G & Buckley, C 1990, 'Improving Retrieval Performance by Relevance Feedback', *Journal of the American Society for Information Science,* vol. 41, no. 4, pp. 288-297.

Salton, G & Lesk, ME 1968, 'Computer Evaluation of Indexing and Text Processing', *Journal of the Association for Computing Machinery,* vol. 15, no. 1, pp. 8-36.

Salton, G, Allan, J & Singhal, A 1996, 'Automatic Text Decomposition and Structuring', *Information Processing & Management,* vol. 32, no. 2, pp. 127-138.

Sandbox of Lucene, 2006, *Apache Lucene.* http://lucene.apache.org/java/docs/lucene-sandbox/

Saracevic, T 1996, 'Relevance Reconsidered', *Information Science: Integration in Perspective, Proceedings of the Second Conference on Conceptions of Library and Information Science (CoLIS 2)*, pp. 201-218.

Schapire, RE, Singer, Y & Singhal, A 1998, 'Boosting and Rocchio Applied to Text Filtering', *Proceedings of the 21st annual international ACM SIGIR conference on Research and Development in Information Retrieval*, ACM Press, New York, NY, pp. 215-223.

Sebastiani, F 1999, 'A Tutorial on Automated Text Categorisation', in A Amandi & R Zunino (eds.), *Proceedings of the First Argentinian International Symposium on Artificial Intelligence (ASAI-99)*, pp. 7-35.

Sebastiani, F 2002, 'Machine Learning in Automated Text Categorization', *ACM Computing Surveys*, vol. 34, no. 1, pp. 1-47.

Sebastiani, F 2005, 'Text Categorization', in A Zanasi (ed.), *Text Mining and its Applications*, WIT Press, Southampton, pp. 109-129.

Sebastiani, F 2006, 'Text Categorization, Automatic', in K Brown (ed.), *The Encyclopedia of Language and Linguistics*, 2nd edn, vol. 14, Elsevier Science Publishers, Amsterdam, NL, pp. 457-462.

Shafi, SM, & Rather, RA 2005, '*Precision* and *Recall* of Five Search Engines for Retrieval of Scholarly Information in the Field of Biotechnology', *Webology*, vol. 2, no. 2, article 12. Retrieved June 6, 2006, from http://www.webology.ir/2005/v2n2/a12.html

Shah, U, Finin, T, Joshi, A, Cost, RS & Mayfield, J 2002, 'Information Retrieval on the Semantic Web', *Proceedings of the eleventh international conference on Information and knowledge management (CIKM'02)*, ACM Press, New York, NY, pp. 461-468.

Sherman, C 2000, 'Humans Do It Better: Inside the Open Directory Project', *Information Today: Online*, July, 2000. Retrieved June 9, 2006 from http://www.onlinemag.net/OL2000/sherman7.html

Singhal, A 2001, 'Modern Information Retrieval: A Brief Overview', *Bulletin of the IEEE Computer Society Technical Committee on Data Engineering*, vol. 24, no. 4, pp. 35-43.

Snowball, 2006, http://snowball.tartarus.org

Sommerville, I 2004, *Software Engineering*, 7th edn, Pearson Education Limited, Harlow.

Spink A, Jansen, BJ, Wolfram, D & Saracevic, T 2002, 'From E-Sex to E-Commerce: Web Search Changes', *IEEE Computer*, vol. 35, no. 3, pp. 107-109.

Straub, DW, David G & Marie-Claude, B 2005 'Quantitative Research,' in D Avison and J Pries-Heje (eds), *Research in Information Systems: A Handbook for Research Supervisors and Their Students*, Elsevier, Amsterdam, pp. 221-238.

Sun Java Studio Creator, http://developers.sun.com/prodtech/javatools/jscreator/index.js

The Open Directory Project, http://www.dmoz.org

Turtle, HR & Croft, WB 1990, 'Inference Networks for Document Retrieval', *Proceedings of the 13th ACM International Conference on Research and Development in Information Retrieval (SIGIR-90)*, ACM Press, New York, NY, pp. 1-24.

Uschold, M & Gruninger, M 1996, 'ONTOLOGIES: Principles, Methods and Applications', *Knowledge Engineering Review*, vol. 11, no. 2, pp. 93-136.

Vaishnavi, V & Kuechler, W 2004/5, *Design Research in Information Systems*. Retrieved: May 18, 2005, from http://www.isworld.org/Researchdesign/drisISworld.htm

Vallet, D, Fernández, M & Castells, P 2005, 'An Ontology-Based Information Retrieval Model', *Proceedings of the Second European Semantic Web Conference, ESWC 2005*, Springer-Verlag, Berlin, pp. 455-470.

Vivisimo, www.vivisimo.com

Voorhees, EM 1998, 'Variations in Relevance Judgments and the Measurement of Retrieval Effectiveness', *Proceedings of the 19th ACM International Conference on Research and Development in Information Retrieval (SIGIR-98)*, ACM Press, New York, NY, pp. 315-323.

Voorhees, EM 2005a, 'Common Evaluation Measures', *Proceedings of the Fourteenth Text Retrieval Conference (TREC 2005)*. Retrieved August 25, 2006 from http://trec.nist.gov/pubs/trec14/t14_proceedings.html

Voorhees, EM 2005b, 'Overview of TREC 2005', *Proceedings of the Fourteenth Text Retrieval Conference (TREC 2005)*. Retrieved August 25, 2006, from http://trec.nist.gov/pubs/trec14/t14_proceedings.html

Wecel, K & Zhdanova, AV 2005, 'Information Delivery for the End User of the Semantic Web', *Proceedings of the Second European Semantic Web Conference, ESWC 2005 Workshop on End User Aspects of the Semantic Web*, pp. 161-175.

Wikipedia, http://en.wikipedia.org

Williams, R 2006, 'The Power of Normalised Word Vectors for Automatically Grading Essays', *Issues in Informing Science and Information Technology*, vol. 3, pp. 721-729. Retrieved April 14, 2006 from http://proceedings.informingscience.org/InSITE2006/IISITWill155.pdf

Wolfram, D, Spink A, Jansen, BJ & Saracevic, T 2001, 'Vox Populi: The Public Searching of the Web', *Journal of the American Society for Information Science and Technology*, vol. 52, no. 12, pp. 1073-1074.

WordNet, http://wordnet.princeton.edu/

Xie, H 2003, 'Supporting ease-of-use and user control: desired features and structure of Web-based online IR systems', *Informing Processing and Management*, vol. 39 (2003), pp. 899-922.

Yahoo! Developers Network: http://developer.yahoo.com/search/index.html

Yang, Y 1994, 'Expert Network: Effective and Efficient Learning from Human Decision in Text Categorization and Retrieval', *Proceedings of the 17th ACM International Conference on Research and Development in Information Retrieval (SIGIR-94)*, ACM Press, New York, NY, pp. 13-22.

Yang, Y 1997, 'An Evaluation of statistical approach to text categorization', Technical Report CMU-CS-97-127, Computer Science Department, Carnegie Mellon University.

Yang, Y 1999, 'An Evaluation of Statistical Approaches to Text Categorization', *Information Retrieval*, vol. 1, no. 2, 1999, pp. 69-90.

Yang, Y & Liu, X 1999, 'A Re-examination of Text Categorization Methods', *Proceedings of the 22nd ACM International Conference on Research and Development in Information Retrieval (SIGIR '99)*, ACM Press, New York, NY, pp. 42-49.

Yang, Y & Pedersen, JO 1997, 'A Comparative Study on Feature Selection in Text Categorization', *Proceedings of the 14th International Conference on Machine Learning (ICML-97)*, Morgan Kaufmann Publishers, San Francisco, CA, pp. 412-420.

Zamir, O & Etzioni, O 1998, 'Web Document Clustering: A Feasibility Demonstration', *Proceedings of the 19th ACM International Conference on Research and Development in Information Retrieval (SIGIR-98)*, ACM Press, New York, NY, pp. 46-54.

Zeng, H, He, Q, Chen, Z, Ma, W & Ma, J 2004, 'Learning to Cluster Web Search Results', *Proceedings of the 27th Annual International ACM SIGIR Conference*, ACM Press, New York, NY, pp. 210-217.

Appendices

Appendix 1: Abbreviation List

AJ	Average Judgment
API	Application Programming Interface
DOM	Document Object Model (http://www.w3.org/DOM)
EJ	Enlarged Judgment
FAQ	Frequently Asked Questions
idf	inverse document frequency
IG	Information Gain
IR	Information Retrieval
JAXP	Java API for XML Processing (http://java.sun.com/webservices/jaxp/index.asp)
MV	Majority Voting
NL	Northern Light search engine
ODP	Open Directory Project
RDF	Resource Description Framework (http://www.w3.org/RDF)
SAX	Simple API for XML (http://www.saxproject.org)
SDK	Software Development Kit
SJ	Strict Judgment
SQL	Structured Query Language
Sqrt	Square root
SS	Summed Scores
SVM	Support Vector Machines
TC	Text Categorization
tf	term frequency
tf-idf	term frequency – inverse document frequency
TSR	Term Space Reduction
TREC	Text Retrieval Conference (http://trec.nist.gov)
VSM	Vector Space Model
WWW	World Wide Web
XML	eXtensible Markup Language (http://www.w3.rog/XML)
XSLT	eXtensible Stylesheet Language Transforms (http://www.w3.org/TR/XSLT)

Appendix 2: Stop Word List of Wikipedia

Source: http://www.dcs.gla.ac.uk/idom/ir_resources/linguistic_utils/stop_words

a, about, above, across, after, afterwards, again, against, all, almost, alone, along, already, also, although, always, am, among, amongst, amoungst, amount, an, and, another, any, anyhow, anyone, anything, anyway, anywhere, are, around, as, at, back, be, became, because, become, becomes, becoming, been, before, beforehand, behind, being, below, beside, besides, between, beyond, bill, both, bottom, but, by, call, can, cannot, cant, co, computer, con, could, couldn't, cry, de, describe, detail, do, done, down, due, during, each, eg, eight, either, eleven, else, elsewhere, empty, enough, etc, even, ever, every, everyone, everything, everywhere, except, few, fifteen, fifty[31], fill, find, fire, first, five, for, former, formerly, forty, found, four, from, front, full, further, get, give, go, had, has, hasn't, have, he, hence, her, here, hereafter, hereby, herein, hereupon, hers, herself, him, himself, his, how, however, hundred, i, ie, if, in, inc, indeed, interest, into, is, it, its, itself, keep, last, latter, latterly, least, less, ltd, made, many, may, me, meanwhile, might, mill, mine, ore, moreover, most, mostly, move, much, must, my, myself, name, namely, neither, never, nevertheless, next, nine, no, nobody, none, noone, nor, not, nothing, now, nowhere, of, off, often, on, once, one, only, onto, or, other, others, otherwise, our, ours, ourselves, out, over, own, part, per, perhaps, please, put, rather, re, same, see, seem, seemed, seeming, seems, serious, several, she, should, show, side, since, sincere, six, sixty, so, some, somehow, someone, something, sometime, sometimes, somewhere, still, such, system, take, ten, than, that, the, their, them, themselves, then, thence, there, thereafter, thereby, therefore, therein, thereupon, these, they, thick, thin, third, this, those, though, three, through, throughout, thru, thus, to, together, too, top, toward, towards, twelve, twenty, two, un, under, until, up, upon, us, very, via, was, we, well, were, what, whatever, when, whence, whenever, where, whereafter, whereas, whereby, wherein, whereupon, wherever, whether, which, while, whither, who, whoever, whole, whom, whose, why, will, with, within, without, would, yet, you, your, yours, yourself, yourselves

---

[31] the original word here is fify, possibly an slip of the pen.

Appendix 3: Search Results of the Five Queries

Mon Aug 21 16:01:03 CST 2006

Search results of Clinton

1. Biography of William J. Clinton (http://www.whitehouse.gov/history/presidents/bc42.html)
Brief biography of the forty-second U.S. President, Bill Clinton.

2. Hillary Rodham Clinton, Senator from New York (http://clinton.senate.gov/)
Official Senate site Hillary Rodham Clinton, the Democratic senator from New York. Includes contact information.

3. Bill Clinton - Wikipedia, the free encyclopedia (http://en.wikipedia.org/wiki/Bill_Clinton)
Hyperlinked, in-depth profile of Bill Clinton, the 42nd President of the United States. Includes notes on his early life and political career, as well as information on his presidency and 1998 impeachment.

4. The Official Site of Clinton, Mississippi (http://www.clintonms.org/)
Official site of Clinton, Mississippi.

5. William J. Clinton Foundation (http://www.clintonfoundation.org/)
Foundation organized by former President Bill Clinton to promote the values of fairness and opportunity for all. Programs include health and HIV/AIDS, economic empowerment, leadership development, and citizen service.

6. Clinton Presidential Materials Project (http://clinton.archives.gov/)
Clinton Presidential Materials Project introduction page. ... The Clinton Presidential Materials Project has become the William J. Clinton Presidential Library ...

7. Clinton County Iowa Home Page (http://www.clintoncountyiowa.com/)
Official site featuring general information and department links.

8. Clinton County welcomes you! — Clinton County, Ohio (http://www.co.clinton.oh.us/)
A growing community answering the challenges of merging rural and urban ideals. ... CLINTON COUNTY OHIO WAR TIME LOSSES/VETERANS BURIALS. Probation Staff ...

9. Welcome to Clinton, Massachusetts (http://www.clintonmass.com/)
The Town of Clinton's original community website - Since 1997 ... 50 great things about Clinton As chosen by our readers... The Clinton Water Department's ...

10. Amazon.com: My Life: Books: Bill Clinton (http://www.amazon.com/exec/obidos/tg/detail/-/0375414576?v=glance)
Amazon.com: My Life: Books: Bill Clinton by Bill Clinton ... Bill Clinton discusses his life goals and how his parents met ... Bill Clinton describes his ...

11. Clinton - Wikipedia, the free encyclopedia (http://en.wikipedia.org/wiki/Clinton)
... Charles Clinton (1690 – 1773) French and Indian War Colonel, father of ... George Clinton (1739 – 1812) first and third Governor of New York, ...

12. Clinton, Oklahoma (http://www.clintonok.org/)
Clinton Chamber of Commerce-Clinton, Oklahoma's leading business organization ... ? 2005 Clinton Chamber of Commerce ...

13. OpinionJournal - Extra (http://www.opinionjournal.com/extra/?id=110004632)
... than word gets out that Bill Clinton was flying down to Washington to plan ... Behind the scenes, Clinton servitors run the Democratic Party, beginning at the ...

14. Bill Clinton Jokes - Clinton Humor and Clinton Jokes (http://politicalhumor.about.com/od/billclinton)
Bill Clinton jokes, political cartoons, parodies, and other classic Clinton humor. ... Political Humor> Democrats> Bill Clinton. Entertainment. Political Humor ...

15. Official Websit of Clinton City (http://www.clintoncity.com/)
... Clinton has grown rapidly over the last ten years. ... Clinton City offers the finest in police and fire protection, professional court ...

16. Clinton County Geneological Information (http://www.kcnet.org/~history/)
... 1870 Clinton County Census ... For those looking for a more detailed map of the Clinton County area, click here... Clinton County. Pat Lowery Family ...

17. Welcome to Clinton County, NY! (http://www.co.clinton.ny.us/)
Official site for the county.

18. USA: biography of William Jefferson Clinton (1946 - (http://odur.let.rug.nl/~usa/P/bc42/about/clintonbio.htm)
USA-project, presidents-area, biographical data of William Jefferson Clinton ... Bill Clinton was born William Jefferson Blythe IV on August 19, 1946, in Hope, ...

19. Clinton County Government (http://www.clintoncountypa.com/)
... Welcome to Clinton County. Local Government Publications. 2006 CLINTON COUNTY RE-ELECTION SCHEDULE FOR CLINTON COUNTY ELECTED ROW OFFICES ...

20. City of Clinton (http://www.cityofclintonnc.com/)
find information about the history and government of Clinton, and the various departments. ... Box 199. 221 Lisbon Street.
Clinton, NC 28329 (910) 592-1961 ...

21. Welcome to Clinton County, Michigan (http://www.clinton-county.org/)
... Clinton County is situated in Michigan's central lower peninsula. ... governor of New York, De Witt Clinton, who was
responsible for organizing the ...

22. William J. Clinton Presidential Library (http://www.clintonlibrary.gov/)
Extensive collection of Clinton Administration documents. Includes research facilities, exhibits, events, and educational
programs on the life and presidency of Bill Clinton.

23. Clinton Industries (http://www.clinton-ind.com/)
... on exacting standards, that's why Clinton Industries has been among the top ... And because Clinton handles a wide range of
products, fulfilling your ...

24. Village of Clinton (http://www.villageofclinton.org/)
A little town with a big heart. ... On behalf of the residents of Clinton, I would like to extend a very warm and sincere
welcome. ...

25. Town of Clinton -- It's Summer in Maine's Dairy Capital!!! (http://www.clinton-me.us/)
Clinton, ME ... Did you know that nearly 13% of Maine's milk is produced in the town of Clinton? ... The Clinton Town Office
Staff will be more than ...

26. Town of Clinton (http://www.townofclinton.com/) Official site of Clinton, NY.

27. American Presidents: Life Portraits (http://www.americanpresidents.org/presidents/president.asp?PresidentNumber=41)
Facts, trivia, a 1969 letter to his local R.O.T.C. program officer expressing his feelings about the war, and the text to his 1993 and
1997 Inaugural Addresses.

28. Clinton, Wisconsin (http://www.clintonwi.us/)
Official Website for the Village of Clinton, Rock County Wisconsin ... Search WWW Search www.clintonwi.us. free hit
counter ...

29. frontline: the clinton years | PBS (http://www.pbs.org/wgbh/pages/frontline/shows/clinton)
Presents a look at the Bill Clinton era. From ABC News's Nightline and PBS's Frontline. Includes interviews, photos, and
anecdotes.

30. Clinton School District Homepage (http://clinton.k12.ar.us/)
(Clinton) Calendar, district history, school sites, employment opportunities, ... Clinton Chamber of Commerce. Van Buren
County. Van Buren County Democrat Newspaper ...

31. Clinton County Election & Voter Information (http://www.clinton-county.org/clerk/election_info.htm)
... Annual School Election (All Clinton County Schools) Members of the Board of Education ... Villages (All Clinton County
Villages) State and Local Proposals ...

32. bill clinton (http://www.discoverthenetwork.org/individualProfile.asp?indid=644)
... Absolute Power: The Legacy of Corruption in the Clinton-Reno Justice Department ... Eyewitness Account Of How Bill
Clinton Compromised America's National Security ...

33. TLC :: What Not to Wear :: Clinton Kelly (http://tlc.discovery.com/fansites/whatnottowear/stylegurus/clinton.html)
What Not to Wear ... Clinton honed his fashion sensibilities and expertise with his tenure as a ... Clinton is also no stranger to
television. ...

34. Bill Clinton - MSN Encarta (http://encarta.msn.com/encyclopedia_761564341/Clinton_Bill.html)
Biographical article from the online encyclopedia Encarta. ... Bill Clinton, born in 1946, 42nd president of the United States
(1993-2001), who ...

35. Clinton, IA Chamber of Commerce (http://www.clintonia.com/index.cfm)
Community information, calendar of events, tourism, and more.

36. Clinton Presidential Library - Home Document (http://www.clinton-library.com/)
Clinton Library, the nation's interactive tribute to President Bill Clinton, is ... Clinton Presidential Center is both an act of faith
and of confidence. ...

37. CNN - Clinton: Iraq has abused its last chance - December 16, 1998 (http://www.cnn.com/US/9812/16/clinton.iraq.speech/)
... From the Oval Office, President Clinton told the nation Wednesday evening ... Clinton also stated that, while other countries
also had weapons of mass ...

38. Bill Clinton A Model Patient - CBS News (http://www.cbsnews.com/stories/2004/10/20/health/main650222.shtml)
The former president is getting a little better "every day," recovering from heart surgery, and has been on the phone with advice
for John Kerry. Mr. Clinton hasn't yet gotten a green light to actually hit the campaign trail for Kerry.

39. Untitled Document (http://www.clintontn.net/)
... The Clinton 12 Documentary Premier. Click here for dates and times. ... the Mission of the City of Clinton government to provide for the safety, ...

40. City of Clinton Oklahoma (http://www.clintonokla.org/)
City of Clinton, Oklahoma community information and events ... Clinton is located in western Oklahoma at the intersection of Interstate 40 and ...

41. Welcome to Clinton, CT! (http://www.clintonct.com/)
Information on events, local merchants, and local government.

42. Township of Clinton, New Jersey (http://www.township.clinton.nj.us/)
... Township of Clinton, New Jersey. The latest revised Windy Acres Settlement Agreement can be found here. ... The four exhibits are also available for ...

43. Clinton County, NY Genealogy (http://www.usgennet.org/usa/ny/county/clinton)
Clinton County, NY: Genealogy and Local History- towns, surnames, queries, online records, discussion boards, topics, links, and more!

44. Senator Hillary Rodham Clinton: Contact Senator Clinton (http://clinton.senate.gov/contact/)
... Senator Clinton sincerely appreciates the interest of her constituents wishing ... Senator Hillary Rodham Clinton. United States Senate. 476 Russell Senate ...

45. Project Vote Smart - Senator Clinton - Interest Group Ratings (http://www.vote-smart.org/issue_rating_category.php?can_id=WNY99268)
Project Vote Smart ... 2004 Senator Clinton supported the interests of the American Society for the ... in 2003, Senator Clinton voted their preferred position ...

46. Clinton County Schools (http://www.clinton.k12.ky.us/)
Mission of the Clinton County Public Schools with links of district interest. ... Clinton County Schools Route 4 Box 100 Albany, KY 42602 606 387 - 6480 ...

47. Clinton, Bill. The Columbia Encyclopedia, Sixth Edition. 2001-05 (http://www.bartleby.com/65/cl/ClintonB.html)
Clinton, Bill. The Columbia Encyclopedia, Sixth Edition. 2001-05 ... 12 acquitted Clinton. ... During both his terms Clinton took an active interest in environmental ...

48. Clinton Group (http://www.clinton.com/)
Managing investment funds for individual, institutional, and sovereign investors.

49. Clinton County, Illinois--Home Page (http://www.clintonco.org/)
Information about local government, offices, and elected officials.

50. Clinton Community College (http://clintoncc.suny.edu/)

Mon Aug 21 16:18:01 CST 2006

Search results of ford

1. Ford Vehicles: Ford Vehicles Official Site: learn about Ford cars, trucks, and SUVs. (http://www.fordvehicles.com/)
Learn about Ford cars, trucks, minivans, and SUVs. Get price quotes, search dealer inventory, compare vehicles, and find out about incentives and financing.

2. Ford Motor Company Home Page (http://www.ford.com/en/default.htm)
The corporate website for Ford Motor Company and its vehicle (car and truck) and service brands, featuring investor, career, news and media information.

3. Ford Motor Company (http://www.ford.com/)
Official site for the Ford Motor Company, manufacturer of SUVs, cars, trucks, and wagons. The Ford family brand includes Lincoln, Mercury, Mazda, Volvo, Jaguar, Land-Rover, and Aston Martin. Find vehicles in the interactive showroom and learn more about Ford services including financing, parts, and sales.

4. Ford :: home (http://www.ford.co.uk/)
... Ford Power Products ... Ford GT. ST Performance Vehicle. Car configurator. Request a brochure.... Ford Direct used cars. Accessories ...

5. ......::::: FORD MODELS :::::..... (http://www.fordmodels.com/)
Official site for the international modeling agency. Offers details of Ford offices around the world, including New York, Los Angeles, Paris, and Toronto.

6. Ford Australia (http://www.ford.com.au/) Official Australian site.

7. Ford Motor Company of Canada, Limited (http://www.ford.ca/) Official Canadian site.

8. Henry Ford Museum & Greenfield Village (http://www.hfmgv.org/)
Collection of Americana that depicts the ever-changing worlds of transportation, manufacturing, home life, entertainment, and technology.

9. Ford Truck Enthusiasts, 1948-2006 Ford trucks, F150, Super Duty & SUV owners community and. ... (http://www.ford-trucks.com/)

Extensive resource for Ford truck owners featuring discussion groups, technical articles, events, and more. Find advice and information for the F-150, F-250 Super Duty, Explorer, Ranger, and other models.

10. Ford - Viva o Novo (http://www.ford.com.br/) ... Ford - Viva o Novo ...

11. Ford :: Startseite (http://www.ford.de/) Official German site.

12. Ford Racing: Home (http://www.fordracing.com/) Offers Ford racing news, links to race results, history, merchandise, and more.

13. Media.Ford.com: (http://media.ford.com/) EXECUTIVE BIO'S, PRESS RELEASES - Ford, Volvo, Mazda, Lincoln, Jaguar, Aston ... Ford snags 4 awards for concept cars ... FORD FOCUS FUEL CELL VEHICLE STARS AT ...

14. Ford Foundation (http://www.fordfound.org/) Providing grants and loans to projects that strengthen democratic values, reduce poverty and injustice, promote international cooperation, and advance human achievement.

15. ford motor company (http://www.mycareer.ford.com/main.asp)
The corporate website for Ford Motor Company. ... Ford Motor Company was recognized as one of the top American corporations on ...

16. Ford Motor Company - Wikipedia, the free encyclopedia (http://en.wikipedia.org/wiki/Ford) ... automaker was founded by an American legend, Henry Ford and incorporated in 1903. Ford now encompasses many brands globally, including Lincoln and Mercury in the ...

17. Harrison Ford (I) (http://www.imdb.com/name/nm0000148) Pictures, biography, and filmography for Harrison Ford -- the mega movie star whose famous movies include the original Star Wars trilogy, Indiana Jones movies, Blade Runner, Clear and Present Danger, and Witness.

18. Media.Ford.com: FORD LEADS WITH BIO-ETHANOL POWERED CARS FOR EUROPE (http://media.ford.com/article_display.cfm?article_id=21101)
BIO&146;S, PRESS RELEASES - Ford, Volvo, Mazda, Lincoln, Jaguar, Aston Martin, ... FORD UNVEILS GREEN FOCUS COUP?-CABRIOLET CONCEPT. FORD IN UK TO INVEST ?1 ...

19. Ford Motor Company of Canada, Limited (http://www.ford.ca/english/default_flash.asp)
Ford Motor Company of Canada, cars and trucks ... vehicles (excluding Mustang Shelby GT 500, SVT, Ford GT, Edge, MKX, F-Series ...

20. Ford Accessories (http://www.fordaccessories.com/) Offers Ford accessories and merchandise.

21. Ford (http://www.ford.co.za/) Official South African site.

22. Ford Vehicles: Ford Mustang - See pricing details, car options, V6 GT (http://www.fordvehicles.com/cars/mustang/)
Official site for the popular muscle car, the Mustang. Offers photos, feature information, specs, and more.

23. Henry Ford - Wikipedia, the free encyclopedia (http://en.wikipedia.org/wiki/Henry_Ford)
... As sole owner of the Ford Company he became one of the richest and... Ford, though poorly educated, had a global vision, with consumerism as ...

24. The Henry Ford: The Life of Henry Ford (http://www.hfmgv.org/exhibits/hf)
From his childhood through the founding of Ford Motor Company and beyond.

25. Ford Fleet - Fleet Vehicles For Any Size Business (https://www.fleet.ford.com/)
to the dedication of our people, Ford Fleet can meet the vehicle needs of any. ... Not at the right site? Please visit Ford.com for retail information. ...

26. Ford (http://www.india.ford.com/) Official site for India.

27. Gerald R. Ford Presidential Library and Museum (http://www.ford.utexas.edu/)
Promotes popular interest and scholarly research in U.S. history during the post-World War II era, especially the Ford presidency (1974-77).

28. Ford :: Ford Team RS :: Ford Team RS home (http://www.ford.co.uk/teamrs_home)
... Ford Power Products ... Ford GT. ST Performance Vehicle. Car configurator. Request a brochure. Request... Ford Direct used cars. Accessories. ...

29. Ford of Belgium (http://www.ford.be/)
Online showroom van Ford Belgie met de nieuwste modellen, nieuws, dealers en Ford over Ford.

30. John Ford (I) (http://www.imdb.com/name/nm0000406/)
John Ford (I) - Filmography, Awards, Biography, Agent, Discussions, Photos, News Articles, Fan Sites ... A Gun Fightin' Gentleman (1919) (as Jack Ford) ...

31. New 2006 and 2007 Ford Cars on Yahoo! Autos (http://autos.yahoo.com/newcars/ford.html) Features information on the year's current models.

32. Biography of Gerald R. Ford (http://www.whitehouse.gov/history/presidents/gf38.html)
Biography of Gerald R. Ford, the former U.S. president, from the official White House web site. Includes highlights of Ford's two years as president, following the resignation of Richard Nixon.

33. Ford Malaysia (http://www.ford.com.my/) Ford vehicles including cars, trucks, 4X4s and vans. Includes services for ... Ford Extended Warranty. Scheduled Service Plan. Total Maintenance Plan. Genuine Parts ...

34. Ford Credit - Auto financing for Ford, Lincoln and Mercury cars and trucks (http://www.fordcredit.com/)
Automotive leasing, loans, and financing options from Ford Credit. Manage your vehicle finance account online, apply for credit, and get estimated payments.

35. Ford | Ford Dealer | Car Quotes and Reviews | 2006 2007
(http://www.autosite.com/content/research/makesearch/index.cfm/action/SelectModel2/make_vch/Ford)
Ford reviews, pictures, and invoice pricing. Get a free no-obligation price ... 2007 Ford Explorer Sport Trac Photo Gallery ... Ford keeps interest in the ...

36. Ford | Free Price Quotes | Ford Dealer | Ford Car | Car.com
(http://www.car.com/content/research/makesearch/index.cfm/action/SelectModel2/make_vch/Ford)
Ford price quotes and reviews. Free no-obligation quote from a local dealer. ... 2007 Ford Explorer Sport Trac Photo Gallery ... Ford keeps interest in the ...

37. Ford :: home :: rotating home (http://www.ford.com.ve/) Show room, modelos, características técnicas; listado de concesionarios y noticias.

38. Ford | Free Price Quotes | Ford Car Dealer | 2006 2007
(http://www.autoweb.com/content/research/makesearch/index.cfm/action/SelectModel2/make_vch/Ford)
Ford reviews and price quotes from a local. ... 2007 Ford Explorer Sport Trac Photo Gallery. Ford looks to gain traction with this sporty Explorer derivative ...

39. Career Programs (http://www.mycareer.ford.com/CareerPrograms.asp)
The corporate website for Ford Motor Company. ... the rapid career development you can find in our Ford College Graduate programs. ...

40. Ford - Research All Models and Prices - MSN Autos (http://autos.msn.com/browse/Ford.aspx)
Ford prices, reviews, used Ford classifieds, and more on MSN Autos ... The Ford Motor Company was incorporated in 1903 with ten people and $28,000. ...

41. Ford Search Results (http://www.autobytel.com/content/research/detail/Ford.htm)
Ford Pricing Guide - Buy your next new or used Ford here using our... The 2007 Ford Crown Victoria is a 4-door, 6-passenger family sedan, available in ...

42. Ford New Zealand (http://www.ford.co.nz/) Official site for New Zealand.

43. Ford Commercial Truck (http://www.commtruck.ford.com/) ... Internet Explorer version 3.0+ Netscape Navigator version 2.0 ...

44. Ford County, KS (http://skyways.lib.ks.us/counties/FO/)
An overview of Ford County, Kansas. ... History of Kansas, first published in 1883, tells about early Ford County. ... data for Ford County online including ...

45. Ford :: Accueil :: voiture neuve, achat voiture, achat auto. (http://www.ford.fr/)
Le site officiel de Ford France avec nouvelles conceptions des voitures. ... Ford Power Products. Sport automobile. Championnat du monde des rallyes ...

46. Oy Ford Ab (http://www.ford.fi/) Oy Ford Ab ... Ford omistajalle. Rahoitus. Vaihtoautot. Tietoa Fordista. Asiakaslehti. Ota yhteytt?. Henry-takuuvaihtoautot. Luotettava ja huoleton vaihtoehto. Oy Ford ...

47. FORD: Summary for FORWARD INDS INC - Yahoo! Finance (http://finance.yahoo.com/q?s=FORD)
information on FORWARD INDS INC (FORD) including quote performance, Real-Time ... Trading Report for (FORD) Detailed Technical Analysis + Free Market Timing Report ...

48. Ford Parts - Always In Stock (http://www.racepages.com/oem/ford.html)
Get your Ford Replacement Parts questions answered in seconds when you call our Customer Service Center.

49. Ford :: home :: rotating home (http://www.ford.es/) Gama de modelos, novedades, historia, prototipos, taller virtual, red de ... Recambios originales Ford. Llantas y neumáticos. Seguridad. Talleres Independientes ...

50. Ford Madox Ford Society (http://www.rialto.com/fordmadoxford_society)
Provides news of recent and future activities, publications, a gallery of first editions, and membership information.

Mon Aug 21 16:29:40 CST 2006
Search results of health
1. Medical Dictionary, Diseases, Healthy Living, Drugs & Medicines on Yahoo! Health (http://health.yahoo.com/)   Provides health research, expert advice, healthy recipes, and more.
2. Health in the Yahoo! Directory (http://dir.yahoo.com/Health/)   health, including diseases and conditions, medications, sexual health, fitness, ... Health Sciences (36) Hospitals and Medical Centers (44) Hygiene (17) ...
3. CNN.com - Health (http://www.cnn.com/HEALTH)   ... More Health Video. ? Mandatory HIV testing (1:43) ? Sudden cardiac arrest (1:14) ... Time.com Science & Health. Search for jobs @ International Edition ...
4. Open Directory - Health (http://dmoz.org/Health/)   ... Occupational Health and Safety (684) Organizations (69) Pharmacy (3,794) ... Harvard Medical School's consumer health information, journal databases, a ...
5. Health News - New York Times (http://www.nytimes.com/pages/health/index.html)   health news on medicine, fitness, nutrition, health care, mental health, drugs, ... Personal Health: Scientists Cast Misery of Migraine in a New Light ...
6. World Health Organization (WHO/OMS) (http://www.who.int/)   Directing and coordinating authority on international health work that strives to bring the highest level of health to all peoples.
7. WebMD - Better Information. Better Health. (http://www.webmd.com/)   Provides medical information and services for consumers, physicians, and other health providers.
8. BBC NEWS	Health (http://news.bbc.co.uk/1/hi/health/default.stm) perspectives. Also entertainment, business, science, technology and health news. ... Health experts' heatwave warning. Glaxo pays $70m in price row. Patient dies ...
9. MSNBC - Health News: Medical news, fitness topics and more - Front Page (http://www.msnbc.msn.com/id/3032076)   ... Receive a daily update with the top health news stories and special reports ... health officials are counting on barbershops to help screen men who wouldn't ...
10. National Institutes of Health (NIH) (http://www.nih.gov/)   Focal point for biomedical research in the U.S.
11. Health.com :: (http://www.health.com/)   Covers health, fitness, beauty, wellness, and food.
12. www.health.gov (http://www.health.gov/)   List of governmental sites related to health issues and topics.
13. Health News - AOL Health (http://health.aol.com/)   Find health advice, information about diseases, diet tips, calorie and body mass ... Health, your destination for in depth information about diseases and conditions, ...
14. C-Health: Your Health and Wellness Source - powered by MediResource (http://chealth.canoe.ca/)   Health and wellness source with links to information on a variety of health-related topics.
15. The top health news articles from Yahoo! News (http://news.yahoo.com/i/751)   Use Yahoo! News to find health news headlines and health articles on weight loss, medications, diseases, aging and more. ... Sexual Health News ...
16. BBC - Health (http://www.bbc.co.uk/health)   In-depth resource on health, diseases, and relationships.
17. Men's Health (http://www.menshealth.com/)   Magazine for men containing information on health, fitness, weight loss, and more.
18. AARP - Health	People Age 50 & Over (http://www.aarp.org/health/) Learn about health programs for people age 50 and over at AARP. We are dedicated to enhancing quality of life for all as we age. Information, advocacy and service.
19. Kaiser Permanente: Thrive - Health Insurance Plans, Healthcare Information, Health Advice (http://www.kaiserpermanente.org/)   Includes health information, members area, details of health plans, news, locations, and more.
20. WHO	World Health Organization (http://www.who.int/en) WHO	World Health Organization WHO	World Health Organization 1 April 2005 -- WHO's new programme to train the next generation of health leaders has welcomed its first eight recruits this week. Over the next few years, the Health Leadership ...

21. Drug and alcohol abuse, treatment, prevention at SAMHSA's National Clearinghouse for Alcohol and Drug Information (http://www.health.org/)
Resource for information about substance abuse prevention and addiction treatment. Includes an FAQ on substance abuse, articles, news, and related resources.

22. InteliHealth: InteliHealth Home (http://www.intelihealth.com/)
Comprehensive collection of consumer health information.

23. Centers for Disease Control and Prevention (http://www.cdc.gov/)
Includes information on disease outbreaks, health topics, and emergency preparedness.

24. Home Page - MSN Health & Fitness (http://health.msn.com/)
... MSN Videos on Health. Find a Therapist. Heart Attack Risk. BMI Calculator. Test Your Stress Level ... About Health & Fitness ...

25. Join AARP: Benefits & Information I People Age 50 and Over (http://www.aarp.org/)
Excels as a dynamic presence in every community, shaping and enriching the experience of aging for each member and for society.

26. C-Health : Seniors' Health (http://chealth.canoe.ca/channel_main.asp?channel_id=10)
they come with their own set of health problems, as if you hadn't lived through ... View health videos about a variety of diseases, conditions and treatment options. ...

27. Breaking Health and Fitness News Stories and Video - CBSNews.com (http://www.cbsnews.com/sections/health/main204.shtml)
s Health, Men&lsquo;s Health, and Health and Fitness Headlines and Information. ... Survey: Most Want Health Care Overhaul ... due to health violations. Couple ...

28. azcentral.com I health & fitness (http://www.azcentral.com/health/)
women's, kids' and men's health to diet, wellness and fitness. ... condition Allergy Alternative Health Alzheimer's Disease Anemia Arthritis ...

29. Florida Department of Health Home Page (http://www.doh.state.fl.us/)
Provides information about disease control and prevention, environmental health, health statistics, alerts and more.

30. U.S. News & World Report: Best Health (http://www.usnews.com/usnews/health/hehome.htm)
Get health information, including our annual list of the best hospitals in ... Health News. Recent Articles. Diseases & Conditions. Allergy & Asthma Center ...

31. AllRefer Health (http://health.allrefer.com/)
Health resource provides reliable and comprehensive information and news on ... Health Topics: A-Al Am-Az B C-Cj Ck-Cz D E F G H I J K L M N O P-Pl Pm-Pz Q R ...

32. Discovery Health :: Discovery Health :: Homepage (http://health.discovery.com/)
Offers health news and in-depth features, show information, and health library.

33. healthfinder? - your guide to reliable health information (http://www.healthfinder.gov/)
Offers consumer health and human services information.

34. U.S. Department of Labor Occupational Safety and Health Organization: OSHA. (http://www.osha.gov/)
Official site for the government agency that establishes protective standards, enforces those standards, and reaches out to employers and employees through technical assistance and consultation programs.

35. Health - Wex (http://www.law.cornell.edu/topics/health.html)
Information about U.S. health law from the Legal Information Institute.

36. Health (http://www.washingtonpost.com/wp-dyn/content/health/)

... Health Discussions ... Scientists, health workers and activists find hope at 16th International AIDS Conference. ... South African Health Chief's Ouster ...

37. Health - Wikipedia, the free encyclopedia (http://en.wikipedia.org/wiki/Health)
... are four general determinants of health which he called "human biology" ... smoking and other substance abuse are examples of steps to improve one's health. ...

38. United States Department of Health and Human Services (http://www.hhs.gov/)
Leading America to better health, safety, and well-being.

39. Travelers' Health I CDC (http://www.cdc.gov/travel)
Includes information on outbreaks, specific diseases, recommended vaccinations, and traveling with children and pets. Presented by the National Center for Infectious Diseases.

40. Health Care, Health Care Guide, Medical Advice, Primary Health Care, Mental Health, Home Health Care (http://health.indiamart.com/)
Includes general health information, news, yellow pages, and advice.

41. Excite - Health (http://health.excite.com/index/id/ap.html)
Whether you're sick as a dog or healthy as an ox, our comprehensive health section can help you live a better, healthier life.

42. DenverPost.com (http://denverpost.healthology.com/)
articles, womens health issues and general health information. ... Copyright Healthology, Inc., an iVillage Company providing health education ...

43. Healthcentral.com - Trusted, Reliable and Up To Date Health Information (http://www.healthcentral.com/)
Providing consumer health information.

44. New York State Department of Health (http://www.health.state.ny.us/)
Home page for the New York State Department of Health ... State Health Department Urges Early Identification and Appropriate Treatment for ...

45. Health:Topic (http://www.oecd.org/topic/0,2686,en_2649_37407_1_1_1_1_37407,00.html)
Good health is necessary for individuals to flourish as citizens, family members, ... Scientific, Industrial and Health Applications of Biotechnology ...

46. National Library of Medicine - National Institutes of Health (http://www.nlm.nih.gov/)
Extensive collection of online information for the public and health care professionals dealing with clinical care, toxicology and environmental health, and basic research.

47. Women's Health Interactive (http://www.womens-health.com/)
Place for women to proactively learn about their health and health-related issues.

48. Health & Fitness Tips - Information, News, Products (http://www.health-fitness-tips.com/)
Specializing in health and fitness information including weight loss, diet, and nutrition.

49. Mayo Clinic medical information and tools for healthy living - MayoClinic.com (http://www.mayoclinic.com/)
The Mayo Clinic's health resource web site offers information on diseases and conditions, healthy living, drugs, and self-care.

50. Health Information - National Institutes of Health (NIH) (http://health.nih.gov/)
Browse health topics alphabetically.

Mon Aug 21 15:45:30 CST 2006
Search results of jaguar
1. jaguar (http://www.jaguar.com/) Official site of the Ford Motor Company division featuring new Jaguar models and local dealer information.
2. One World Journeys | Jaguar: Lord of the Mayan Jungle (http://www.oneworldjourneys.com/jaguar) A multimedia expedition into the heart of the Mexican jungle, searching for the elusive jaguar.
3. Jaguar (http://www.bluelion.org/jaguar.htm) Compares jaguars and leopards and provides information about the animal's shrinking habitat and relationship with man.
4. Jag-lovers - the Jaguar Enthusiasts' premier Internet site (http://www.jag-lovers.org/) Offers model pages, mailing lists, book reviews, and more for the Jaguar car enthusiast.
5. Title: Jaguar Enthusiasts' Club Main Page (http://www.jec.org.uk/) Offers information on activities. Based in the U.K., but offers memberships worldwide.
6. jaguars.com >> The official website of the NFL's Jacksonville Jaguars. (http://www.jaguars.com/) Official site of the Jaguars. Includes schedule, news, multimedia, photos, player information, statistics, team store, tickets, and more.
7. Jaguar UK - Jaguar Cars (http://www.jaguar.co.uk/) ... Vehicles. Tools and Services. Finance. Owners. About Jaguar. Home. X-TYPE. S-TYPE. XJ. XK. Accessories ... Site Map. FAQ. Privacy Policy. Terms & Conditions ...
8. Jaguar US - Jaguar USA Home (http://www.jaguarusa.com/us/en/home.htm) Jaguar USA Official Home Page ... From $62,495. From $62,495. From $75,500. From $75,500. Build Your Jaguar. Request a Brochure ...
9. Jaguar AU - Jaguar Cars (http://www.jaguar.com.au/) Official Australian site for the Ford Motor Company division. Includes model specifications and general information.
10. Jaguar - The British Metal Band - Home Page (http://www.jaguar-online.com/) Jaguar are a British rock band who have been very influential within... Jaguar Collectors CD Project. The band have announced an exciting project and ...
11. Jaguar - Wikipedia, the free encyclopedia (http://en.wikipedia.org/wiki/Jaguar) ... a b c d e "Jaguar (panthera onca) ... The jaguar (Panthera onca) are mammals of the Felidae family and one of four " ... (European jaguar) and panthera ...
12. Jaguar -- Kids' Planet -- Defenders of Wildlife (http://www.kidsplanet.org/factsheets/jaguar.html) Jaguar -- Kids' Planet -- Defenders of Wildlife Jaguar -- Kids' Planet -- Defenders of Wildlife ...
13. Jaguar UK - R is for Racing (http://www.jaguar.co.uk/uk/en/vehicles/r-performance/overview/r_racing.htm) ... bred into the bloodline of every Jaguar, particularly the very special range of ... create the essence of the Jaguar breed – rare, beautiful, refined, and ...
14. Jagúar (http://www.jaguar.is/) Groove-oriented music with influences in funk, latin, soul, and rock.
15. Jaguar DE - Jaguar Cars (http://www.jaguar.de/) ... Corporate Sales. Suche. Jaguar Weltweit. Inhalt. H?ufig gestellte Fragen. DAT Leitfaden. Kraftstoffverbrauch & CO2-Emissionen. Nutzungsbedingungen. Kontakt. Barrierefreiheit ...
16. Jaguar Models - Main Page (resin model kits) (http://www.jaguarmodels.com/) Jaguar Models, 12 ... Contacting Information. Jaguar Models, Inc. 18229 Railroad Street, City of Industry, CA 91748 ... We have added product listings of ...
17. Jaguar CA - Jaguar Cars (http://www.jaguar.com/ca/en/home.htm) ... Request a Brochure. Locate a Dealer. Request a Test Drive. Search. Site Map. Contact Us. FAQ. Fran?ais ... X-TYPE. S-TYPE. XJ. XK. Welcome to. JAGUAR CANADA ...
18. Jaguar Search Results (http://www.autobytel.com/content/research/detail/Jaguar.htm) Jaguar Pricing Guide - Buy your next new or used Jaguar here using our pricing ... The 2006 Jaguar S-Type is a 4-door, 5-passenger luxury sedan, or luxury...
19. Jaguar NL - Home (http://www.jaguar.nl/) Official Dutch site for the Ford Motor Company division.
20. Jaguar | Free Price Quotes | Jaguar Dealer | Jaguar Car | Car.com (http://www.car.com/content/research/makesearch/index.cfm/action/SelectModel2/make_vch/Jaguar) Jaguar,Jag price quotes and reviews. Free no-obligation quote from a local dealer. ... 2007 Jaguar XK Preview. Aiming to set the luxury performance...
21. Apple - Apple - Mac OS X - Leopard Sneak Peek (http://www.apple.com/macosx/leopard/index.html) Sneak peak from Apple of some of the features in the next generation of their Macintosh OS X, codenamed Leopard.

22. AtariAge - Atari Jaguar History (http://www.atariage.com/Jaguar/history.html)
AtariAge - News, message boards, rarity guides, game database, manuals, pictures, ... Atari Jaguar with CD-ROM ... program and publish Jaguar games, and has ...

23. Jaguar (http://dialspace.dial.pipex.com/agarman/jaguar.htm) Key facts and information on the jaguar's habitat, diet and status as a near threatened species.

24. Jaguar (car) - Wikipedia, the free encyclopedia (http://en.wikipedia.org/wiki/Jaguar_(car))
... Jaguar E-types are featured in the films The Italian Job, Robbery, The Odessa ... Harold, of Harold and Maude, had a Jaguar E-Type hearse. ...

25. Jaguar (http://www.fas.org/man/dod-101/sys/ac/row/jaguar.htm)
... and tactical support aircraft, the Jaguar has been transformed into a potent fighter-bomber. ... The Jaguar strike fighter was equipped also with Magic air ...

26. Jaguar (http://www.bigcatrescue.org/jaguar.htm)
Jaguar Facts, Jaguar Photos and Jaguars in the news at the world's largest big ... The Jaguar and the Leopard are often confused with one another in zoos. ...

27. Jaguar (http://www.thewildones.org/Animals/jaguar.html)

... The jaguar (Panthera onca) is the only member of the 'big cat' family that lives ... and is about the same size as the jaguar, but it is classified as a small cat ...

28. San Diego Zoo's Animal Bytes: Jaguar (http://www.sandiegozoo.org/animalbytes/t-jaguar.html)
Get fun and interesting jaguar facts in an easy-to-read style from the San Diego ... over 85 species in the jaguar diet, including peccaries, deer, tapirs, ...

29. Jaguar | Free Price Quotes | Jaguar Car Dealer | 2006 2007
(http://www.autoweb.com/content/research/makesearch/index.cfm/action/SelectModel2/make_vch/Jaguar)
Jaguar,Jag reviews and price quotes from a local dealer. ... 2007 Jaguar XK Preview. Aiming to set the luxury performance standard ...

30. Jaguar - Java Access to Generic Underlying Architectural Resources (http://www.eecs.harvard.edu/~mdw/proj/old/jaguar/)
... Jaguar is an extension of the Java runtime environment which enables direct Java ... Unlike the JNI, however, Jaguar does not require copying of data ...

31. The Jaguar - Houston Zoo {N A HURY} (http://users.netropolis.net/nahury1/jaguar.htm) General overview of the species.

32. Yahooligans! Animals: Jaguar (http://yahooligans.yahoo.com/content/animals/species/6638.html)
A picture and description of this animal. ... The Jaguar is the biggest and most powerful North American wildcat, and the only ...

33. New 2006 and 2007 Jaguar Cars on Yahoo! Autos (http://autos.yahoo.com/newcars/jaguar/index.html)
new Jaguar pictures, specs, reviews and more from the most comprehensive online automotive site. ... Find Used Jaguar Cars Near You. Check Yahoo! ...

34. Jaguar | Jaguar Dealer | Car Quotes and Reviews | 2006 2007
(http://www.autosite.com/content/research/makesearch/index.cfm/action/SelectModel2/make_vch/Jaguar)
Jaguar,Jag reviews, pictures, and invoice pricing. Get a free no-obligation ... 2006 Jaguar XJ Super V8 Portfolio Quick Spin. Preferred 10 to 1 over a corner...

35. Jaguar car quote, dealer prices, dealer quotes, MSRP prices, invoice prices
(http://www.autobytel.com/content/buy/lm/new/search/index.cfm/action/SelectModel/make_vch/Jaguar)
Jaguar,Jag car quote, dealer prices, dealer quotes, MSRP prices, invoice prices ... Jaguar XK. ABOUT AUTOBYTEL " ... Powered by AIC - Automotive Information Center ...

36. Schr?dinger -> Site Map (http://www.schrodinger.com/Products/jaguar.html) A general purpose ab initio electronic structure package ... Jaguar Chem3D EULA. Script Center. Script Downloads. Seminar Center. June 1st 2006. May 25th 2006 ...

37. Animal Fact Sheets (http://www.zoo.org/educate/fact_sheets/jaguar/jaguar.htm) ... which includes four species of "big cats", the jaguar, tiger, lion and leopard. ... Jaguar cubs are usually born with their eyes closed, weigh about 25-29 ounces ...

38. Jaguar - Research All Models and Prices - MSN Autos (http://autos.msn.com/browse/Jaguar.aspx)
Jaguar prices, reviews, used Jaguar classifieds, and more on MSN Autos ... Jaguar was founded in 1922 as the Swallow Sidecar Company of Blackpool,. ...

39. Jaguar Performance Products, Georgia (http://www.jaguarkarts.com/) Jaguar Performance Karts is a manufacture of racing kart chassis in Georgia, ... Jaguar Performance had a record breaking season in the year 2001 and 2002 is ...

40. Used Jaguar Prices & Reviews (http://auto.consumerguide.com/Search/index.cfm/type/used/make/1608/name/Jaguar/)
Search results for used Jaguar reviews. Results include car name, vehicle class, ... Jaguar was then purchased by Ford in 1989, and is now a division in the ...

41. Jaguar (http://www.co.pima.az.us/cmo/sdcp/sdcp2/fsheets/jaguar.html)

... The jaguar (Panthera onca) is the largest cat native to the Western. ... The jaguar can be a far ranging animal, traveling distances up to 500 miles. ...

42. JAGUAR cologne (http://www.4-fragrances.com/men/jaguar-m.htm) Jaguar ... JAGUAR BLUE Eau de Toilette Spray 3.4 oz New $48.00 $39.99. FREE US SHIPPING ON ORDERS OVER $60 ... discount JAGUAR jaguar mark 2 jaguar,cologne, ...

43. Media.Ford.com: The Products :Jaguar (http://media.ford.com/products/index.cfm?make_id=95)
Ford, Volvo, Mazda, Lincoln, Jaguar, Aston Martin, Mercury, Land Rover ... Jaguar North America today announced Manufacturer's Suggested Retail Prices ...

44. Jaguar History (http://www.exoticcarrental.com/JaguarHistory.htm)
Information about the history of the Jaguar. ... the company name to Jaguar. In 1948 at the Earls Court Motor Show the XK 120 Roadster was introduced by Jaguar. ...

45. J A G U A R - ?ndice (http://jaguar.edu.co/)
Taller-escuela dedicado a la educación, producción y publicación de artes ... comercial educativo ...

46. NatureWorks - Jaguar (http://www.nhptv.org/natureworks/jaguar.htm)
NatureWorks ... The jaguar is the largest cat in North America and the third largest cat in the world. ... The Jaguar, unlike most big cats, loves the water. ...

47. Flickr: Photos tagged with jaguar (http://www.flickr.com/photos/tags/jaguar)
Flickr is almost certainly the best online photo management and sharing ... Jaguar Luxury Automobile. Official Site-Jaguar vehicle specs, pictures, options and ...

48. Jaguar (http://www.pansophist.com/jag.htm)
An owner discusses his XJ6.

49. Jaguar Printout- EnchantedLearning.com
(http://www.enchantedlearning.com/subjects/mammals/cats/jaguar/Jaguarprintout.shtml)
Jaguar Printout. Jaguar are medium-sized cats that live in South and Central ... As a bonus, site members have access to a banner-ad-free version of the site, ...

50. USS Jaguar (http://www.worldkids.net/jaguar)
Star Trek club for kids with chat, message board, stories, and more.

Mon Aug 21 15:54:39 CST 2006

Search results of ups

1. UPS Package Tracking (http://www.ups.com/tracking/tracking.html)
UPS Package Tracking service lets you track your package across the world, including multiple packages, airmail, or freight, and offering updates on the Web or by email.

2. UPS Global Home (http://www.ups.com/)
Worldwide express carrier and package delivery company. UPS is a global provider of specialized transportation and logistics services.

3. Cash Flow, International Trade & Small Business Lending : UPS Capital (http://www.upscapital.com/) UPS offers businesses worldwide the opportunity to integrate supply chain ... combined with the broad capabilities of UPS help enhance operations

4. UPS Careers (https://ups.managehr.com/) Job opportunities from United Parcel Services. Jobs range from package handlers, delivery drivers, and warehouse management to administration, communications, information systems, and logistics.

5. UPS Calculate Time and Cost (http://wwwapps.ups.com/calTimeCost?loc=en_US)
... of, and services requested for, packages actually tendered to UPS. ... have specially negotiated rates, contact your UPS account executive for a rate quote. ...

6. UPS Careers (http://upsjobs.com/)
Job opportunities from United Parcel Services. Jobs range from package handlers, delivery drivers, and warehouse management to administration, communications, information systems, and logistics.

7. Welcome to UPS Supply Chain Solutions (http://www.ups-scs.com/)
UPS delivery solutions for businesses, providing logistics, global freight, financial services, mail services, and consulting to business customers.

8. Uninterruptible power supply - Wikipedia, the free encyclopedia (http://en.wikipedia.org/wiki/Uninterruptible_power_supply)
... An uninterruptible power supply (UPS), sometimes called an uninterruptible power ... particular type of equipment, a UPS is typically used to protect ...

9. APC Product Information for UPS (http://www.apc.com/products/category.cfm?id=13)
... Back-UPS HS ... Smart-UPS XL ... GUTOR Industrial UPS and DC Systems ...

10. RACING.UPS.COM - Home Page (http://www.racing.ups.com/)
UPS Racing NASCAR teams, with current stats and standings, photos and video, details about the cars, the drivers, and the crew, and a NASCAR tutorial for racing newbies.

11. The UPS Store: Packaging, Shipping, Passport Photos & Printing Service (http://www.upsstore.com/)
Find out how the UPS Store can help. Track packages, estimate shipping costs, get your US passport photo, print and finish documents, purchase moving supplies & more. Find The UPS Store near you!

12. UPS Community (http://community.ups.com/) ... UPS teamed up with students in Dubai to raise environmental awareness about ... UPS provided collection points for recycling waste. ...

13. UPS: Summary for UNITED PARCEL SVC - Yahoo! Finance (http://finance.yahoo.com/q?s=ups)
information on UNITED PARCEL SVC (UPS) including quote performance, Real-Time ... Designers Selected to Show in the UPS Hub at Olympus Fashion Week is Available ...

14. UPS Lithuania (http://www.ups-lithuania.com/)
... UPS 2nd QUARTER PRODUCES SOLID EARNINGS ON 15% REVENUE GAIN ... Neteis?tas UPS pavadinimo ir ?enklo naudojimas ... UPS 2nd Quarter Earnings Climb over 18 ...

15. UPS Wireless (http://mobile.ups.com/omnisky/index.jsp)
... Welcome to UPS Wireless services. ? Tracking. ? Quick Cost. ? Transit Time. ? Drop-off Locator. Email Customer Services at. customer.service@ups.com ...

16. UPS Pressroom: Current Press Releases (http://www.pressroom.ups.com/pressreleases/current/0,1088,4454,00.html)
... UPS Expands Real-World Testing of Hydrogen Fuel Cell Technology ... achievement," said Chris Mahoney, UPS senior vice president of global transportation services. ...

17. UPS Sustainability (http://www.sustainability.ups.com/) ... UPS is the world's largest package delivery company and a global leader in ... Headquartered in Atlanta, UPS serves more than 200 countries and territories ...

18. UPS Pressroom: Current Press Releases (http://www.pressroom.ups.com/pressreleases/current/0,1088,4402,00.html)
... The UPS Foundation in partnership with the Corporation for National and ... Press Releases. Sign Up for Email Updates. Current Press Releases. UPS Worldwide ...

19. University of Puget Sound :: Home (http://www.ups.edu/) Welcome to the University of Puget Sound home page. ... 07.13.06 Harned Hall dedication to include lecture by Pulitzer Prize-winning ...

20. UPS Trade Direct - UPS Supply Chain Solutions (http://www.ups-scs.com/tradedirect)
UPS Trade Direct provides integrated freight and package delivery allowing you to bypass distribution centers by shipping directly to retail stores or customers' doors.

21. What is UPS? - A Word Definition From the Webopedia Computer Dictionary
(http://www.webopedia.com/TERM/U/UPS.html)
This page describes the term UPS and lists other pages on the Web where you can ... Information about batteries used in computer UPS ...

22. UPS Power Protection and Battery Backup by Minuteman - Official Website (http://www.minutemanups.com/)
Line of remote-controllable uninterruptible power protection (UPS) products for telephones, computers, and data communication devices.

23. UPS (http://mobile.ups.com/) ... UPS Wireless Services ...

24. the f-ups news (http://www.thefups.com/) ... F-Ups Announce Tour With Tsunami Bomb, Over It. Mar 17, 2005 "All The Young Dudes" on FUSE! ... People ask us all the time what type of music we classify ...

25. UPS (http://web.belkin.com/support/download/download.asp?category=2&lang=1&mode=)
... UPS. Desktop Accessories. Audio Video. Cables. Computer Accessories. Mice and Keyboards ... Home Office 375VA UPS With Automatic Shutdown Software. F6H375-USB ...

26. RACING.UPS.COM Race Summary Article
(http://www.racing.ups.com/racing/news_results/article.cgi?file=post_20010408_20010408)
Racing.UPS.com, the source for #88 UPS Racing information and The Official ... Speedway, but his third in just eight events with UPS as the primary. ...

27. THE ups DEBUGGER (http://ups.sourceforge.net/) The ups debugger for C, C++ and Fortran - unofficial home page ... 3.37 released. Archive of ups-users mailing list. ups in print. Fortran support. MP3 of ups song ...

28. UPS Careers (http://ups.softshoe.com/) ... career or a part-time position to pay for college, UPS is right for you. ... UPS kudos for being a world class employer? Find out. Welcome to UPS Careers ...

29. United Parcel Service - Wikipedia, the free encyclopedia (http://en.wikipedia.org/wiki/United_Parcel_Service)
... Historically, UPS only faced competition from USPS for the inexpensive... UPS entered the heavy freight business with its purchase of Menlo Worldwide ...

30. Underground Punk Support (http://go.to/upspunk) an undergound punk distro and zine

31. OPTI-UPS Protect and Serve (http://www.opti-ups.com/) Manufactures UPS power management products.

32. UPS - UPS Manufacturers, UPS Factories, UPS Suppliers, China UPS (http://hotproducts.alibaba.com/manufacturers-exporters/Ups.html) Start here to find prequalified UPS suppliers from China and around the world ... (AVR), uninterruptible power supply (UPS), battery chargers, flashlights, and ...

33. Uninterruptible Power Supply (UPS) FAQ (http://www.jetcafe.org/~npc/doc/ups-faq.html)
Frequently Asked Questions (FAQ) about Uninterruptible Power Supplies (UPSs) ... 13: Can I really count on a UPS protecting my equipment? ...

34. Howstuffworks "How does a computer's uninterruptible power supply (UPS) work?"
(http://computer.howstuffworks.com/question28.htm) How does a computer's uninterruptible power supply (UPS) work? Does the computer always run from the battery? ... A UPS generally protects a computer against ...

35. The DIY (or, if you must, "Ghetto") UPS (http://www.dansdata.com/diyups.htm)
How to build your own ugly and awkward uninterruptible power supply! ... contraption works in basically the same way as a normal "dual conversion" UPS. ...

36. Urban Legends Reference Pages: Rumors of War (Uniform Behavior) (http://www.snopes.com/rumors/ups.asp)
Have terrorists acquired missing or stolen UPS uniforms? ... adding to their stock, former UPS employees acquiring old uniforms out of ...

37. UPS Capital Visa ? Business Rewards Card (http://www.capital.ups.com/solutions/visa_card.html)
... The NEW UPS Capital business card is a great place to begin a... The UPS Capital Visa? Business Rewards Card is offered and issued by Chase Bank ...

38. UPS - Investor Relations (http://investor.shareholder.com/ups/index.cfm)
... UPS 2nd Quarter Produces Solid Earnings On 15% Revenue Gain ... UPS, Pilots Reach Accord In Contract... UPS Board Sets Dividend. COLOGNE, ...

39. UPS Careers: Job Search (https://ups.iiserve.com/chicago/)
... through the UPS Earn & Learn Program. Benefits (Life/Health/401K) Paid Vacations & Holidays ... One UPS Way, Hodgkins, IL 60525. Ph: 888-4UPS-JOB. Package ...

40. UPS Careers: Opportunities: Part-time: Job Search (https://ups.iiserve.com/peakjobs.htm)
... with UPS in your area. Package Handler. Search All ... UPS Global I UPS Corporate. Copyright ? 2002 United Parcel Service, Inc. All rights reserved. ...

41. The UPS Store: Locations (http://go.mappoint.net/ups/PrxInput.aspx)
Search over 3,300 locations to find The UPS Store ... The UPS Store? locations are independently owned and operated by
franchisees of Mail Boxes Etc. ...

42. UPS Selector Sizing Applications (http://www.apcc.com/tools/ups_selector/pso/rslr/index.cfm?ISOCountryCode=US)
to specify your required runtime and other options, and recommend a UPS solution. ... easy way to finding the right UPS product
for a single home or office ...

43. Welcome To Air Cargo World -- Breaking News (http://www.aircargoworld.com/break_news/04212006e.htm)
... UPS said its freight forwarding business lost customers in the past two quarters, ... UPS has been spending money and attention
on new technology for the Menlo ...

44. Business Week Online: Personal Investing
(http://host.businessweek.com/businessweek/Corporate_Snapshot.html?Symbol=UPS)
BusinessWeek magazine: The most-read source of global ... Get Fund Prospectus. CORPORATE SNAPSHOT. UNITED PARCEL
SERVICE INC CL B (NYSE:UPS) LAST. CHANGE ...

45. UPS Israel (http://www.ups-israel.com/index.cfm)
... UPS 2nd QUARTER PRODUCES SOLID EARNINGS ON 15% REVENUE GAIN ... UPS 2nd Quarter Earnings Climb over
18% as Package Business Grows Worldwide ...

46. United Package Smashers - The Truth About United Parcel Service, UPS and the Big Brown Turd
(http://www.unitedpackagesmashers.com/)
Resources and information for unhappy and disgruntled UPS customers and employees. ... plaintiffs for lawsuits against UPS for
any alleged unlawful, ...

47. UPS: Headlines for UNITED PARCEL SVC - Yahoo! Finance (http://finance.yahoo.com/q/h?s=UPS)
Find out the latest news headlines for UNITED PARCEL SVC (UPS) ... Designers Selected to Show in the UPS Hub at Olympus
Fashion Week is Available ...

48. UPS (Uninterruptible power supply) and DC Power systems from Powerware (http://www.powerware.com/)
Power system protection, Powerware UPS, Telecom power systems and ... Site map. UPS from Powerware; Your source for UPS
Power surge protectors, UPS Power ...

49. Cover Pages: UPS OnLine Toolbox Supports XML for Tracking Shipments to Your Office. (http://xml.coverpages.org/ni2001-
03-16-b.html)
... "significant enhancements" to the UPS OnLine Tools, which "offer advanced ... Announcement: "UPS Adds Two New Tools to
Its Online Toolbox. ...

50. InformationWeek.com (http://www.informationweek.com/841/ups_side.htm)
Logistics company redoes its infrastructure to put wireless technology to the test ... Prior to 1989, UPS was shipping 8 million to 9
million packages a day and ...

Appendix 4: The First Two Levels of the ODP Categories

Arts

Animation, Architecture, Art History, Awards, Bodyart, Chats and Forums, Classical Studies, Comics, Costumes, Crafts, Cultures and Groups, Design, Digital, Directories, Education, Entertainment, Events, Genres, Graphic Design, Humanities, Illustration, Literature, Magazines and E-zines, Movies, Music, News and Media, Online Writing, Organizations, People, Performing Arts, Periods and Movements, Photography, Radio, Regional, Television, Video, Visual Arts, Weblogs.

Business

Accounting, Aerospace and Defense, Agriculture and Forestry, Arts and Entertainment, Associations, Automotive, Biotechnology and Pharmaceuticals, Business and Society, Business Services, Chemicals, Construction and aintenance, Consumer Goods and Services, Cooperatives, Customer Service, Directories, E-Commerce, Education and Training, Electronics and Electrical, Employment, Energy and Environment, Financial Services, Food and Related Products, Healthcare, Hospitality, Human Resources, Industrial Goods and Services, Information Services, Information echnology, International Business and Trade, Investing, Major Companies, Management, Marketing and Advertising, Materials, Mining and Drilling, News and Media, Opportunities, Publishing and Printing, Real Estate, Regional, Resources, Retail Trade, Small Business, Telecommunications, Textiles and Nonwovens, Transportation and Logistics, Wholesale Trade.

Computers

Algorithms, Artificial Intelligence, Artificial Life, Bulletin Board Systems, CAD and CAM, Chats and Forums, Companies, Computer Science, Consultants, Data Communications, Data Formats, Desktop Publishing, Directories, E-books, Education, Emulators, Ethics, Graphics, Hacking, Hardware, History, Home Automation, Human-Computer nteraction, Internet, Intranet, Mailing Lists, Mobile Computing, Multimedia, News and Media, Open Source, Organizations, Parallel Computing, Performance and Capacity, Programming, Robotics, Security, Shopping, Software, Speech Technology, Supercomputing, Systems, Usenet, Virtual Reality.

Games

Board Games, Card Games, Coin-Op, Conventions, Developers and Publishers, Dice, Gambling, Game Studies, Hand-Eye Coordination, Hand Games, History, Miniatures, Online, Paper and Pencil, Party Games, Play-By-Mail, Play Groups, Puzzles, Resources, Roleplaying, Tile Games, Trading Card Games, Video Games, Yard, Deck, and Table Games.

Health

Addictions, Aging, Alternative, Animal, Beauty, Child Health, Conditions and Diseases, Conferences, Dentistry, Directories, Education, Fitness, Home Health, Medicine, Men's Health, Mental Health, News and Media, Nursing, Nutrition, Occupational Health and Safety, Organizations, Pharmacy, Products and Shopping, Professions, Public Health and Safety, Regional, Reproductive Health, Resources, Search Engines, Senior Health, Senses, Services, Specific Substances, Support Groups, Teen Health, Weight Loss, Women's Health.

Home

Apartment Living, Consumer Information, Cooking, Do-It-Yourself, Domestic Services, Emergency Preparation, Entertaining, Family, Gardening, Homemaking, Homeowners, Home Improvement, Moving and Relocating, News and Media, Personal Finance, Personal Organization, Rural Living, Software, Urban Living.

Kids and Teens

Arts, Computers, Directories, Entertainment, Games, Health, International, News, People and Society, Pre-School, School Time, Sports and Hobbies, Teen Life, Your Family.

News

Alternative, Analysis and Opinion, Breaking News, By Subject, Chats and Forums, Colleges and Universities, Current Events, Directories, Extended Coverage, Internet Broadcasts, Magazines and E-zines, Media, Museums and Archives, Newspapers, Online Archives, Personalized News, Regional, Satire, Weather, Weblogs.

Recreation

Antiques, Audio, Autos, Aviation, Birding, Boating, Camps, Climbing, Collecting, Directories, Drugs, Food, Guns, Humor, Kites, Knives, Living History, Models, Motorcycles, Nudism, Outdoors, Parties, Pets, Picture Ratings, Radio, Roads and Highways, Scouting, Theme Parks, Tobacco, Trains and Railroads, Travel, Whips.

Reference

Almanacs, Archives, Ask an Expert, Bibliography, Biography, Books, Dictionaries, Directories, Education, Encyclopaedias, Flags, Journals, Knots, Knowledge Management, Libraries, Maps, Museums, Open Access Resources, Parliamentary Procedure, Quotations, Thesauri, Time, World Records.

Regional

A, Africa, Asia, B, C, Caribbean, Central America, Countries, D, E, Europe, F, G, H, I, J, K, L, M, Middle East, N, North America, O, Oceania, P, Polar Regions, Q, R, S, South America, T, U, V, W, Y, Z.

Science

A, Agriculture, Anomalies and Alternative Science, Astronomy, B, Biology, C, Chats and Forums, Chemistry, Conferences, D, Directories, E, Earth Sciences, Educational Resources, Employment, Environment, F, G, H, I, Institutions, Instruments and Supplies, J, K, L, M, Math, Methods and Techniques, N, News and Media, O, P, Physics, Publications, Q, R, Reference, S, Science in Society, Search Engines, Social Sciences, Software, T, Technology, U, V, W, X, Y, Z.

Shopping

Antiques and Collectibles, Auctions, By Region, Children, Classifieds, Clothing, Consumer Electronics, Crafts, Death Care, Directories, Entertainment, Ethnic and Regional, Flowers, Food, General Merchandise, Gifts, Health, Holidays, Home and Garden, Jewelry, Music, Niche, Office Products, Pets, Photography, Publications, Recreation, Sports, Tobacco, Tools, Toys and Games, Travel, Vehicles, Visual Arts, Weddings.

Society

Activism, Advice, Crime, Death Disabled, Ethnicity, Folklore, Future, Gay, Lesbian, and Bisexual, Genealogy, Government, History, Holidays, Issues, Law, Lifestyle Choices, Military, Organizations, Paranormal, People, Philanthropy, Philosophy, Politics, Relationships, Religion and Spirituality, Sexuality, Subcultures, Support Groups, Transgendered, Work.

Sports

A, Adventure Racing, Airsoft, Animal Sports, Archery, B, Badminton, Baseball, Basketball, Billiards, Bocce, Boomerang, Bowling, Boxing, C, Cheerleading, College and University, Cricket, Croquet, Cycling, D, Darts, Disabled, E, Equestrian, Events, Extreme Sports, F, Fantasy, Fencing, Flying Discs, Footbag, Football, G, Gaelic, Goalball, Golf, Greyhound Racing, Gymnastics, H, Handball, Hockey, I, Informal Sports, J, Jai Alai, K, Kabbadi, Korfball, L, Lacrosse, Laser Games, Lumberjack, M, Martial Arts, Motorsports, Multi-Sports, N, Netball, O, Officiating, Organizations, Orienteering, P, Paddleball, Paintball, People, Pesapallo, Petanque, Q, R, Racquetball, Resources, Rodeo, Rope, kipping, Rounders, Running, S, Sepak Takraw, Skateboarding, Skating, Soccer, Softball, Software, Squash, Strength Sports, T, Table Tennis, Tchoukball, Team Handball, Team Spirit, Tennis, Track and Field, U, V, Volleyball, W, Walking, Water Sports, Winter Sports, Women, Wrestling, X, Y, Youth and High School, Z.

Appendix 5: Index Structure of Lucene

This section includes two main sections intended to delve into the index structure of Lucene. The first part is about the overall index structure of Lucene, and the index files in Lucene; the second part focuses on the inverted index file employed by Lucene. This section is a summary of appendix B of Gospodnetić and Hatcher (2005, pp. 393-407)

A5.1 Lucene Index Structure

A5.1.1 Multifile index Structure

An index of Lucene can be taken as a black-box from a software developer's perspective. The index is represented by an abstract *Directory* class; indexing process is to create an instance of the *Directory* class and populate it with the *Fields* class which is composed of name and value pairs. The indexing process is performed by calling the *IndexWriter.addDocument* (*Document*) method which takes the abstract *Directory* class as the parameter to represent the index. The searching process also needs this *Document* class and passes it to the *IndexSearcher* class, and then finds the *Documents* that match a given query.

Lucene supports two index structures: *multifile indexes* and *compound* indexes. After the indexing process is finished, the *index files* of multifile indexes may looks like:

deletable	1KB	file	2006-8-17 12:55
_lfyc.f1	10 KB	file	2006-8-17 12:55
_lfyc.f2	10 KB	file	2006-8-17 12:55
_lfyc.fnm	1k KB	file	2006-8-17 12:55
_lfyc.frq	100 KB	file	2006-8-17 12:55
_lfyc.fdx	110 KB	file	2006-8-17 12:55
_lfyc.prx	120 KB	file	2006-8-17 12:55
_gabh.f1	10 KB	file	2006-8-17 12:55
_ gabh.f2	10 KB	file	2006-8-17 12:55
_ gabh.fnm	1k KB	file	2006-8-17 12:55
_ gabh.frq	100 KB	file	2006-8-17 12:55
_ gabh.fdx	110 KB	file	2006-8-17 12:55
segments	1 KB	file	2006-8-17 12:55

A Lucene index is made up of *segments* which contain one or more documents; each *segment* is composed of index files which share a common prefix and differ in the suffix. The above example demonstrates an index with two segments, _lfyc and _gabh; and each segment contains some index files. The exact number of files that constitute an index and each segment varies from index to index and depends on the number of fields the index contains. Segment information, such as the names of all existing index segments, is stored in a file named 'segments' which Lucene consults first before accessing any files in the index directory, and thus ensures that even if a non-Lucene file is also stored in the same directory with Lucene (this is strongly not suggested), Lucene can identify the non-Lucene created file. The file *deletable* contains information about documents that have been marked for deletion. The files with an .fN extension, where N is a number, correspond to the indexed fields present in the indexed documents. In the above example, the index has two indexed fields. Therefore, the corresponding files are lfyc.f1, lfyc.f2 and gabh.f1 and gabh.f2 for the two segments. Furthermore, the size of an .fN file of a segment reflects the number of *Documents* with that field.

Lucene supports *incremental indexing*. When new documents are added to the index, Lucene does not have to reindex the whole corpus; on the other hand, Lucene creates a new segment for these new added documents, and thus makes the new added contents immediately searchable. After an index is fully built, the number of index files and segments remains steady.

To create a *multifile* index structure, the *setUseCompoundFile()* method of class *IndexWriter* is needed, as shown below.

> *IndexWriter writer = new IndexWriter(indexDir, new StandardAnalyzer(), true);*
> *writer.setUseCompoundFile(false); //indicates a multiindex index is created*

A5.1.2 Compound Index Structure

A *multifile* index creates a large number of segments as documents are added to an index. Because contemporary operating systems limit the number of files in a system that can be opened at the same time, therefore, *multifile* index may reach the limit of open files of the operating system when lots of indexes are being searched or indexed simultaneously. To solve the problem, Lucene introduces the *compound index structure* in which each segment contains only one .cfs file, compared with the *multifile index* in which each segment contains seven different files. However, the concepts of segments, documents, fields and terms still apply in compound index structure.

To create a compound index, there is no need to call the *IndexWriter's setUseCompoundFile()* method because by default, Lucene creates a compound index structure.

A5.2 Inverted Index File

Lucene uses an inverted index file structure (Chapter 2 section 2.2.4) to arrange documents such that terms take centre stage, where each term refers to the documents that contain it.

Figure A5-1 illustrates a sample book index with a single segment name. Each of the files shown in this figure is described as following.

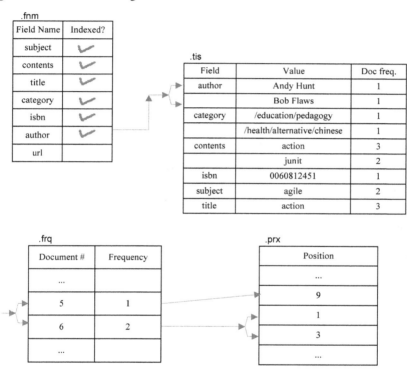

Figure A5-1 Lucene index format

Adaption of: Gospodnetić and Hatcher 2005, p. 405

Field Names (.fnm)

The field names used by documents in the associated segment are contained in this file. The column *indexed* indicates whether the field is indexed. The order of field names in the .fnm file is not necessarily alphabetical. In this example, the segment contains six indexed fields, and the field *url* is not indexed.

Term Directory (.tis)

This file contains all terms (tuples of field name and value) appeared in a segment. Terms are first sorted by field name, and then by value within a field. Document frequency, the number of documents that contain this term within the segment, is also contained in this file. In this sample index, term "junit" appears in two books' *contents* field, therefore, Field *contents* contains the *Value* "junit" with document frequent (*doc freq.*) equals two.

Term Frequencies (.frq)

Term frequencies in each document are listed in this file. In this sample index, the term frequency file shows that term "junit" appears in two files – document #5 and document #6, and the term frequencies are one and two for these two documents respectively.

Term Position (.prx)

For each term within a document, this file presents the position(s) of the term in the document. The figure above indicates that the term "junit" appears in document #5 at position nine, and at position one and three in document #6. The position information is used when queries demand it. For tokenized fields, position information comes directly from the token position.

Summary

Maximum performance and minimum resource utilization are two principles for designing an index structure. Lucene uses an inverted file structure to organize its indexes. Term is the atom element in the Lucene index; terms are contained in a Document, documents form a segment, and an index includes one or more segments. Multifile index and compound index are two index forms of Lucene while the latter is suitable for environments with large number of indexes, indexes with a large number of fields, or where large numbers of indexes are used. Lucene's inverted index file structure is supported by four associated files, namely field names, term directory, term frequencies, and term position, where details of index information format are provided in http://lucene.apache.org/java/docs/fileformats.html

Appendix 6: Consent Form

Title of Project: Improving the Relevance of Search Results via Search-term Disambiguation and Ontological Filtering.

Investigator: Dengya Zhu, School of Information Systems, Curtin Business School, Curtin University of Technology, Western Australia

Tel: 0432 261 516   email:
dengya.zhu@postgrad.curtin.edu.au

Supervisor: Dr Heinz Dreher, Senior Lecturer, Curtin University of Technology, Western Australia

Tel: (08) 9266-2117   email: Heinz.dreher@cbs.curtin.edu.au

You are of your own accord making a decision whether or not to participate in this research study. Your signature verifies that you have decided to participate in the study, having read and understood all the information accessible. Your signature also officially states that you have had adequate opportunity to discuss this study with the investigators and all your questions have been answered to your satisfaction.

I, (the undersigned) _____

                                  Please PRINT

of _____

Postcode _____   Phone _____

consent to involvement in this study and give my authorisation for any results from this study to be used in any research paper, on the understanding that confidentiality will be maintained. I comprehend that I may withdraw from the study at any time without discrimination. If so, I undertake to contact the investigator (Tel. 0432 261 516) at the earliest opportunity.

Signature _____   Date _____

                   Subject

I have explained to the subject the procedures of the study to which the subject has consented their involvement and have answered all questions. In my appraisal the subject has voluntarily and intentionally given informed consent and possesses the legal capacity to give informed consent to participate in this research study.

Investigator: Date:

Appendix 7: Information Form

Title of Project: Improving the Relevance of Search Results via Search-term Disambiguation and Ontological Filtering.
Investigator: Dengya Zhu, School of Information Systems, Curtin Business School, Curtin University of Technology, Western Australia, Tel: 0432 261 516; email: dengya.zhu@postgrad.curtin.edu.au

Supervisor: Dr Heinz Dreher, Senior Lecturer, Curtin University of Technology, Western Australia, Tel: (08) 9266-2117; email: Heinz.dreher@cbs.curtin.edu.au

Purpose of study
The purpose of the research is to develop an ontology based visualized browser, which combines both keyword queries and visualized lightweight ontology based navigator into a single user interface. A novel strategy has been proposed which focuses on the improvement of *precision* of Web search results by disambiguating query with the interaction of users. A browser prototype will be proposed and a trial of the proposed prototype is conducted then. Evaluation of the developed browser is fulfilled by analyzing the experiment data collected and the *precision* improvement will be calculated.
To help us evaluate the proposed browser, you are invited to participate in the study to give your opinion about if the retrieved information is relevant to the given information need based on your knowledge and experience. The *precision* improvement will be derived according to the relevance judgment of yours.
Procedures
If you are prepared to be involved in the study, I will present you a copy of the retrieved search results (a list of returned items that similar to the one returned by Google/Yahoo) and the information need. You are asked to tick if the retrieved item is "relevant", "partially relevant", "insufficient information" or "irrelevant" to the corresponding information need. There are all 15 queries relating to the 15 categories in Open Directory Project (www.dmoz.com). For each query, the search-term may have more then one meanings, information need is therefore defined to be used as the based of relevant judgment. For each query, 50 returned search results (if applicable and the maximum) are considered. A maximum of 750 items therefore need to be take into account. It will take you around 2 hours time. Finally, you three experts' (anonymous) opinions will be combined together to decide if the returned results is relevant to the information need.
To make a final decision, we assign an item 3 points if it is judged as relevant, 1 point if it is partially relevant, 0 point if the information is insufficient, and -3 point if the item is judged as irrelevant. The points of your three experts' will be added together and if the sum is bigger than 0, the returned item will be treated as "relevant", less then 0, the item will be treated as "irrelevant", 0, neutral.
Risks, discomforts and benefits
If you feel uncomfortable judging the relevant of any returned search items, feel free to express your concerns. You are, of course, free to decline to judge any of the items. The judgment that you give will be of value to the final conclusion of the relevance of the items to the given information need. You three experts' opinions are treated equally important in reaching the final relevance conclusion of each item. **The evaluation of the project is not affected by the number of relevant or irrelevant or other kinds of items returned, please feel free to make your decision.**
Confidentiality
Any information that you give will remain completely confidential. During analysis, you will be completely anonymous. You will be asked to sign on the document for the purpose of authority of the relevance judgment only. The signature document will be treated as raw documents, and with all records being kept for a period of 5 years with the project supervisor in a secure place. After this period all document will be destroyed. This is a requirement of Curtin University of Technology.
Requests for more information
You are encouraged to discuss any concerns regarding the study with the Investigator or the Supervisor at any time, and to ask any questions you may have.
Refusal or withdrawal
You may refuse to participate in the study. If you change your mind once you have agreed to participate and withdraw your consent, then you will be free to withdraw at any time and without fear of prejudice. If you decide to withdraw from the study then please contact the Investigator at the earliest opportunity. In the event that you withdraw, all your data will be destroyed.
Approval
This study has been approved by the Curtin University Human Research Ethics Committee. If needed, verification of approval can be obtained by either writing to the Curtin University Human Research Ethics Committee, c/- Office for Research and Development, Curtin University of Technology, GPO Box U1987, Perth, 6845 or by telephoning (08) 9266 2784.

Appendix 8: Relevance Judgment Survey Form

R = Relevant; P = Partially relevant; I = Irrelevant N = Not sufficient to make a judgment

Please mark (x) under columns R, P, I or N.

Search-term 5: Ups

Information need: Information about how UPS (Uninterruptible Power Supply) works, key specification of UPS

INFORMATION SNIPPET	R	P	I	N
1. jaguar (http://www.jaguar.com/) Official site of the Ford Motor Company division featuring new Jaguar models and local dealer information.				
2. One World Journeys | Jaguar: Lord of the Mayan Jungle (http://www.oneworldjourneys.com/jaguar) A multimedia expedition into the heart of the Mexican jungle, searching for the elusive jaguar.				
3. Jaguar (http://www.bluelion.org/jaguar.htm) Compares jaguars and leopards and provides information about the animal's shrinking habitat and relationship with man.				
4. Jag-lovers - the Jaguar Enthusiasts' premier Internet site (http://www.jag-lovers.org/) Offers model pages, mailing lists, book reviews, and more for the Jaguar car enthusiast.				
5. Title: Jaguar Enthusiasts' Club Main Page (http://www.jec.org.uk/) Offers information on activities. Based in the U.K., but offers memberships worldwide.				
6. jaguars.com >> The official website of the NFL's Jacksonville Jaguars. (http://www.jaguars.com/) Official site of the Jaguars. Includes schedule, news, multimedia, photos, player information, statistics, team store, tickets, and more.				
7. Jaguar UK - Jaguar Cars (http://www.jaguar.co.uk/) ... Vehicles. Tools and Services. Finance. Owners. About Jaguar. Home. X-TYPE. S-TYPE. XJ. XK. Accessories ... Site Map. FAQ. Privacy Policy. Terms & Conditions ...				
8. Jaguar US - Jaguar USA Home (http://www.jaguarusa.com/us/en/home.htm) Jaguar USA Official Home Page ... From $62,495. From $62,495. From $75,500. From $75,500. Build Your Jaguar. Request a Brochure ...				
9. Jaguar AU - Jaguar Cars (http://www.jaguar.com.au/) Official Australian site for the Ford Motor Company division. Includes model specifications and general information.				
10. Jaguar - The British Metal Band - Home Page (http://www.jaguar-online.com/) Jaguar are a British rock band who have been very influnetial within the rock ... Jaguar Collectors CD Project. The band have announced an exciting project and ...				
11. Jaguar - Wikipedia, the free encyclopedia (http://en.wikipedia.org/wiki/Jaguar) ... a b c d e "Jaguar (panthera onca) ... The jaguar (Panthera onca) are mammals of the Felidae family and one of four " ... (European jaguar) and panthera ...				
12. Jaguar -- Kids' Planet -- Defenders of Wildlife (http://www.kidsplanet.org/factsheets/jaguar.html) Jaguar -- Kids' Planet -- Defenders of Wildlife Jaguar -- Kids' Planet -- Defenders of Wildlife ...				
13. Jaguar UK - R is for Racing (http://www.jaguar.co.uk/uk/en/vehicles/r-performance/overview/r_racing.htm) ... bred into the bloodline of every Jaguar, particularly the very special range of ... create the essence of the Jaguar breed "C rare, beautiful, refined, and ...				
14. Jag"²ar (http://www.jaguar.is/) Groove-oriented music with influences in funk, latin, soul, and rock.				

INFORMATION SNIPPET	R	P	I	N
15. Jaguar DE - Jaguar Cars (http://www.jaguar.de/) ... Corporate Sales. Suche. Jaguar Weltweit. Inhalt. H?ufig gestellte Fragen. DAT Leitfaden. Kraftstoffverbrauch & CO2-Emissionen. Nutzungsbedingungen. Kontakt. Barrierefreiheit ...				
16. Jaguar Models - Main Page (resin model kits) (http://www.jaguarmodels.com/) Jaguar Models, 12 ... Contacting Information. Jaguar Models, Inc. 18229 Railroad Street, City of Industry, CA 91748 ... We have added product listings of ...				
17. Jaguar CA - Jaguar Cars (http://www.jaguar.com/ca/en/home.htm) ... Request a Brochure. Locate a Dealer. Request a Test Drive. Search. Site Map. Contact Us. FAQ. Fran?ais ... X-TYPE. S-TYPE. XJ. XK. Welcome to. JAGUAR CANADA ...				
18. Jaguar Search Results (http://www.autobytel.com/content/research/detail/Jaguar.htm) Jaguar Pricing Guide - Buy your next new or used Jaguar here using our pricing ... The 2006 Jaguar S-Type is a 4-door, 5-passenger luxury sedan, or luxury sports ...				
19. Jaguar NL - Home (http://www.jaguar.nl/) Official Dutch site for the Ford Motor Company division.				
20. Jaguar I Free Price Quotes I Jaguar Dealer I Jaguar Car I Car.com (http://www.car.com/content/research/makesearch/index.cfm/action/SelectModel2/make_vch/Jaguar) Jaguar,Jag price quotes and reviews. Free no-obligation quote from a local dealer. ... 2007 Jaguar XK Preview. Aiming to set the luxury performance standard ...				
21. Apple - Apple - Mac OS X - Leopard Sneak Peek (http://www.apple.com/macosx/leopard/index.html) Sneak peak from Apple of some of the features in the next generation of their Macintosh OS X, codenamed Leopard.				
22. AtariAge - Atari Jaguar History (http://www.atariage.com/Jaguar/history.html) AtariAge - News, message boards, rarity guides, game database, manuals, pictures, ... Atari Jaguar with CD-ROM ... program and publish Jaguar games, and has ...				
23. Jaguar (http://dialspace.dial.pipex.com/agarman/jaguar.htm) Key facts and information on the jaguar's habitat, diet and status as a near threatened species.				
24. Jaguar (car) - Wikipedia, the free encyclopedia (http://en.wikipedia.org/wiki/Jaguar_(car)) ... Jaguar E-types are featured in the films The Italian Job, Robbery, The Odessa ... Harold, of Harold and Maude, had a Jaguar E-Type hearse. ...				
25. Jaguar (http://www.fas.org/man/dod-101/sys/ac/row/jaguar.htm) ... and tactical support aircraft, the Jaguar has been transformed into a potent fighter-bomber. ... The Jaguar strike fighter was equipped also with Magic air ...				
26. Jaguar (http://www.bigcatrescue.org/jaguar.htm) Jaguar Facts, Jaguar Photos and Jaguars in the news at the world's largest big ... The Jaguar and the Leopard are often confused with one another in zoos. ...				
27. Jaguar (http://www.thewildones.org/Animals/jaguar.html) ... The jaguar (Panthera onca) is the only member of the 'big cat' family that lives ... and is about the same size as the jaguar, but it is classified as a small cat ...				
28. San Diego Zoo's Animal Bytes: Jaguar (http://www.sandiegozoo.org/animalbytes/t-jaguar.html) Get fun and interesting jaguar facts in an easy-to-read style from the San Diego ... over 85 species in the jaguar diet, including peccaries, deer, tapirs, ...				
29. Jaguar I Free Price Quotes I Jaguar Car Dealer I 2006 2007 (http://www.autoweb.com/content/research/makesearch/index.cfm/action/SelectModel2/make_vch/J aguar) Jaguar,Jag reviews and price quotes from a local dealer. ... 2007 Jaguar XK Preview. Aiming to set the luxury performance standard ...				

INFORMATION SNIPPET	R	P	I	N
30. Jaguar - Java Access to Generic Underlying Architectural Resources (http://www.eecs.harvard.edu/~mdw/proj/old/jaguar/) ... Jaguar is an extension of the Java runtime environment which enables direct Java ... Unlike the JNI, however, Jaguar does not require copying of data ...				
31. The Jaguar - Houston Zoo {N A HURY} (http://users.netropolis.net/nahury1/jaguar.htm) General overview of the species.				
32. Yahooligans! Animals: Jaguar (http://yahooligans.yahoo.com/content/animals/species/6638.html) A picture and description of this animal. ... The Jaguar is the biggest and most powerful North American wildcat, and the only ...				
33. New 2006 and 2007 Jaguar Cars on Yahoo! Autos (http://autos.yahoo.com/newcars/jaguar/index.html) new Jaguar pictures, specs, reviews and more from the most comprehensive online automotive site. ... Find Used Jaguar Cars Near You. Check Yahoo! ...				
34. Jaguar I Jaguar Dealer I Car Quotes and Reviews I 2006 2007 (http://www.autosite.com/content/research/makesearch/index.cfm/action/SelectModel2/make_vch/Jaguar) Jaguar,Jag reviews, pictures, and invoice pricing. Get a free no-obligation ... 2006 Jaguar XJ Super V8 Portfolio Quick Spin. Preferred 10 to 1 over a corner office ...				
35. Jaguar car quote, dealer prices, dealer quotes, MSRP prices, invoice prices (http://www.autobytel.com/content/buy/lm/new/search/index.cfm/action/SelectModel/make_vch/Jaguar)				
Jaguar,Jag car quote, dealer prices, dealer quotes, MSRP prices, invoice prices ... Jaguar XK. ABOUT AUTOBYTEL " ... Powered by AIC - Automotive Information Center ...				
36. Schr?dinger -> Site Map (http://www.schrodinger.com/Products/jaguar.html) A general purpose ab initio electronic structure package ... Jaguar Chem3D EULA. Script Center. Script Downloads. Seminar Center. June 1st 2006. May 25th 2006 ...				
37. Animal Fact Sheets (http://www.zoo.org/educate/fact_sheets/jaguar/jaguar.htm) ... which includes four species of "big cats", the jaguar, tiger, lion and leopard. ... Jaguar cubs are usually born with their eyes closed, weigh about 25-29 ounces ...				
38. Jaguar - Research All Models and Prices - MSN Autos (http://autos.msn.com/browse/Jaguar.aspx) Jaguar prices, reviews, used Jaguar classifieds, and more on MSN Autos ... Jaguar was founded in 1922 as the Swallow Sidecar Company of Blackpool, England. ...				
39. Jaguar Performance Products, Georgia (http://www.jaguarkarts.com/) Jaguar Performance Karts is a manufacture of racing kart chassis in Georgia, ... Jaguar Performance had a record breaking season in the year 2001 and 2002 is ...				
40. Used Jaguar Prices & Reviews (http://auto.consumerguide.com/Search/index.cfm/type/used/make/1608/name/Jaguar/) Search results for used Jaguar reviews. Results include car name, vehicle class, ... Jaguar was then purchased by Ford in 1989, and is now a division in the ...				
41. Jaguar (http://www.co.pima.az.us/cmo/sdcp/sdcp2/fsheets/jaguar.html) ... The jaguar (Panthera onca) is the largest cat native to the Western Hemisphere. ... The jaguar can be a far ranging animal, traveling distances up to 500 miles. ...				
42. JAGUAR cologne (http://www.4-fragrances.com/men/jaguar-m.htm) Jaguar ... JAGUAR BLUE Eau de Toilette Spray 3.4 oz New $48.00 $39.99. FREE US SHIPPING ON ORDERS OVER $60 ... discount JAGUAR jaguar mark 2 jaguar,cologne, ...				
43. Media.Ford.com: The Products :Jaguar (http://media.ford.com/products/index.cfm?make_id=95) Ford, Volvo, Mazda, Lincoln, Jaguar, Aston Martin, Mercury, Land Rover ... Jaguar North America today announced Manufacturer's Suggested Retail Prices ...				

INFORMATION SNIPPET	R	P	I	N
44. Jaguar History (http://www.exoticcarrental.com/JaguarHistory.htm) Information about the history of the Jaguar. ... the company name to Jaguar. In 1948 at the Earls Court Motor Show the XK 120 Roadster was introduced by Jaguar. ...				
45. J A G U A R - ?ndice (http://jaguar.edu.co/) Taller-escuela dedicado a la educací¨®n, producci¨®n y publicací¨®n de artes ... comercial educativo ...				
46. NatureWorks - Jaguar (http://www.nhptv.org/natureworks/jaguar.htm) NatureWorks ... The jaguar is the largest cat in North America and the third largest cat in the world. ... The Jaguar, unlike most big cats, loves the water. ...				
47. Flickr: Photos tagged with jaguar (http://www.flickr.com/photos/tags/jaguar) Flickr is almost certainly the best online photo management and sharing ... Jaguar Luxury Automobile. Official Site-Jaguar vehicle specs, pictures, options and ...				
48. Jaguar (http://www.pansophist.com/jag.htm) An owner discusses his XJ6.				
49. Jaguar Printout- EnchantedLearning.com (http://www.enchantedlearning.com/subjects/mammals/cats/jaguar/Jaguarprintout.shtml) Jaguar Printout. Jaguar are medium-sized cats that live in South and Central ... As a bonus, site members have access to a banner-ad-free version of the site, ...				
50. USS Jaguar (http://www.worldkids.net/jaguar) Star Trek club for kids with chat, message board, stories, and more.				

Appendix 9: Statistical Results of the Five Judges

Description for Relevance judgment

R=Relevant

P=Partially Relevant

I=Irrelevant

N=Not enough information to make a decision

If judge one judges search result one is relevant, then the number onw will be put in the cell located by column "R" and the row of search result one. The same search result may be judged partially relevant by judge four. Consequently, number four will be put in the cell located by column "P" and the row of search result one.

A relevance judgment contributes three points for the search result, partially relevant adds one point, irrelevant judgment adds minus three points to the search result, and N has no effect on the final judgment.

SS=Summed Score (add the points assigned to each search result) AJ=Average-score-based Judge (SS>0 Relevant, SS<0 irrelevant, SS=0, special case) SJ=Strict Judge (the search result is considered irrelevant if any of the judges make an irrelevance judgment) EJ=Enlarged Judge (if any judge make a R or P decision, the result is taken as relevant)

Description for *Precision* at Standard *Recall* Levels

Based on AJ, each search-term may have a different number of relevant documents. For example, the search-term "Clinton" has 15 relevant information snippets. An actual *precision* at the 15 *recall* point is first calculated. The calculated results are then used to compute *precisions* at the standard interpolated 11 *recall* levels.

Relevance judgment for Search-term 1: Clinton

INFORMATION SNIPPET/SEARCH RESULT	R	P	I	N	SS	AJ	SJ	EJ
1. Biography of William J. Clinton	1 2 3 5	4			13	R	R	R
2. Hillary Rodham Clinton, Senator	3	1 5	2 4		-1	I	I	R
3. Bill Clinton - Wikipedia, the free	1 2 3 4 5				15	R	R	R
4. The Official Site of Clinton, site of	4		1 2 3 5		-9	I	I	R
5. William J. Clinton Foundation (	3 4	1 2	5		5	R	I	R
						3	2	5
6. Clinton Presidential Materials	1 3 4 5	2			13	R	R	R
7. Clinton County Iowa Home			1 2 3 4 5		-15	I	I	I
8. Clinton County welcomes you! ¡a			1 2 3 4 5		-15	I	I	I
9. Welcome to Clinton, Massach			1 2 3 4 5		-15	I	I	I
10. Amazon.com: My Life:	1 2 3 4	5			13	R	R	R
						5	4	7
11. Clinton - Wikipedia, the free enc	3 4		1 2 5		-3	I	I	R
12. Clinton, Oklahoma (http://www.	4		1 2 3 5		-9	I	I	R
13. OpinionJournal - Extra	3 4 5	2		1	10	R	R	R
14. Bill Clinton Jokes - Clinton	3	1 2	4 5		-1	I	I	R
15. Official Websit of Clinton			1 2 3 4 5		-15	I	I	I
						6	5	11
16. Clinton County Geneological			1 2 3 4 5		-15	I	I	I
17. Welcome to Clinton County,			1 2 3 4 5		-15	I	I	I
18. USA: biography of William -	1 2 3 4 5				15	R	R	R
19. Clinton County Government			1 2 3 4 5		-15	I	I	I
20. City of Clinton (http://www.			1 2 3 4 5		-15	I	I	I
						7	6	12
21. Welcome to Clinton County,			1 2 3 4 5		-15	I	I	I
22. William J. Clinton Presidential	1 2 3 5		4		9	R	I	R
23. Clinton Industries (http://www.			1 2 3 4 5		-15	I	I	I
24. Village of Clinton (http://www.			1 2 3 4 5		-15	I	I	I
25. Town of Clinton -- It's			1 2 3 4 5		-15	I	I	I
26. Town of Clinton (http://www.			1 2 3 4 5		-15	I	I	I
27. American Presidents: Life Por	2 3 4 5	1			13	R	R	R
28. Clinton, Wisconsin (http://www.			1 2 3 4 5		-15	I	I	I
29. frontline: the clinton years	PBS	2 4 5	1 3			11	R	R	R
30. Clinton School District Home			1 2 3 4 5		-15	I	I	I
						10	8	15
31. Clinton County Election &			1 2 3 4 5		-15	I	I	I

INFORMATION SNIPPET/SEARCH RESULT	R	P	I	N	SS	AJ	SJ	EJ
32. bill clinton	2 3 4	1		5	10	R	R	R
33. TLC :: What Not to Wear ::			1 2 3 4	5	-12	I	I	I
34. Bill Clinton - MSN Encarta	1 2 3 4	5			13	R	R	R
35. Clinton, IA Chamber of			1 2 3 4 5		-15	I	I	I
36. Clinton Presidential Library -	2 3		1 5		8	R	R	R
37. CNN - Clinton: Iraq has abused	2 3 4 5			1	12	R	R	R
38. Bill Clinton A Model Patient -	2 3		5	1 4	3	R	I	R
39. Untitled Document (http://		4	1 2 3 5		-11	I	I	R
40. City of Clinton Oklahoma (http			1 2 3 4 5		-15	I	I	I
41. Welcome to Clinton, CT! (http			1 2 3 4 5		-15	I	I	I
42. Township of Clinton, New			1 2 3 4 5		-15	I	I	I
43. Clinton County, NY Genealogy			1 2 3 4 5		-15	I	I	I
44. Senator Hillary Rodham Clinton		3 4	1 2 5		-7	I	I	R
45. Project Vote Smart - Senator	4	3	2 5	1	-2	I	I	R
46. Clinton County Schools (http://			1 2 3 4 5		-15	I	I	I
47. Clinton, Bill. The Columbia	2 3		4 5	1	0	N		
48. Clinton Group (http://www.			1 2 3 4 5		-15	I	I	I
49. Clinton County, Illinois--Ho			1 2 3 4 5		-15	I	I	I
50. Clinton Community College			1 2 3 4 5		-15	I	I	I
						15	12	23

Precisions at actual *recall* levels (%)

Position	1	3	5	6	10	13	18	21	27	29	32	34	36	37	38
Recall	6.7	13.3	20	26.7	33.3	40	46.7	53.3	60	66.7	73.3	80	86.7	93.3	100
Precision	100	66.7	60	66.7	50	46.2	38.9	38.14	33.3	34.5	34.4	35.3	36.1	37.8	39.5

Precision at the 11 Standard *Recall* Levels

Recall	0	0.1	0.2	0.3	0.4	0.5	0.6	0.7	0.8	0.9	1.0
Precision	100	66.7	60	50	46.2	38.1	33.3	34.4	35.3	37.8	39.5

Search-term 2: Ford

INFORMATION SNIPPET	R	P	I	N	SS	AJ	SJ	EJ
1. Ford Vehicles: Ford Vehicles		5	1 2 3	4	-8	I	I	R
2. Ford Motor Company Home	4	1 5	2 3		-1	I	I	R
3. Ford Motor Company (http://.	4	5	2 3	1	-2	I	I	R
4. Ford :: home (http://www		4 5	1 2 3		-7	I	I	R
5. ......::::: FORD MODELS		4 5	1 2 3		-7	I	I	R
						0	0	5
6. Ford Australia (			2 3 4 5	1	-12	I	I	I
7. Ford Motor Company of Canad			2 3 4 5	1	-12	I	I	I
8. Henry Ford Museum & Gr	3 4	1 2 5			9	R	R	R
9. Ford Truck Enthusiasts, 1948-		4	1 2 3 5		-11	I	I	R
10. Ford - Viva o Novo (http://			1 2 3 4 5		-15	I	I	I
						1	1	7
11. Ford :: Startseite (http://www			2 3 4 5	1	-12	I	I	I
12. Ford Racing: Home (http://w		1	2 3 4 5		-11	I	I	R
13. Media.Ford.com: (http://media.			1 2 3 4 5		-15	I	I	I
14. Ford Foundation (http://www.	4	1 3 5	2		3	R	I	R
15. ford motor company (http://		1	2 3 4 5		-11	I	I	R
						2	1	1 0
16. Ford Motor Company - Wiki	3 5	1 2 4			9	R	R	R
17. Harrison Ford (I) (http://www.			1 2 3 4 5		-15	I	I	I
18. Media.Ford.com: FORD LE			1 2 3 4 5		-15	I	I	I
19. Ford Motor Company of Can			1 2 3 4 5		-15	I	I	I
20. Ford Accessories (http://www.			1 2 3 4 5		-15	I	I	I
						3	2	1 1
21. Ford (http://www.ford.co.za/)			1 2 3 4 5		-15	I	I	I
22. Ford Vehicles: Ford Mustang -			1 2 3 4 5		-15	I	I	I
23. Henry Ford - Wikipedia, the fr	1 2 3 4 5				15	R	R	R
24. The Henry Ford: The Life of	1 2 3 4 5				15	R	R	R
25. Ford Fleet - Fleet Vehicles For			1 2 3 4 5		-15	I	I	I
26. Ford (http://www.india.ford.			1 2 3 4 5		-15	I	I	I
27. Gerald R. Ford Presidential			1 2 3 4 5		-15	I	I	I
28. Ford :: Ford Team RS :: Ford			1 2 3 4 5		-15	I	I	I
29. Ford of Belgium (http://www.			1 2 3 4 5		-15	I	I	I
30. John Ford (I) (http://www.i			1 2 3 4 5		-15	I	I	I

INFORMATION SNIPPET	R	P	I		N	SS	AJ	SJ	EJ
							5	4	1 3
31. New 2006 and 2007 Ford Cars			1 2 3 4 5			-15	I	I	I
32. Biography of Gerald R. Ford		4	1 2 3 5			-11	I	I	R
33. Ford Malaysia (http://www.f			1 2 3 4 5			-15	I	I	I
34. Ford Credit - Auto financing			1 2 3 4 5			-15	I	I	I
35. Ford I Ford Dealer I Car Quo			1 2 3 4 5			-15	I	I	I
36. Ford I Free Price Quotes I For			1 2 3 4 5			-15	I	I	I
37. Ford :: home :: rotating home			1 2 3 4 5			-15	I	I	I
38. Ford I Free Price Quotes I			1 2 3 4 5			-15	I	I	I
39. Career Programs http://www.			1 2 3 4 5			-15	I	I	I
40. Ford - Research All Models			1 2 3 4 5			-15	I	I	I
41. Ford Search Results (http://w			1 2 3 4 5			-15	I	I	I
42. Ford New Zealand (			1 2 3 4 5			-15	I	I	I
43. Ford Commercial Truck (htt			1 2 3 4 5			-15	I	I	I
44. Ford County, KS (http://			1 2 3 4 5			-15	I	I	I
45. Ford :: Accueil :: voiture ne			1 2 3 4 5			-15	I	I	I
46. Oy Ford Ab (http://www.ford			1 2 4 5	3		-12	I	I	I
47. FORD: Summary for FORW			1 2 3 4 5			-15	I	I	I
48. Ford Parts - Always In Stock			1 2 3 4 5			-15	I	I	I
49. Ford :: home :: rotating home			1 2 4 5	3		-12	I	I	I
50. Ford Madox Ford Society			1 2 3 4 5			-15	I	I	I
							5	4	1 3

*Precision*s at actual *recall* levels (%)

Position	8	14	16	23	24
Recall	20	40	60	80	100
Precision	12.5	14.3	18.8	17.4	20.8

Precision at the 11 Standard *Recall* Levels

Recall	0	0.1	0.2	0.3	0.4	0.5	0.6	0.7	0.8	0.9	1.0
Precision	12.5	12.5	12.5	14.3	14.3	18.8	18.8	17.4	17.4	20.8	20.8

Search-term 3: Health

INFORMATION SNIPPET	R	P	I	N	SS	AJ	SJ	EJ
1. Medical Dictionary, Diseases,	1 2	3 4 5			9	R	R	R
2. Health in the Yahoo! Directory (	1 2	3 4 5			9	R	R	R
3. CNN.com - Health (http://www.		2 3 4 5	1		1	R	I	R
4. Open Directory - Health (http://	2	1 3 4		5	6	R	R	R
5. Health News - New York Times (	2 5	1 3 4			9	R	R	R
					5	4	5	
6. World Health Organization (WHO/	3	2	1 4 5		-5	I	I	R
7. WebMD - Better Information. Better	1 2 5	3 4			11	R	R	R
8. BBC NEWS I Health (http://news.	5	1 2 3 4			7	R	R	R
9. MSNBC - Health News: Medical	2	1 3 4 5			7	R	R	R
10. National Institutes of Health (NIH)	1 2	4	3 5		1	R	I	R
					9	7	10	
11. Health.com :: (http://www.health.	1 2 3 5	4			13	R	R	R
12. www.health.gov (http://www.	1 2 3 5	4			13	R	R	R
13. Health News - AOL Health (http://	1 2 3 4 5				15	R	R	R
14. C-Health: Your Health and	2 4 5	1 3			11	R	R	R
15. The top health news articles	1 2 4 5	3			13	R	R	R
					14	12	15	
16. BBC - Health (http://www.bbc.co.	1 2 3 5	4			13	R	R	R
17. Men's Health (http://www.	2 4 5	1 3			11	R	R	R
18. AARP - Health I People Age 50 &	5	1 2 3 4			7	R	R	R
19. Kaiser Permanente: Thrive -	5	1 2 3 4			7	R	R	R
20. WHO I World Health			2 3 4 5	1	-12	I	I	I
					13	16	19	
21. Drug and alcohol abuse,	5	2	1 3 4		-5	I	I	R
22. InteliHealth: InteliHealth	2 3 5	1 4			11	R	R	R
23. Centers for Disease Control and		1 2 3 5	4		1	R	I	R
24. Home Page - MSN Health &	1 2 5	3 4			11	R	R	R
25. Join AARP: Benefits &		1 2 3 5	4		1	R	I	R
26. C-Health : Seniors' Health	2 5	1	3 4		1	R	I	R
27. Breaking Health and Fitness	2	4 5	1 3		-1	I	I	R
28. azcentral.com I health & fit	2 5	1 3	4		5	R	I	R
29. Florida Department of Health		1 2 3 5	4		1	R	I	R
30. U.S. News & World Report:	1 2 5	4	3		7	R	I	R
					26	18	29	
31. AllRefer Health (http://health.	1 2 4 5	3			13	R	R	R

INFORMATION SNIPPET	R	P	I	N	SS	AJ	SJ	EJ
32. Discovery Health :: Discovery	1 2 4 5	3			13	R	R	R
33. healthfinder? - your guide to	1 2 5	3	4		7	R	I	R
34. U.S. Department of Labor	1	2 5	3 4		-1	I	I	R
35. Health - Wex (http://www.law.		1 2 5	3 4		-3	I	I	R
36. Health (http://www.		1 2 5	3 4		-3	I	I	R
37. Health - Wikipedia, the free	1 3 4 5	2			13	R	R	R
38. United States Department of	2 5	1 3	4		5	R	I	R
39. Travelers' Health I CDC (http://	2	1 5	3 4		-1	I	I	R
40. Health Care, Health Care Guide,	1 2 4 5		3		9	R	I	R
41. Excite - Health (http://health.	1 2 5		3 4		3	R	I	R
42. DenverPost.com (http://	1 4 5	2	3		7	R	I	R
43. Healthcentral.com - Trusted,	1 2 4 5		3		9	R	I	R
44. New York State Department of	2	1 5	3 4		-1	I	I	R
45. Health:Topic (http://www.oecd.or	1 2 5		3 4		3	R	I	R
46. National Library of Medicine -	1	2 5	3 4		-1	I	I	R
47. Women's Health Interactive (http://	5	1 2 4	3		3	R	I	R
48. Health & Fitness Tips -	2 5	1 3 4			9	R	R	R
49. Mayo Clinic medical information	2 4 5	1 3			11	R	R	R
50. Health Information - National	2 5	1 3 4			9	R	R	R
						40	24	49

Precisions at actual *recall* levels (%)

Po	1	2	3	4	5	7	8	9	10	11	12	13	14	15
Re	2.5	5	7.5	10	12.5	15	17.5	20	22.5	25	27.5	30	32.5	35
Pr	100	100	100	100	100	85.7	87.5	88.9	90	90.9	91.7	92.3	92.9	93.3
Po	16	17	18	19	22	23	24	25	26	28	29	30	31	32
Re	37.5	40	42.5	45	47.5	50	52.5	55	57.5	60	62.5	65	67.5	70
pr	93.8	94.1	94.4	94.7	86.4	87	87.5	88	88.5	85.7	86.2	86.7	87.1	87.5
Po	33	37	38	40	41	42	43	45	47	48	49	50		
Re	72.5	75	77.5	80	82.5	85	87.5	90	92.5	95	97.5	100		
pr	87.9	81.1	81.6	80	80.5	81	81.4	80	78.7	79.2	79.6	80		

Note: Po=position Re=recall Pr=precision

Precision at the 11 Standard *Recall* Levels

Recall	0	0.1	0.2	0.3	0.4	0.5	0.6	0.7	0.8	0.9	1.0
Precision	100	100	88.9	92.3	94.1	87	85.7	87.5	80	80	80

Search-term 4: Jaguar

INFORMATION SNIPPET	R	P	I	N	SS	AJ	SJ	EJ
1. jaguar (http://www.jaguar.com			1 2 3 4 5		-15	I	I	I
2. One World Journeys I Jaguar: L	1 2 5	3 4			11	R	R	R
3. Jaguar (http://www.bluelion. a)	1 2 3 5	4			13	R	R	R
4. Jag-lovers - the Jaguar Enthus			1 2 3 4 5		-15	I	I	I
5. Title: Jaguar Enthusiasts' Club			1 2 3 4 5		-15	I	I	I
						2	2	2
6. jaguars.com >> The off			1 2 3 4 5		-15	I	I	I
7. Jaguar UK - Jaguar Cars (			1 2 3 4 5		-15	I	I	I
8. Jaguar US - Jaguar USA Hom			1 2 3 4 5		-15	I	I	I
9. Jaguar AU - Jaguar Cars (			1 2 3 4 5		-15	I	I	I
10. Jaguar - The British Meta			1 2 3 4 5		-15	I	I	I
						2	2	2
11. Jaguar - Wikipedia, the free.	1 2 3 4 5				15	R	R	R
12. Jaguar -- Kids' Planet -- De	1 4 5	3		2	10	R	R	R
13. Jaguar UK - R is for Racing (			1 2 3 4 5		-15	I	I	I
14. Jag'²ar (http://www.jaguar.is			1 2 3 4 5		-15	I	I	I
15. Jaguar DE - Jaguar Cars (htt			1 2 3 4	5	-12	I	I	I
						4	4	4
16. Jaguar Models - Main Page			1 2 3 4 5		-15	I	I	I
17. Jaguar CA - Jaguar Cars			1 2 3 4 5		-15	I	I	I
18. Jaguar Search Results			1 2 3 4 5		-15	I	I	I
19. Jaguar NL - Home (h			1 2 3 4 5		-15	I	I	I
20. Jaguar I Free Price Quotes I			1 2 3 4 5		-15	I	I	I
						4	4	4
21. Apple - Apple - Mac OS X -			1 2 3 4 5		-15	I	I	I
22. AtariAge - Atari Jaguar			1 2 3 4 5		-15	I	I	I
23. Jaguar (http://dialspace.dial.	1 2 3 4 5				15	R	R	R
24. Jaguar (car) - Wikipedia, the			1 2 3 4 5		-15	I	I	I
25. Jaguar (http://www.fas.org/			1 2 3 4 5		-15	I	I	I
26. Jaguar (http://www.bigcatr	1 2 3 4		5		9	R	I	R
27. Jaguar (http://www.	1 2 3 5	4			13	R	R	R
28. San Diego Zoo's Animal By	1 2 3 5	4			13	R	R	R
29. Jaguar I Free Price Quotes I			1 2 3 4 5		-15	I	I	I
30. Jaguar - Java Access to Gen			1 2 3 4 5		-15	I	I	I
						8	7	8
31. The Jaguar - Houston Zoo {	1 2 3 5	4			13	R	R	R

INFORMATION SNIPPET	R	P	I	N	SS	AJ	SJ	EJ
32. Yahooligans! Animals: Jag	1 2 **5**	3 4			11	R	R	R
33. New 2006 and 2007 Jaguar			1 2 3 4 **5**		-15	I	I	I
34. Jaguar	Jaguar Dealer	C			1 2 3 4 **5**		-15	I	I	I
35. Jaguar car quote, dealer			1 2 3 4 **5**		-15	I	I	I
36. Schr?dinger -> Site			1 2 2 4 **5**		-15	I	I	I
37. Animal Fact Sheets ttp://w	1 2 3 **5**	4			13	R	R	R
38. Jaguar - Research All Mode			1 2 3 4 **5**		-15	I	I	I
39. Jaguar Performance Produc			1 2 3 4 **5**		-15	I	I	I
40. Used Jaguar Prices &			1 2 3 4 **5**		-15	I	I	I
41. Jaguar (http://www.co.	1 2 3 **5**	4			13	R	R	R
42. JAGUAR cologne (http://w			1 2 3 4 **5**		-15	I	I	I
43. Media.Ford.com: The Produ			1 2 3 4 **5**		-15	I	I	I
44. Jaguar History (http://www.			1 2 3 4 **5**		-15	I	I	I
45. J A G U A R - ?ndice (			1 4	2 3 **5**	-6	I	I	I
46. NatureWorks - Jaguar (http:	1 2 3 **5**	4			13	R	R	R
47. Flickr: Photos tagged with ja			1 2 3 4 **5**		-15	I	I	I
48. Jaguar (http://www.)			1 2 3 4 **5**		-15	I	I	I
49. Jaguar Printout-	1 2 3 **5**	4			13	R	R	R
50. USS Jaguar (http://www.			1 2 3 4 **5**		-15	I	I	I
						14	13	14

Precisions at actual *recall* levels (%)

Position	2	3	11	12	23	26	27	28	31	32	37	41	46	49
Recall	7.1	14.3	21.4	28.6	35.7	42.9	50	57.1	64.3	71.4	78.6	85.7	92.9	100
Precision	50	66.7	27.3	33.3	21.7	23.1	25.9	28.6	29	31.3	29.7	29.3	28.3	28.6

Precision at the 11 Standard *Recall* Levels

Recall	0	0.1	0.2	0.3	0.4	0.5	0.6	0.7	0.8	0.9	1.0
Precision	50	66.7	27.3	21.7	23.1	25.9	29	31.3	29.3	28.3	28.6

Search-term 5: Ups

INFORMATION SNIPPET	R	P	I	N	SS	AJ	SJ	EJ
1. UPS Package Tracking (http://			1 2 3 4 5		-15	I	I	I
2. UPS Global Home (http://ww			1 2 3 4 5		-15	I	I	I
3. Cash Flow, International Trad			1 2 3 4 5		-15	I	I	I
4. UPS Careers (https://ups.			1 2 3 4 5		-15	I	I	I
5. UPS Calculate Time and			1 2 3 4 5		-15	I	I	I
						0	0	0
6. UPS Careers (http://upsjobs			1 2 3 4 5		-15	I	I	I
7. Welcome to UPS Supply			1 2 3 4 5		-15	I	I	I
8. Uninterruptible power	1 2 3 4 5				15	R	R	R
9. APC Product Information	4	2		135	4	R	R	R
10. RACING.UPS.COM -			1 2 3 4 5		-15	I	I	I
						2	2	2
11. The UPS Store: Packaging			1 2 3 4 5		-15	I	I	I
12. UPS Community (http://			1 2 3 4 5		-15	I	I	I
13. UPS: Summary for			1 2 3 4 5		-15	I	I	I
14. UPS Lithuania (http://			1 2 3 4 5		-15	I	I	I
15. UPS Wireless (http://			2 3 4 5	1	-12	I	I	I
						2	2	2
16. UPS Pressroom: Current			1 2 3 4 5		-15	I	I	I
17. UPS Sustainability (http			1 2 3 4 5		-15	I	I	I
18. UPS Pressroom:			1 2 3 4 5		-15	I	I	I
19. University of Puget Sound			1 2 3 4 5		-15	I	I	I
20. UPS Trade Direct - UPS			1 2 3 4 5		-15	I	I	I
						2	2	2
21. What is UPS? - A Word	1 2 4	3		5	10	R	R	R
22. UPS Power Protection and	1 3 4 5	2			13	R	R	R
23. UPS (http://mobile.ups.	1		2 3 4 5		-9	I	I	R
24. the f-ups news (http://			2 3 4 5	1	-12	I	I	I
25. UPS (http://web.belkin.		1 2 3 4 5			5	R	R	R
26. RACING.UPS.COM Race			1 2 3 4 5		-15	I	I	I
27. THE ups DEBUGGER (http://			1 2 3 4 5		-15	I	I	I
28. UPS Careers (http://ups.			1 2 3 4 5		-15	I	I	I
29. United Parcel Service -			1 2 3 4 5		-15	I	I	I
30. Underground Punk			1 2 3 4 5		-15	I	I	I
						5	5	6
31. OPTI-UPS Protect and	1 3 5	2	4		7	R	I	R

INFORMATION SNIPPET	R	P	I	N	SS	AJ	SJ	EJ
32. UPS - UPS Manufacturers,	1 5	2 3	4		5	R	I	R
33. Uninterruptible Power	1 2 3 5	4			13	R	R	R
34. Howstuffworks "How	1 2 3 5	4			13	R	R	R
35. The DIY (or, if you must, "	2 3 5	1 4			11	R	R	R
36. Urban Legends Reference			1 2 3 4 5		-15	I	I	I
37. UPS Capital Visa ? Business			1 2 3 4 5		-15	I	I	I
38. UPS - Investor Relations (/			1 2 3 4 5		-15	I	I	I
39. UPS Careers: Job Search (			1 2 3 4 5		-15	I	I	I
40. UPS Careers: Opportunities:			1 2 3 4 5		-15	I	I	I
41. The UPS Store: Locations		1	2 3 4	5	-8	I	I	R
42. UPS Selector Sizing Applic		1 2 4		3 5	3	R	R	R
43. Welcome To Air Cargo			1 2 3 4 5		-15	I	I	I
44. Business Week Online:			1 2 3 4 5		-15	I	I	I
45. UPS Israel (http://www.ups			1 2 3 4 5		-15	I	I	I
46. United Package Smashers -			1 2 3 4 5		-15	I	I	I
47. UPS: Headlines for UNITED			1 2 3 4 5		-15	I	I	I
48. UPS (Uninterruptible power	3 5	1 2 4			9	R	R	R
49. Cover Pages: UPS OnLine		1	2 3 4	5	-8	I	I	R
50. InformationWeek.com (http://			1 2 3 4 5		-15	I	I	I
						12	10	15

*Precision*s at actual *recall* levels (%)

Position	8	9	21	22	25	31	32	33	34	35	42	48
Recall	8.3	16.7	25	33.3	41.7	50	58.3	66.7	75	83.3	91.7	100
Precision	12.5	22.2	14.3	18.2	20	19.4	21.9	24.2	26.5	28.6	26.2	25

Precision at the 11 Standard *Recall* Levels

Recall	0	0.1	0.2	0.3	0.4	0.5	0.6	0.7	0.8	0.9	1.0
Precision	12.5	22.2	14.3	18.2	20	19.4	24.2	26.5	28.6	26.2	25

Average *Precision*s at the 11 Standard *Recall* Levels for all the five search-terms

Recall	0	0.1	0.2	0.3	0.4	0.5	0.6	0.7	0.8	0.9	1.0
Precision	55	53.6	40.6	39.3	39.5	37.8	38.2	39.4	38.1	38.6	38.8

Appendix 10: Classified Search Results of "Clinton"

Marked Categories: Business, Kids & Teens, News, Regional, Society.

There are 15 relevant research results which are categorized into: Kids & Teens, News, Society.

Society	AJ
History 1. Biography of William J. Clinton Brief biography of the forty-second U.S. President, Bill Clinton.	R
History 2. Hillary Rodham Clinton, Senator from New York Official Senate site Hillary Rodham Clinton, the Democratic senator from New York. Includes contact information.	
History 3. Bill Clinton - Wikipedia, the free encyclopedia Hyperlinked, in-depth profile of Bill Clinton, the 42nd President of the United States. Includes notes on his early life and political career, as well as information on his presidency and 1998 impeachment.	R
History 4. William J. Clinton Foundation Foundation organized by former President Bill Clinton to promote the values of fairness and opportunity for all. Programs include health and HIV/AIDS, economic empowerment, leadership development, and citizen service.	R
History 5. Clinton Presidential Materials Project Clinton Presidential Materials Project introduction page. ... The Clinton Presidential Materials Project has become the William ...	R
History 6. Amazon.com: My Life: Books: Bill Clinton Amazon.com: My Life: Books: Bill Clinton by Bill Clinton ... Bill Clinton discusses his life goals and how his parents met ... Bill Clinton describes his ...	R
History 7. Bill Clinton Jokes - Clinton Humor and Clinton Jokes Bill Clinton jokes, political cartoons, parodies, and other classic Clinton humor. ... Political Humor> Democrats> Bill Clinton. Entertainment. Political Humor ...	
History 8. USA: biography of William Jefferson Clinton (1946 - USA-project, presidents-area, biographical data of William Jefferson Clinton ... Bill Clinton was born William Jefferson Blythe IV on August 19, 1946, in Hope, ...	R
History 9. William J. Clinton Presidential Library (http://uk.wrs.yahoo.com/_ylt=A0Je5VsRZ. Extensive collection of Clinton Administration documents. Includes research facilities, exhibits, events, and educational programs on the life and presidency of Bill Clinton.	R
History 10. frontline: the clinton years I PBS Presents a look at the Bill Clinton era. From ABC News's Nightline and PBS's Frontline. Includes interviews, photos, and anecdotes.	R
History 11. TLC :: What Not to Wear :: Clinton Kelly What Not to Wear ... Clinton honed his fashion sensibilities and expertise with his tenure as a ... Clinton is also no stranger to television. ...	
History 12. Bill Clinton - MSN Encarta Biographical article from the online encyclopedia Encarta. ... Bill Clinton, born in 1946, 42nd president of the United States (1993-2001), who ...	R
History 13. Clinton Presidential Library - Home Document Clinton Library, the nation's interactive tribute to President Bill Clinton, is ... Clinton Presidential Center is both an act of faith and of confidence. ...	R
History 14. Senator Hillary Rodham Clinton: Contact Senator Clinton... Senator Clinton sincerely appreciates the interest of her constituents wishing ... Senator Hillary Rodham Clinton. United States Senate. 476 Russell Senate ...	
History 15. Clinton, Bill. The Columbia Encyclopedia, Sixth Edition. 2001-05 Clinton, Bill. The Columbia Encyclopedia, Sixth Edition. 2001-05 ... 12 acquitted Clinton. ... During both his terms Clinton took an active interest in environmental ...	N

*Precision*s at actual *recall* levels (%) "Society"

Position	1	3	4	5	6	8	9	10	12	13
Recall	6.7	13.3	20	26.7	33.3	0.4	46.7	53.3	60	66.7
Precision	100	66.7	75	80	83.3	75	77.8	80	75	76.9

Precision at the 11 Standard *Recall* Levels "Society"

Recall	0	0.1	0.2	0.3	0.4	0.5	0.6	0.7	0.8	0.9	1.0
Precision	100	66.7	75	83.3	75	80	75	76.9	0	0	0

News	AJ
Online Archives 1. Clinton - Wikipedia, the free encyclopedia ... Charles Clinton (1690 – 1773) French and Indian War Colonel, father of James and ... George Clinton (1739 – 1812) first and third Governor of New York, ...	
Online Archives 2. OpinionJournal - Extra ... than word gets out that Bill Clinton was flying down to Washington to plan ... Behind the scenes, Clinton servitors run the Democratic Party, beginning at the ...	R
Online Archives 3. Official Websit of Clinton City ... Clinton has grown rapidly over the last ten years. ... Clinton City offers the finest in police and fire protection, professional ...	
Online Archives 4. Clinton Industries ... on exacting standards, that's why Clinton Industries has been among the top ... And because Clinton handles a wide range of products, fulfilling your ...	
Online Archives 5. Village of Clinton A little town with a big heart. ... On behalf of the residents of Clinton, I would like to extend a very warm and sincere welcome. ...	
Online Archives 6. Town of Clinton -- It's Summer in Maine's Dairy Capital Clinton, ME ... Did you know that nearly 13% of Maine's milk is produced in the town of Clinton? ... The Clinton Town Office Staff will be more than happy to ...	
Online Archives 7. Clinton, Wisconsin Official Website for the Village of Clinton, Rock County Wisconsin ... Search WWW Search www.clintonwi.us. free hit counter ...	
Online Archives 8. bill clinton ... Absolute Power: The Legacy of Corruption in the Clinton-Reno Justice Department ... Eyewitness Account Of How Bill Clinton Compromised America's National Security ...	R
Online Archives 9. CNN - Clinton: Iraq has abused its last chance - December 16, 1998 ... From the Oval Office, President Clinton told the nation Wednesday evening why ... Clinton also stated that, while other countries also had weapons of mass ...	R
Online Archives 10. Bill Clinton A Model Patient - CBS News The former president is getting a little better "every day," recovering from heart surgery, and has been on the phone with advice for John Kerry. Mr. Clinton hasn't yet gotten a green light to actually hit the campaign trail for Kerry.	R

*Precision*s at actual *recall* levels (%) "News"

Position	2	8	9	10
Recall	6.7	13.3	20	26.7
Precision	50	25	33.3	40

Precision at the 11 Standard *Recall* Levels (%) "News"

Recall	0	0.1	0.2	0.3	0.4	0.5	0.6	0.7	0.8	0.9	1.0
Precision	50	25	33.3	40	0	0	0	0	0	0	0

Kids and Teens	AJ
School Time 1. American Presidents: Life Portraits Facts, trivia, a 1969 letter to his local R.O.T.C. program officer expressing his feelings about the war, and the text to his 1993 and 1997 Inaugural Addresses.	R

*Precision*s at actual *recall* levels (%) "Society" + "News"

Position	1	3	4	5	6	8	9	10	12	13	17	23	24	25
Recall	6.7	13.3	20	26.7	33.3	0.4	46.7	53.3	60	66.7	73.3	80	86.7	93.3
Precision	100	66.7	75	80	83.3	75	77.8	80	75	76.9	64.7	52.2	54.2	56

Precision at the 11 Standard *Recall* Levels (%) "Society" + "News"

Recall	0	0.1	0.2	0.3	0.4	0.5	0.6	0.7	0.8	0.9	1.0
Precision	100	66.7	75	83.3	75	80	75	64.7	52.2	56	0

Appendix 11: Classified Search Results of "Ford"

Marked categories: Arts, Business, Computers, Home, Kids And Teens, Recreation, Reference, Regional, Shopping, Society, Sports.

There are five relevant search results categorized into: Reference, Society and Recreation.

Reference	AJ
Museums 1. Henry Ford Museum & Greenfield Village Collection of Americana that depicts the ever-changing worlds of transportation, manufacturing, home life, entertainment, and technology.	R
Encyclopedias 1. Henry Ford - Wikipedia, the free encyclopedia ... As sole owner of the Ford Company he became one of the richest and best-known ... Ford, though poorly educated, had a global vision, with consumerism as ...	R

Precision at the 11 Standard *Recall* Levels (%) "Reference"

Recall	0	0.1	0.2	0.3	0.4	0.5	0.6	0.7	0.8	0.9	1.0
Precision	100	100	100	100	100	0	0	0	0	0	0

Society	AJ
Philanthropy 1. Ford Foundation Providing grants and loans to projects that strengthen democratic values, reduce poverty and injustice, promote international cooperation, and advance human achievement.	R

Recreation	AJ
Autos 1. Ford Motor Company Home Page The corporate website for Ford Motor Company and its vehicle (car and truck) and service brands, featuring investor, career, news and media information.	
Autos 2. Ford Motor Company of Canada, Limited Official Canadian site.	
Autos 3. Ford Truck Enthusiasts, 1948-2006 Ford trucks, F150, Super Duty & SUV owners community and information source. ... Extensive resource for Ford truck owners featuring discussion groups, technical articles, events, and more. Find advice and information for the F-150, F-250 Super Duty, Explorer, Ranger, and other models.	
Autos 4. Ford :: Startseite Official German site.	
Autos 5. ford motor company The corporate website for Ford Motor Company. ... Ford Motor Company was recognized as one of the top American corporations on ...	
Autos 6. Ford Motor Company - Wikipedia, the free encyclopedia ... automaker was founded by an American legend, Henry Ford and incorporated in 1903. Ford now encompasses many brands globally, including Lincoln and Mercury in the ...	R
Autos 7. Ford Motor Company of Canada, Limited Ford Motor Company of Canada, cars and trucks ... vehicles (excluding Mustang Shelby GT 500, SVT, Ford GT, Edge, MKX, F-Series ...	
Autos 8. Ford Vehicles: Ford Mustang - See pricing details, car options, V6 GT Official site for the popular muscle car, the Mustang. Offers photos, feature information, specs, and more.	
Autos 9. The Henry Ford: The Life of Henry Ford From his childhood through the founding of Ford Motor Company and beyond.	R

Autos 10. Ford Official site for India.	
Autos 11. Ford :: Ford Team RS :: Ford Team RS home ... Ford Power Products ... Ford GT. ST Performance Vehicle. Car configurator. Request a brochure. Request a test drive ... Ford Direct used cars. Accessories ...	
Autos 12. New 2006 and 2007 Ford Cars on Yahoo! Autos Features information on the year's current models.	
Autos 13. Ford I Ford Dealer I Car Quotes and Reviews I 2006 2007 Ford reviews, pictures, and invoice pricing. Get a free no-obligation price ... 2007 Ford Explorer Sport Trac Photo Gallery ... Ford keeps interest in the ...	
Autos 14. Ford I Free Price Quotes I Ford Dealer I Ford Car I Car.com Ford price quotes and reviews. Free no-obligation quote from a local dealer. ... 2007 Ford Explorer Sport Trac Photo Gallery ... Ford keeps interest in the ...	
Autos 15. Ford I Free Price Quotes I Ford Car Dealer I 2006 2007 Ford reviews and price quotes from a local dealer. ... 2007 Ford Explorer Sport Trac Photo Gallery. Ford looks to gain traction with this sporty Explorer derivative ...	
Autos 16. Ford - Research All Models and Prices - MSN Autos Ford prices, reviews, used Ford classifieds, and more on MSN Autos ... The Ford Motor Company was incorporated in 1903 with ten people and $28,000. ...	
Scouting 1. Ford Australia Official Australian site.	
Scouting 2. Ford Official South African site.	
Scouting 3. Ford New Zealand Official site for New Zealand.	

Precision at the 11 Standard *Recall* Levels (%) "Reference" + "Society"

Recall	0	0.1	0.2	0.3	0.4	0.5	0.6	0.7	0.8	0.9	1.0
Precision	100	100	100	100	100	100	100	0	0	0	0

Appendix 12: Classified Search Results of "health"

Marked Categories: Arts, Business, Computers, Health, Kids & Teens, News, Regional, Science, Society

There are 40 relevant research results which are categorized into: Arts, Business, Computers, Health, Kids & Teens, News, Regional and Society.

Society	AJ
Issues 1. BBC NEWS I Health perspectives. Also entertainment, business, science, technology and health news. ... Health experts' heatwave warning. Glaxo pays $70m in price row. Patient dies ...	R
Law 1. Health - Wex Information about U.S. health law from the Legal Information Institute.	

Regional	AJ
North America 1. Health in the Yahoo! Directory health, including diseases and conditions, medications, sexual health, fitness, ... Health Sciences (36) Hospitals and Medical Centers (44) Hygiene (17) ...	R
North America 2. Health News - New York Times health news on medicine, fitness, nutrition, health care, mental health, drugs, ... Personal Health: Scientists Cast Misery of Migraine in a New Light ...	R
North America 3. National Institutes of Health (NIH) Focal point for biomedical research in the U.S.	R
North America 4. AARP - Health I People Age 50 & Over Learn about health programs for people age 50 and over at AARP. We are dedicated to enhancing quality of life for all as we age. Information, advocacy and service.	R
North America 5. Join AARP: Benefits & Information I People Age 50 and Over Excels as a dynamic presence in every community, shaping and enriching the experience of aging for each member and for society.	R
North America 6. Florida Department of Health Home Page (http://uk.wrs.yahoo.com/_ylt=A0Je5Vy.belErQQAUQvdmMwF;_ylu=X3oDMTEwcmlvNjMyBGNvbG8Dd wRsA1dTMQRwb3MDMjkEc2VjA3NyBHZ0aWQD/SIG=11ffke4os/EXP=1156235070/**http%3a//www.do h.state.fl.us/) Provides information about disease control and prevention, environmental health, health statistics, alerts and more.	R
North America 7. healthfinder? - your guide to reliable health information Offers consumer health and human services information.	R
North America 8. United States Department of Health and Human Services Leading America to better health, safety, and well-being.	R
North America 9. New York State Department of Health Home page for the New York State Department of Health ... State Health Department Urges Early Identification and Appropriate Treatment for ...	
Africa 1. Health ... Health Discussions ... Scientists, health workers and activists find hope at 16th International AIDS Conference. ... South African Health Chief's Ouster ...	
Europe 1. Health Care, Health Care Guide, Medical Advice, Primary Health Care, Mental Health, Home Health Care Includes general health information, news, yellow pages, and advice.	R

*Precision*s at actual *recall* levels (%) "Regional"

Position	1	2	3	4	5	6	7	8	11
Recall	2.5	5	7.5	10	12.5	15	17.5	20	22.5
Precision	100	100	100	100	100	100	100	100	81.8

Precision at the 11 Standard *Recall* Levels "Regional"

Recall	0	0.1	0.2	0.3	0.4	0.5	0.6	0.7	0.8	0.9	1.0
Precision	100	100	100	0	0	0	0	0	0	0	0

News	AJ
Online Archives 1. CNN.com - Health ... More Health Video. ? Mandatory HIV testing (1:43) ? Sudden cardiac arrest (1:14) ... Time.com Science & Health. Search for jobs @ International Edition ...	R

Kids and Teens	AJ
Health 1. azcentral.com I health & fitness women's, kids' and men's health to diet, wellness and fitness. ... condition Allergy Alternative Health Alzheimer's Disease Anemia Arthritis ...	R

Health	AJ
Resources 1. Medical Dictionary, Diseases, Healthy Living, Drugs & Medicines on Yahoo! Health Provides health research, expert advice, healthy recipes, and more.	R
Resources 2. WebMD - Better Information. Better Health. Provides medical information and services for consumers, physicians, and other health providers.	R
Resources 3. MSNBC - Health News: Medical news, fitness topics and more - Front Page ... Receive a daily update with the top health news stories and special reports ... health officials are counting on barbershops to help screen men who wouldn't ...	R
Resources 4. Healthcentral.com - Trusted, Reliable and Up To Date Health Information Providing consumer health information.	R
Resources 5. Mayo Clinic medical information and tools for healthy living - MayoClinic.com The Mayo Clinic's health resource web site offers information on diseases and conditions, healthy living, drugs, and self-care.	R
Occupational Health and Safety 1. Open Directory - Health ... Occupational Health and Safety (684) Organizations (69) Pharmacy (3,794) ... Harvard Medical School's consumer health information, journal databases, a ...	R
Occupational Health and Safety 2. U.S. Department of Labor Occupational Safety and Health Organization: OSHA. Official site for the government agency that establishes protective standards, enforces those standards, and reaches out to employers and employees through technical assistance and consultation programs.	
Public Health and Safety 1. World Health Organization (WHO/OMS) Directing and coordinating authority on international health work that strives to bring the highest level of health to all peoples.	
Public Health and Safety 2. WHO I World Health Organization WHO I World Health Organization WHO I World Health Organization 1 April 2005 -- WHO's new programme to train the next generation of health leaders has welcomed its first eight recruits this week. Over the next few years, the Health Leadership ...	
Public Health and Safety 3. Health:Topic Good health is necessary for individuals to flourish as citizens, family members, ... Scientific, Industrial and Health Applications of Biotechnology ...	R

Fitness 1. Health.com :: Covers health, fitness, beauty, wellness, and food.	R
Fitness 2. The top health news articles from Yahoo! News Use Yahoo! News to find health news headlines and health articles on weight loss, medications, diseases, aging and more. ... Sexual Health News ...	R
Fitness 3. Men's Health Magazine for men containing information on health, fitness, weight loss, and more.	R
Fitness 4. Breaking Health and Fitness News Stories and Video - CBSNews.com s Health, Men&lsquo;s Health, and Health and Fitness Headlines and Information. ... Survey: Most Want Health Care Overhaul ... due to health violations. Couple ...	
Mental Health 1. C-Health: Your Health and Wellness Source - powered by MediResource Health and wellness source with links to information on a variety of health-related topics.	R
Conditions and Diseases 1. BBC - Health In-depth resource on health, diseases, and relationships.	R
Conditions and Diseases 2. InteliHealth: InteliHealth Home Comprehensive collection of consumer health information.	R
Conditions and Diseases 3. Centers for Disease Control and Prevention Includes information on disease outbreaks, health topics, and emergency preparedness.	R
Conditions and Diseases 4. Home Page - MSN Health & Fitness ... MSN Videos on Health. Find a Therapist. Heart Attack Risk. BMI Calculator. Test Your Stress Level ... About Health & Fitness ...	R
Conditions and Diseases 5. C-Health : Seniors' Health they come with their own set of health problems, as if you hadn't lived through ... View health videos about a variety of diseases, conditions and treatment options. ...	R
Conditions and Diseases 6. U.S. News & World Report: Best Health Get health information, including our annual list of the best hospitals in ... Health News. Recent Articles. Diseases & Conditions. Allergy & Asthma Center ...	R
Addictions 1. Drug and alcohol abuse, treatment, prevention at SAMHSA's National Clearinghouse for Alcohol and Drug Information Resource for information about substance abuse prevention and addiction treatment. Includes an FAQ on substance abuse, articles, news, and related resources.	
Addictions 2. Health - Wikipedia, the free encyclopedia ... are four general determinants of health which he called "human biology" ... smoking and other substance abuse are examples of steps to improve one's health. ...	R
Education 1. Excite - Health Whether you're sick as a dog or healthy as an ox, our comprehensive health section can help you live a better, healthier life.	R
Pharmacy 1. Health Information - National Institutes of Health (NIH) Browse health topics alphabetically.	R

Precisions at actual *recall* levels (%) "Health"

Position	1	2	3	4	5	6	10	11	12	13
Recall	2.5	5	7.5	10	12.5	15	17.5	20	22.5	25
Precision	100	100	100	100	100	100	70	72.7	75	76.9
Position	15	16	17	18	19	20	21	23	24	25
Recall	27.5	30	32.5	35	37.5	40	42.5	45	47.5	50
Precision	73.3	75	76.5	77.8	78.9	80	81	78.3	79.2	80

Precision at the 11 Standard *Recall* Levels "Health"

Recall	0	0.1	0.2	0.3	0.4	0.5	0.6	0.7	0.8	0.9	1.0
Precision	100	100	72.7	75	80	80	0	0	0	0	0

Computers	AJ
Internet 1. AllRefer Health Health resource provides reliable and comprehensive information and news on ... Health Topics: A-Al Am-Az B C-Cj Ck-Cz D E F G H I J K L M N O P-Pl Pm-Pz Q R ...	R

Business	AJ
Financial Services 1. Kaiser Permanente: Thrive - Health Insurance Plans, Healthcare Information, Health Advice. Includes health information, members area, details of health plans, news, locations, and more.	R

Arts	AJ
Television 1. Discovery Health :: Discovery Health :: Homepage Offers health news and in-depth features, show information, and health library.	R

*Precision*s at actual *recall* levels (%) "Health" + "Regional"

Position	1	2	3	4	5	6	10	11	12	13
Recall	2.5	5	7.5	10	12.5	15	17.5	20	22.5	25
Precision	100	100	100	100	100	100	70	72.7	75	76.9
Position	15	16	17	18	19	20	21	23	24	25
Recall	27.5	30	32.5	35	37.5	40	42.5	45	47.5	50
Precision	73.3	75	76.5	77.8	78.9	80	81	78.3	79.2	80
Position	26	27	28	29	30	31	32	33	36	
Recall	52.5	55	57.5	60	62.5	65	67.5	70	72.5	
Precision	80.8	81.5	82.1	82.8	83.3	83.9	84.4	84.8	80.6	

Precision at the 11 Standard *Recall* Levels "Health" + "Regional"

Recall	0	0.1	0.2	0.3	0.4	0.5	0.6	0.7	0.8	0.9	1.0
Precision	100	100	72.7	75	80	80	82.8	84.8	0	0	0

*Precision*s at actual *recall* levels (%) "Regional" + "Health"

Position	1	2	3	4	5	6	7	8	11	12
Recall	2.5	5	7.5	10	12.5	15	17.5	20	22.5	25
Precision	100	100	100	100	100	100	100	100	81.8	83.3
Position	13	14	15	16	17	21	22	23	24	26
Recall	27.5	30	32.5	35	37.5	40	42.5	45	47.5	50
Precision	84.6	85.7	86.7	87.5	88.2	76.2	77.2	78.3	79.2	76.9
Position	27	28	29	30	31	32	34	35	36	
Recall	52.5	55	57.5	60	62.5	65	67.5	70	72.5	
Precision	77.8	78.6	79.3	80	80.6	81.3	79.4	80	80.6	

Precision at the 11 Standard *Recall* Levels "Regional" + "Health"

Recall	0	0.1	0.2	0.3	0.4	0.5	0.6	0.7	0.8	0.9	1.0
Precision	100	100	100	85.7	76.2	76.9	80	80	80.6	0	0

Appendix 13: Classified Search Results of "jaguar"

Marked Categories: Arts, Business, Computers, Games, Home, Kids & Teens, Regional, Science, Shopping, Society, Sports.

There are 12 relevant research results which are categorized into: Game, Kids & Teens and Science

Science	AJ
Biology 1. One World Journeys I Jaguar: Lord of the Mayan Jungle A multimedia expedition into the heart of the Mexican jungle, searching for the elusive jaguar.	R
Biology 2. Jaguar - Wikipedia, the free encyclopedia ... a b c d e "Jaguar (panthera onca) ... The jaguar (Panthera onca) are mammals of the Felidae family and one of four " ... (European jaguar) and panthera ...	R
Biology 3. Jaguar Key facts and information on the jaguar's habitat, diet and status as a near threatened species.	R
Biology 4. Jaguar ... The jaguar (Panthera onca) is the only member of the 'big cat' family that lives ... and is about the same size as the jaguar, but it is classified as a small cat ...	R
Institutions 1. The Jaguar - Houston Zoo {N A HURY} General overview of the species.	R

Precisions at actual *recall* levels (%)

Position	1	2	3	4	5
Recall	7.1	14.3	21.4	28.6	35.7
Precision	100	100	100	100	100

Precision at the 11 Standard *Recall* Levels

Recall	0	0.1	0.2	0.3	0.4	0.5	0.6	0.7	0.8	0.9	1.0
Precision	100	100	100	100	100	0	0	0	0	0	0

Kids and Teens	AJ
School Time 1. Jaguar Jaguar Facts, Jaguar Photos and Jaguars in the news at the world's largest big ... The Jaguar and the Leopard are often confused with one another in zoos. ...	R
School Time 2. San Diego Zoo's Animal Bytes: Jaguar Get fun and interesting jaguar facts in an easy-to-read style from the San Diego ... over 85 species in the jaguar diet, including peccaries, deer, tapirs, ...	R
School Time 3. Yahooligans! Animals: Jaguar A picture and description of this animal. ... The Jaguar is the biggest and most powerful North American wildcat, and the only ...	R
School Time 4. Animal Fact Sheets ... which includes four species of "big cats", the jaguar, tiger, lion and leopard. ... Jaguar cubs are usually born with their eyes closed, weigh about 25-29 ounces ...	R
School Time 5. Jaguar ... The jaguar (Panthera onca) is the largest cat native to the Western Hemisphere. ... The jaguar can be a far ranging animal, traveling distances up to 500 miles. ...	R

School Time 6. NatureWorks - Jaguar NatureWorks ... The jaguar is the largest cat in North America and the third largest cat in the world. ... The Jaguar, unlike most big cats, loves the water. ...	R
International 1. J A G U A R - ?ndice Taller-escuela dedicado a la educación, producción y publicación de artes ... comercial educativo ...	

Precisions at actual *recall* levels (%)

Position	1	2	3	4	5	6	7
Recall	7.1	14.3	21.4	28.6	35.7	42.9	50
Precision	100	100	100	100	100	100	100

Precision at the 11 Standard *Recall* Levels

Recall	0	0.1	0.2	0.3	0.4	0.5	0.6	0.7	0.8	0.9	1.0
Precision	100	100	100	100	100	85.7	0	0	0	0	0

Games	AJ
Video Games 1. Jaguar Compares jaguars and leopards and provides information about the animal's shrinking habitat and relationship with man.	R
Video Games 2. Jaguar -- Kids' Planet -- Defenders of Wildlife Jaguar -- Kids' Planet -- Defenders of Wildlife Jaguar -- Kids' Planet -- Defenders of Wildlife ...	R
Video Games 3. AtariAge - Atari Jaguar History AtariAge - News, message boards, rarity guides, game database, manuals, pictures, ... Atari Jaguar with CD-ROM ... program and publish Jaguar games, and has ...	

Precisions at actual *recall* levels (%) for clicking "science" + "Kids & Teens"

Position	1	2	3	4	5	6	7	8	9	10	11
Recall	7.1	14.3	21.4	28.6	35.7	42.9	50	57.1	64.3	71.4	78.6
Precision	100	100	100	100	100	100	100	100	100	100	100

Precision at the 11 Standard *Recall* Levels for clicking "science" + "Kids & Teens"

Recall	0	0.1	0.2	0.3	0.4	0.5	0.6	0.7	0.8	0.9	1.0
Precision	100	100	100	100	100	100	100	100	100	0	0

Appendix 14: Classified Search Results of "UPS"

Marked Categories: Business, Computers, Health, Home, News, Reference, Regional, Science, Society, Sports.

There are 12 relevant research results which are categorized into: Computers and Business.

Computers	AJ
Software 1. The UPS Store: Packaging, Shipping, Passport Photos & Printing Service Find out how the UPS Store can help. Track packages, estimate shipping costs, get your US passport photo, print and finish documents, purchase moving supplies & more. Find The UPS Store near you!	
Software 2. UPS Selector Sizing Applications to specify your required runtime and other options, and recommend a UPS solution. ... easy way to finding the right UPS product for a single home or office ...	R
Internet 1. UPS Pressroom: Current Press Releases ... The UPS Foundation in partnership with the Corporation for National and ... Press Releases. Sign Up for Email Updates. Current Press Releases. UPS Worldwide ...	
Data Formats 1. What is UPS? - A Word Definition From the Webopedia Computer Dictionary This page describes the term UPS and lists other pages on the Web where you can ... Information about batteries used in computer UPS ...	R
Hardware 1. UPS. ... UPS. Desktop Accessories. Audio Video. Cables. Computer Accessories. Mice and Keyboards ... Home Office 375VA UPS With Automatic Shutdown Software. F6H375-USB ...	R
Programming 1. THE ups DEBUGGER The ups debugger for C, C++ and Fortran - unofficial home page ... 3.37 released. Archive of ups-users mailing list. ups in print. Fortran support. MP3 of ups song ...	
Systems 1. The DIY (or, if you must, "Ghetto") UPS How to build your own ugly and awkward uninterruptible power supply! ... contraption works in basically the same way as a normal "dual conversion" UPS. ...	R

Precisions at actual *recall* levels (%) "Computers"

Position	2	4	5	7
Recall	8.3	16.7	25	33.3
Precision	50	50	60	57.1

Precision at the 11 Standard *Recall* Levels "Computers"

Recall	0	0.1	0.2	0.3	0.4	0.5	0.6	0.7	0.8	0.9	1.0
Precision	50	50	60	57.1	0	0	0	0	0	0	0

Business	AJ
Transportation and Logistics 1. UPS Package Tracking UPS Package Tracking service lets you track your package across the world, including multiple packages, airmail, or freight, and offering updates on the Web or by email.	
Transportation and Logistics 2. UPS Global Home Worldwide express carrier and package delivery company. UPS is a global provider of specialized transportation and logistics services.	
Transportation and Logistics 3. UPS Careers Job opportunities from United Parcel Services. Jobs range from package handlers, delivery drivers, and warehouse management to administration, communications, information systems, and logistics.	

Transportation and Logistics 4. UPS Calculate Time and Cost ... of, and services requested for, packages actually tendered to UPS. ... have specially negotiated rates, contact your UPS account executive for a rate quote. ...	
Transportation and Logistics 5. UPS Careers Job opportunities from United Parcel Services. Jobs range from package handlers, delivery drivers, and warehouse management to administration, communications, information systems, and logistics.	
Transportation and Logistics 6. Welcome to UPS Supply Chain Solutions (http://uk.wrs.yahoo.com/_ylt= UPS delivery solutions for businesses, providing logistics, global freight, financial services, mail services, and consulting to business customers.	
Transportation and Logistics 7. UPS Trade Direct - UPS Supply Chain Solutions UPS Trade Direct provides integrated freight and package delivery allowing you to bypass distribution centers by shipping directly to retail stores or customers' doors.	
Transportation and Logistics 8. United Parcel Service - Wikipedia, the free encyclopedia ... Historically, UPS only faced competition from USPS for the inexpensive ground ... UPS entered the heavy freight business with its purchase of Menlo Worldwide ...	
Transportation and Logistics 9. Welcome To Air Cargo World -- Breaking News ... UPS said its freight forwarding business lost customers in the past two quarters, ... UPS has been spending money and attention on new technology for the Menlo ...	
Financial Services 1. Cash Flow, International Trade & Small Business Lending : UPS Capital UPS offers businesses worldwide the opportunity to integrate supply chain ... combined with the broad capabilities of UPS help enhance operations as well as ...	
Financial Services 2. UPS Capital Visa ? Business Rewards Card ... The NEW UPS Capital business card is a great place to begin a long-term ... The UPS Capital Visa? Business Rewards Card is offered and issued by Chase Bank ...	
Electronics and Electrical 1. Uninterruptible power supply - Wikipedia, the free encyclopedia ... An uninterruptible power supply (UPS), sometimes called an uninterruptible power ... particular type of equipment, a UPS is typically used to protect ...	R
Electronics and Electrical 2. APC Product Information for UPS ... Back-UPS HS ... Smart-UPS XL ... GUTOR Industrial UPS and DC Systems ...	R
Electronics and Electrical 3. UPS Power Protection and Battery Backup by Minuteman - Official Website Line of remote-controllable uninterruptible power protection (UPS) products for telephones, computers, and data communication devices. From Para Systems, Inc.	R
Electronics and Electrical 4. OPTI-UPS Protect and Serve Manufactures UPS power management products.	R
Electronics and Electrical 5. UPS - UPS Manufacturers, UPS Factories, UPS Suppliers, China UPS Start here to find prequalified UPS suppliers from China and around the world ... (AVR), uninterruptible power supply (UPS), battery chargers, flashlights, and ...	R
Electronics and Electrical 6. Uninterruptible Power Supply (UPS) FAQ Frequently Asked Questions (FAQ) about Uninterruptible Power Supplies (UPSs) ... 13: Can I really count on a UPS protecting my equipment? ...	R
Electronics and Electrical 7. Howstuffworks "How does a computer's uninterruptible power supply (UPS) work?" How does a computer's uninterruptible power supply (UPS) work? Does the computer always run from the battery? ... A UPS generally protects a computer against ...	R
Electronics and Electrical 8. UPS (Uninterruptible power supply) and DC Power systems from Powerware Power system protection, Powerware UPS, Telecom power systems and ... Site map. UPS from Powerware; Your source for UPS Power surge protectors, UPS Power ...	R
Employment 1. UPS Careers ... career or a part-time position to pay for college, UPS is right for you. ... UPS kudos for being a world class employer? Find out. Welcome to UPS Careers ...	

| Employment 2. UPS Careers: Job Search ... through the UPS Earn & Learn Program. Benefits (Life/Health/401K) Paid Vacations & Holidays ... One UPS Way, Hodgkins, IL 60525. Ph: 888-4UPS-JOB. Package ... |
| Employment 3. UPS Careers: Opportunities: Part-time: Job Search ... job openings with UPS in your area. Package Handler. Search All ... UPS Global I UPS Corporate. Copyright ? 2002 United Parcel Service, Inc. All rights reserved. ... |
| Investing 1. Business Week Online: Personal Investing BusinessWeek magazine: The most-read source of global ... Get Fund Prospectus. CORPORATE SNAPSHOT. UNITED PARCEL SERVICE INC CL B (NYSE:UPS) LAST. CHANGE ... |

*Precision*s at actual *recall* levels (%) "Business"

Position	12	13	14	15	16	17	18	19
Recall	8.3	16.7	25	33.3	41.7	50	58.3	66.7
Precision	8.3	15.4	21.4	26.7	31.3	35.3	38.9	42.1

Precision at the 11 Standard *Recall* Levels "Business"

Recall	0	0.1	0.2	0.3	0.4	0.5	0.6	0.7	0.8	0.9	1.0
Precision	8.3	15.4	21.4	26.7	31.3	35.3	42.1	42.1	0	0	0

*Precision*s at actual *recall* levels (%) "Computers" + "Business"

Position	2	4	5	7	19	20	21	22	23	24	25	26
Recall	8.3	16.7	25	33.3	41.7	50	58.3	66.7	75	83.5	91.7	100
Precision	50	50	60	57.1	26.3	30	33.3	36.4	39.1	41.7	44	46.2

Precision at the 11 Standard *Recall* Levels (%) "Computers" + "Business"

Recall	0	0.1	0.2	0.3	0.4	0.5	0.6	0.7	0.8	0.9	1.0
Precision	50	50	60	57.1	26.3	30	36.4	39.1	41.7	44	46.2

*Precision*s at actual *recall* levels (%) "Computers" + "Business: Electronics and Electrical"

Position	2	4	5	7	8	9	10	11	12	13	14	15
Recall	8.3	16.7	25	33.3	41.7	50	58.3	66.7	75	83.5	91.7	100
Precision	50	50	60	57.1	62.5	66.7	70	72.7	75	76.9	78.6	80

Precision at the 11 Standard *Recall* Levels (%) "Computers" + "Business: Electronics and Electrical"

Recall	0	0.1	0.2	0.3	0.4	0.5	0.6	0.7	0.8	0.9	1.0
Precision	50	50	60	57.1	62.5	66.7	72.7	75	76.9	78.6	80

Appendix 15: An Example to Illustrate VSM as a Classifier

This appendix uses real data from the ODP to illustrate how the VSM as a classifier approach works.

1. Using the ODP data to build category-documents

Four documents are formed based on the ODP data. However, not all the information in the corresponding ODP page is utilized to form the category-document to reduce the computation complex and workload.

Document 1 (D1)

Recreation: Autos: Makes and Models: Jaguar. Jag Lovers Web Site - Large and well-known resource. Includes extensive collection of brochures ranging from 1930s to present, mailing list, photo albums and other features. Jaguar - Official worldwide Web site of Jaguar Cars

Document 2 (D2)

Shopping: Vehicles: Parts and Accessories: Makes and Models: European: British: Jaguar. AJ6 Engineering - Company in the UK that manufacturers and fits performance parts for Jaguar cars.

Document 3 (D3)

Science: Biology: Flora and Fauna: Animalia: Chordata: Mammalia: Carnivora: Felidae: Panthera: Jaguar. Jaguar - General information and facts from Big Cats Online. Jaguar Facts - Woodland Park Zoo's fact sheet on Jaguars.

Document 4 (D4)

Science: Math: Algebra. Algebra Links - From Spartanburg County School District Two.
Algebra Universalis List of Researchers - Compiled by ...
Document repository D = {D1, D2, D3, D4}.

2. Tokenizing Vocabulary to Create the Vocabulary

The vocabulary of the four documents is:
1930, accessories, AJ6, albums, algebra, and, animalia, autos, big, biology, british, brochures, by, carnivora, cars, cats, chordate, collection, company, complied, county, district, engineering, European, extensive, facts, fauna, features, felidae, fits, flora, for, from, general, in, includes, information, jag, jaguar, large, links, list, lover, mailing, makes, mammalia, manufacturers, math, models, of, official, on, online, other, panthera, park, parts, performance, photo, present, ranging, recreation, researchers, resource, school, science, sheet, shopping, site, spartanburg, that, the, to, two, uk, universalis, vehicles, web, well-known, woodland, worldwide, zoo's.

By removing stopping word and then stemming, the above vocabulary will become:
1930, accessory, AJ6, album, algebra, animal, auto, big, biology, british, brochure, carnivo, car, cat, chordata, collection, company, comply, county, district, engineer, Europe, extensive, fact, fauna, feature, felidae, fit, flora, general, include, information, jag, jaguar, large, link, list, lover, mail, make, mammal, manufact, math, model, office, online, other, panthera, park, part, performance, photo, present, range, recreation, researcher, resource, school, science, sheet, shopping, site, Spartanburg, two, UK, universal, vehicle, web, well-known, woodland, worldwide, zoo. (72 indexing terms)

All of the above vocabulary can form a vector:

T = [1930, accessory, AJ6, album, algebra, animal, auto, big, biology, british, brochure, carnivo, car, cat, chordata, collection, company, comply, county, district, engineer, Europe, extensive, fact, fauna, feature, felidae, fit, flora, general, include, information, jag, jaguar, large, link, list, lover, mail, make, mammal, manufact, math, model, office, online, other, panthera, park, part, performance, photo, present, range, recreation, researcher, resource, school, science, sheet, shopping, site, spartanburg, two, uk, universal, vehicle, web, well-known, woodland, worldwide, zoo]

Each document can also represented by a vector. Suppose in a document, the word "accessory" and "big" appear **one** time, the word "animal" appears in the document **two** times, the word "British" appear in the document **four** times, and so on. Then the vector representation of the document would looks like: **t** = [0, 1, 0, 0, 0, 2, 0, 1, 0, 4, ...]

3. Calculating the Term (Word) Frequency (tf)

Term frequency is calculated by the formula:

$$tf_{i,j} = freq_{i,j} / max_l \ freq_{l,j}$$

$freq_{i,j}$ is the raw frequency of term t_i in document d_j and maximum term frequency in document d_j is $max_l \ freq_{l,j}$
Table A15- shows the calculation results of term frequency of "node document" D1 to D4.

Table A15-1 Term frequency

No.	Terms	D1	D2	D3	D4	N/nt
1	1930	1/3				4
2	Accessory		1/2			4
3	AJ6		1/2			4
4	Album	1/3				4
5	Algebra				1	4
6	Animal			1/4		4
7	Auto	1/3				4
8	Big			1/4		4
9	Biology			1/4		4
10	British		1/2			4
11	Brochure	1/3				4
12	Carnivo			1/4		4
13	Car	1/3	1/2			2
14	Cat			1/4		4
15	Chordata			1/4		4
16	Collection	1/3				4
17	Company		1/2			4
18	Comply				1/3	4
19	County				1/3	4
20	District				1/3	4
21	Engineer		1/2			4
22	Europe		1/2			4
23	Extensive	1/3				4
24	Fact			3/4		4
25	Fauna			1/4		4
26	Feature	1/3				4
27	Felidae			1/4		4
28	Fit		1/2			4
29	Flora			1/4		4
30	General			1/4		4
31	Include	1/3				4
32	Information			1/4		4
33	Jag	1/3				4
34	Jaguar	1	1	1		4/3
35	Large	1/3				4
36	Link				1/3	4
37	List	1/3			1/3	2
38	Lover	1/3				4
39	Mail	1/3				4
40	Make	1/3	1/2			2
41	Mammal			1/4		4

No.	Terms	D1	D2	D3	D4	N/nt
42	Manufacture		1/2			4
43	Math				1/3	4
44	Model	1/3	1/2			2
45	Office	1/3				4
46	Online			1/4		4
47	Other	1/3				4
48	Panthera			1/4		4
49	Park			1/4		4
50	Part		1			4
51	Performance		1/2			4
52	Photo	1/3				4
53	Present	1/3				4
54	Range	1/3				4
55	Recreation	1/3				4
56	Researcher				1/3	4
57	Resource	1/3				4
58	School				1/3	4
59	Science			1/4	1/3	2
60	Sheet			1/4		4
61	Shopping		1/2			4
62	Site	2/3				4
63	Spartanburg				1/3	4
64	Two				1/3	4
65	UK		1/2			4
66	Universal				1/3	4
67	Vehicle		1/2			4
68	Web	2/3				4
69	Well-known	1/3				4
70	Woodland			1/4		4
71	Worldwide	1/3				4
72	Zoo			1/4		4

4. Calculating Inverse Document Frequency (idf)

The idf can be calculated by using the following formula:

$$idf_{d,t} = \log_2 (N/n_t) \quad \ldots\ldots\ldots\ldots\ldots\ldots\ldots \text{ Formula A15-1}$$

where N is the total number of documents in the documents repository. Here $N = 4$; n_t is the number of documents which contains term t.

There are some variations for formula Formula A15-1, for example,

$$idf_{d,t} = \log (N/n_t)$$

Another variation of for calculating idf is

$$idf_{d,t} = N/n_t$$

In this section, formula Formula A15-1 is accepted to compute idf. For this example, if a term appears only once in one of the four documents, idf then equals:

$Log_2(4) = 1.38629$
If a term appears two times in one of the four documents, idf then equals:
$log_2 (2) = 0.69315$
Finally, the term "jaguar" appears in three documents, namely, document one, document two and document three; therefore, the idf of the term "jaguar" equals:
$log_2 (4/3) = 0.28768$

5. Calculating Term Weighting $W_{i,j}$

$W_{i,j}$ is $w_{di,tj}$. It is a weighting strategy to measure the importance of a term t_j in the given document d_i.

The occurrence frequency of a term t in a given document d no doubt implies the importance of the term to the document; the term frequency is therefore one factor to weighting a term.

Another factor to be considered is the so-called inverse term frequency, which reveals the relative importance of a term among the whole document repository, not only in one given document. For example, a word may appears among 80 per cent of the document repository, the importance of this word, compared to the term which only appears among eight per cent of the document repository, is relatively low. Thus, idf measures overall importance of a term among the whole document set.

The term-weighting strategy of Vector Space Model does not consider the mutual relationship among index terms; it only considers single word. Although some believe this is a disadvantage of this model, experiments have approved only marginal improvement can be obtained at the cost of heavy computation load (Baeza-Yates and Ribeiro-Neto 1999, p. 30).
Term weight can be calculated by the Formula A15-2:

$$W_{d_i,t_j} = tf_{d_i,t_j} \times idf_{D,t_j}$$ ....Formula A15-2

The results are shown in Table A15-. The value in the blank area is zero.

Table A15-2 Term weighting

No.	Terms	Doc1	Doc2	Doc3	Doc4	Log2(N/nt)
1	1930	0.46210				1.38629
2	Accessory		0.69315			1.38629
3	AJ6		0.69315			1.38629
4	Album	0.46210				1.38629
5	Algebra				1.38629	1.38629
6	Animal			0.34657		1.38629
7	Auto	0.46210				1.38629
8	Big			0.34657		1.38629
9	Biology			0.34657		1.38629
10	British		0.69315			1.38629
11	Brochure	0.46210				1.38629
12	Carnivo			0.34657		1.38629
13	Car	0.23105	0.34657			0.69315
14	Cat			0.34657		1.38629
15	Chordata			0.34657		1.38629
16	Collection	0.46210				1.38629
17	Company		0.69315			1.38629
18	Comply				0.46210	1.38629
19	County				0.46210	1.38629
20	District				0.46210	1.38629
21	Engineer		0.69315			1.38629

No.	Terms	Doc1	Doc2	Doc3	Doc4	Log2(N/nt)
22	Europe		0.69315			1.38629
23	Extensive	0.46210				1.38629
24	Fact			1.03972		1.38629
25	Fauna			0.34657		1.38629
26	Feature	0.46210				1.38629
27	Felidae			0.34657		1.38629
28	Fit		0.69315			1.38629
29	Flora			0.34657		1.38629
30	General			0.34657		1.38629
31	Include	0.46210				1.38629
32	Information			0.34657		1.38629
33	Jag	0.46210				1.38629
34	Jaguar	0.28768	0.28768	0.28768		0.28768
35	Large	0.46210				1.38629
36	Link				0.46210	1.38629
37	List	0.23105		0.23105		0.69315
38	Lover	0.46210				1.38629
39	Mail	0.46210				1.38629
40	Make	0.23105	0.34657			0.69315
41	Mammal			0.34657		1.38629
42	Manufacture		0.69315			1.38629
43	Math				0.46210	1.38629
44	Model	0.23105	0.34657			0.69315
45	Office	0.46210				1.38629
46	Online			0.34657		1.38629
47	Other	0.46210				1.38629
48	Panthera			0.34657		1.38629
49	Park			0.34657		1.38629
50	Part		1.38629			1.38629
51	Performance		0.69315			1.38629
52	Photo	0.46210				1.38629
53	Present	0.46210				1.38629
54	Range	0.46210				1.38629
55	Recreation	0.46210				1.38629
56	Researcher				0.46210	1.38629
57	Resource	0.46210				1.38629
58	School				0.46210	1.38629
59	Science			0.17329	0.23105	0.69315
60	Sheet			0.34657		1.38629
61	Shopping		0.69315			1.38629
62	Site	0.92420				1.38629

No.	Terms	Doc1	Doc2	Doc3	Doc4	Log2(N/nt)
63	Spartanburg				0.46210	1.38629
64	Two				0.46210	1.38629
65	UK		0.69315			1.38629
66	Universal				0.46210	1.38629
67	Vehicle		0.69315			1.38629
68	Web	0.92420				1.38629
69	Well-known	0.46210				1.38629
70	Woodland			0.34657		1.38629
71	Worldwide	0.46210				1.38629
72	Zoo			0.34657		1.38629

6. Calculating the Similarity by Cosine Coefficient

6.1 Calculating the Similarity by Cosine Coefficient for Search-term "jaguar"

Suppose the search-term is jaguar, then the search-term vector will be $[0,0,\dots,1,0,\dots]$ which indicates the word jaguar appears only one time.

The $W_{i,j}$ of the search-term "jaguar" can be calculated by the same process as described above. The formula for $W_{i,q}$ used here is (Formula A15-3):

$$w_{i,q} = t_q \times idf_q$$
$$= (0.5 + 0.5 \times freq_{i,q} / max_1 \, freq_{1,q}) \times \log_2 (N / n_i) \quad \dots\text{.. Formula A15-3}$$

thus, the query vector is:
$V_q = [0, 0, \dots 0.28768, 0,\dots]$

The similarity of the search-term "jaguar" with each document (for this example, D1, D2, D3, D4) can be calculated by comparing the cosine value of query vector with each document vector. The formula is:

$$sim(v_q, d_j) = \frac{v_q \bullet d_j}{|v_q| \times |d_j|} = \frac{\sum_{i=1,\dots N} w_{i,j} \times w_{i,q}}{\sqrt{\sum_{i=1,\dots N} w_{i,j}^2 \times \sum_{i=1,\dots N} w_{i,q}^2}}$$

The document vectors are:
$V_{D1} = [$

0.46210	0	0	0.46210	0	0	0.46210	0	0	0
0.46210	0	0.23105	0	0	0.46210	0	0	0	0
0	0	0.46210	0	0	0.46210	0	0	0	0
0.46210	0	0.46210	0.28768	0.46210	0	0.23105	0.46210	0.46210	0.23105
0	0	0	0.23105	0.46210	0	0.46210	0	0	0
0	0.46210	0.46210	0.46210	0.46210	0	0.46210	0	0	0
0	0.92420	0	0	0	0	0	0.92420	0.46210	0
0.46210	0								

]

$V_{D2} = [$

0	0.69315	0.69315	0	0	0	0	0	0	0.69315
0	0	0.34657	0	0	0	0.69315	0	0	0
0.69315	0.69315	0	0	0	0	0	0.69315	0	0
0	0	0	0.28468	0	0	0	0	0	0.34657
0	0.69315	0	0.34657	0	0	0	0	0	1.38629

0.69315	0	0	0	0	0	0	0	0	0
0.69315	0	0	0	0.69315	0	0.69315	0	0	0
0	0								

]

$V_{D3} = [$

0	0	0	0	0	0.34657	0	0.34657	0.34657	0
0	0.34657	0	0.34657	0.34657	0	0	0	0	0
0	0	0	1.03972	0.34657	0	0.34657	0	0.34657	0.34657
0	0.34657	0	0.28768	0	0	0	0	0	0.34657
0	0.69315	0	0.34657	0	0	0	0	0	1.38629
0.69315	0	0	0	0	0	0	0	0	0
0.69315	0	0	0	0.69315	0	0.69315	0	0	0
0	0								

]

$V_{D4} = [$

0	0	0	0	1.38629	0	0	0	0	0
0	0	0	0	0	0	0	0.46210	0.46210	0.46210
0	0	0	0	0	0	0	0	0	0
0	0	0	0	0	0.46210	0.23105	0	0	0
0	0	0.46210	0	0	0	0	0	0	0
0	0	0	0	0	0.46210	0	0.46210	0.23105	0
0	0	0.46210	0.46210	0	0.46210	0	0	0	0
0	0								

]

Now, calculating $\sum_{i=1...N} w_{i,q}^2$
$= 0 \times 0 + 0 \times 0 + ... + 0.28768 \times 0.28768 + 0 \times 0 + ...$
$= 0.08276$

Calculating $\sum_{i=1...N} w_{i,j}^2$
V_{D1}
$= 0.46210 \times 0.46210 + 0 \times 0 + 0 \times 0 + 0.46210 \times 0.46210 + 0 \times 0 + 0 \times 0 + 0.46210 \times 0.46210 + 0 \times 0 + 0 \times 0 + 0 \times 0$
$+ 0.46210 \times 0.46210 + 0 \times 0 + 0.23105 \times 0.23105 + 0 \times 0 + 0 \times 0 + 0.46210 \times 0.46210 + 0 \times 0 + 0 \times 0 + 0 \times 0 + 0 \times 0$
$+ 0 \times 0 + 0 \times 0 + 0.46210 \times 0.46210 + 0 \times 0 + 0 \times 0 + 0.46210 \times 0.46210 + 0 \times 0 + 0 \times 0 + 0 \times 0 + 0 \times 0$
$+ 0.46210 \times 0.46210 + 0 \times 0 + 0.46210 \times 0.46210 + 0.28768 \times 0.28768 + 0.46210 \times 0.46210 + 0 \times 0 + 0.23105 \times 0.23105$
$+ 0.46210 \times 0.46210 + 0.46210 \times 0.46210 + 0.23105 \times 0.23105 + 0 \times 0 + 0 \times 0 + 0 \times 0 + 0.23105 \times 0.23105$
$+ 0.46210 \times 0.46210 + 0 \times 0 + 0.46210 \times 0.46210 + 0 \times 0 + 0 \times 0 + 0 \times 0 + 0 \times 0 + 0.46210 \times 0.46210$
$+ 0.46210 \times 0.46210 + 0.46210 \times 0.46210 + 0.46210 \times 0.46210 + 0 \times 0 + 0.46210 \times 0.46210 + 0 \times 0 + 0 \times 0 + 0 \times 0$
$+ 0 \times 0 + 0.92420 \times 0.92420 + 0 \times 0 + 0 \times 0 + 0 \times 0 + 0 \times 0 + 0 \times 0 + 0.92420 \times 0.92420 + 0.46210 \times 0.46210 + 0 \times 0$
$+ 0.46210 \times 0.46210 + 0 \times 0$
$= 6.48885$

V_{D2}
$= 0 \times 0 + 0.69315 \times 0.69315 + 0.69315 \times 0.69315 + 0 \times 0 + 0 \times 0 + 0 \times 0 + 0 \times 0 + 0 \times 0 + 0 \times 0 + 0.69315 \times 0.69315$
$+ 0 \times 0 + 0 \times 0 + 0.34657 \times 0.34657 + 0 \times 0 + 0 \times 0 + 0 \times 0 + 0.69315 \times 0.69315 + 0 \times 0 + 0 \times 0 + 0 \times 0$
$+ 0.69315 \times 0.69315 + 0.69315 \times 0.69315 + 0 \times 0 + 0 \times 0 + 0 \times 0 + 0 \times 0 + 0 \times 0 + 0.69315 \times 0.69315 + 0 \times 0 + 0 \times 0$
$+ 0 \times 0 + 0 \times 0 + 0 \times 0 + 0.28768 \times 0.28768 + 0 \times 0 + 0 \times 0 + 0 \times 0 + 0 \times 0 + 0.34657 \times 0.34657 + 0 \times 0$
$+ 0.69315 \times 0.69315 + 0 \times 0 + 0.34657 \times 0.34657 + 0 \times 0 + 0 \times 0 + 0 \times 0 + 0 \times 0 + 0 \times 0 + 1.38629 \times 1.38629$
$+ 0.69315 \times 0.69315 + 0 \times 0 + 0 \times 0 + 0 \times 0 + 0 \times 0 + 0 \times 0 + 0 \times 0 + 0 \times 0 + 0 \times 0 + 0.69315 \times 0.69315 + 0 \times 0$
$+ 0 \times 0 + 0 \times 0 + 0.69315 \times 0.69315 + 0 \times 0 + 0.69315 \times 0.69315 + 0 \times 0 + 0 \times 0 + 0 \times 0 + 0 \times 0 + 0 \times 0$
$= 8.13038$

V_{D3}
$= 0 \times 0 + 0 \times 0 + 0 \times 0 + 0 \times 0 + 0 \times 0 + 0.34957 \times 0.34657 + 0 \times 0 + 0.34957 \times 0.34657 + 0.34957 \times 0.34657 + 0 \times 0$
$+ 0 \times 0 + 0.34957 \times 0.34657 + 0 \times 0 + 0.34957 \times 0.34657 + 0.34957 \times 0.34657 + 0 \times 0 + 0 \times 0 + 0 \times 0 + 0 \times 0 + 0 \times 0$

$+ 0 \times 0 + 0 \times 0 + 0 \times 0 + 1.03972 \times 1.03972 + 0.34957 \times 0.34657 + 0 \times 0 + 0.34957 \times 0.34657 + 0 \times 0$
$+ 0.34957 \times 0.34657 + 0.34957 \times 0.34657 + 0 \times 0 + 0.34957 \times 0.34657 + 0 \times 0 + 0.28768 \times 0.28768 + 0 \times 0 + 0 \times 0$
$+ 0 \times 0 + 0 \times 0 + 0 \times 0 + 0 \times 0 + 0.34957 \times 0.34657 + 0 \times 0 + 0 \times 0 + 0 \times 0 + 0.34957 \times 0.34657 + 0 \times 0$
$+ 0.34957 \times 0.34657 + 0.34957 \times 0.34657 + 0 \times 0 + 0 \times 0 + 0 \times 0 + 0 \times 0 + 0 \times 0 + 0 \times 0 + 0 \times 0 + 0 \times 0$
$+ 0.17329 \times 0.17329 + 0.34957 \times 0.34657 + 0 \times 0 + 0 \times 0 + 0 \times 0 + 0 \times 0 + 0 \times 0 + 0 \times 0 + 0 \times 0 + 0 \times 0$
$+ 0.34957 \times 0.34657 + 0 \times 0 + 0.34957 \times 0.34657$
$= 3.37452$

V_{D4}
$= 0 \times 0 + 0 \times 0 + 0 \times 0 + 0 \times 0 + 1.38629 \times 1.38629 + 0 \times 0 + 0 \times 0 + 0 \times 0 + 0 \times 0 + 0 \times 0 + 0 \times 0 + 0 \times 0 + 0 \times 0$
$+ 0 \times 0 + 0 \times 0 + 0 \times 0 + 0.46210 \times 0.46210 + 0.46210 \times 0.46210 + 0.46210 \times 0.46210 + 0 \times 0 + 0 \times 0 + 0 \times 0 + 0 \times 0$
$+ 0 \times 0 + 0 \times 0 + 0 \times 0 + 0 \times 0 + 0 \times 0 + 0 \times 0 + 0 \times 0 + 0 \times 0 + 0 \times 0 + 0 \times 0 + 0.46210 \times 0.46210$
$+ 0.23105 \times 0.23105 + 0 \times 0 + 0 \times 0 + 0 \times 0 + 0 \times 0 + 0 \times 0 + 0.46210 \times 0.46210 + 0 \times 0 + 0 \times 0 + 0 \times 0 + 0 \times 0$
$+ 0 \times 0 + 0 \times 0 + 0 \times 0 + 0 \times 0 + 0 \times 0 + 0 \times 0 + 0 \times 0 + 0 \times 0 + 0.46210 \times 0.46210 + 0 \times 0 + 0.46210 \times 0.46210$
$+ 0.23105 \times 0.23105 + 0 \times 0 + 0 \times 0 + 0 \times 0 + 0.46210 \times 0.46210 + 0.46210 \times 0.46210 + 0 \times 0 + 0.46210 \times 0.46210$
$+ 0 \times 0 + 0 \times 0 + 0 \times 0 + 0 \times 0$
$= 4.16392$

Calculating $\mathrm{sqrt}(\sum_{i=1...N} w_{i,q}^2 \times \sum_{i=1...N} w_{i,j}^2)$
$| v_q | \times | d_1 |$
$= \mathrm{sqrt}(0.08276 \times 6.48885)$
$= 0.73281$
$| v_q | \times | d_2 |$
$= \mathrm{sqrt}(0.08276 \times 8.13038)$
$= 0.82029$
$| v_q | \times | d_3 |$
$= \mathrm{sqrt}(0.08276 \times 3.37452)$
$= 0.52846$
$| v_q | \times | d_4 |$
$= \mathrm{sqrt}(0.08276 \times 4.16392)$
$= 0.58703$

Now calculating $V_q \bullet V_{Di}$
$V_q \bullet V_{D1}$
$= 0 \times 0.46210 + 0 \times 0 + ... + 0.28768 \times 0.28768 + 0 \times 0.46210 + 0 \times ...$
$= 0.08276$
$V_q \bullet V_{D2}$
$= 0 \times 0 + 0 \times 0.69315 + ... + 0.28768 \times 0.28768 + 0 \times 0 + 0 \times ...$
$= 0.08276$
$V_q \bullet V_{D3}$
$= 0 \times 0 + 0 \times 0 + ... + 0.28768 \times 0.28768 + 0 \times 0 + 0 \times ...$
$= 0.08276$
$V_q \bullet V_{D4}$
$= 0 \times 0 + 0 \times 0 + ... + 0.28768 \times 0 + 0 \times 0 + 0 \times ...$
$= 0$

Calculate cos-based similarity $\mathrm{sim}(v_q, d_j) = v_q \bullet d_j / | v_q | \times | d_j |$
$\cos(V_q, V_{D1}) = 0.08276 / 0.73281 = 0.11293$
$\cos(V_q, V_{D2}) = 0.08276 / 0.82029 = 0.10089$
$\cos(V_q, V_{D3}) = 0.08276 / 0.52846 = 0.15660$
$\cos(V_q, V_{D4}) = 0 / 0.58703 = 0$
According to the calculation given, the returned document should be:

D3, D1 and D2

To make a comparison of cosine coefficient with the simple term frequent, calculate the frequency jaguar appears in the three documents.
Document one has 28 index terms; jaguar appears three times. Frequency = 3/28 = 0.10714
Document two has 17 index terms; jaguar appears two times. Frequency = 2/17 = 0.11765
Document three has 21 index terms; jaguar appears four times. Frequency = 4/21 = 0.19048

According to this very simple calculation, the order is D3, D2, D1, but for document two, "part" also appears two times. Therefore, when searching for jaguar, the importance of document two should be a "little bit" lower. As can be seen from the above calculation, cosine coefficient is sensitive to this difference, but the simple term frequency is not.

6.2 Calculating the Similarity by Cosine Coefficient for Search-term "jaguar vehicle"

Now, suppose that the search-term is "jaguar vehicle". The query vector based on Formula A15-2 and Formula A15-3 is:

$V_q = [$

0	0	0	0	0	0	0	0	0	0
0	0	0	0	0	0	0	0	0	0
0	0	0	0	0	0	0	0	0	0
0	0	0	0.28768	0	0	0	0	0	0
0	0	0	0	0	0	0	0	0	0
0	0	0	0	0	0	0	0	0	0
0	0	0	0	0	0	1.38629	0	0	0
0	0								

$]$

Note: $\log_2(4/3) = 0.28768$, $\log_2(4) = 1.38629$
$\Sigma_{i=1...N} w_{i,q}^2$
$= 0 \times 0 + 0 \times 0 + ... + 0.28768 \times 0.28768 + 0 \times 0 + ... + 1.38629 \times 1.38629 + 0 \times 0 +$
$= 0.08276 + 1.92181$
$= 2.00457$

Calculating sqrt($\Sigma_{i=1...N} w_{i,j}^2 \times \Sigma_{i=1...N} w_{i,q}^2$)
$| v_q | \times | d_1 |$
$= \mathrm{sqrt}(2.00457 \times 6.48885)$
$= 3.60657$
$| v_q | \times | d_2 |$
$= \mathrm{sqrt}(2.00457 \times 8.13038)$
$= 4.03707$
$| v_q | \times | d_3 |$
$= \mathrm{sqrt}(2.00457 \times 3.37452)$
$= 2.60086$
$| v_q | \times | d_4 |$
$= \mathrm{sqrt}(2.00457 \times 4.16392)$
$= 2.88909$

Calculating $Vq \bullet V_{Di}$
$V_q \bullet V_{D1}$
$= 0 \times 0.46210 + 0 \times 0 + ... + 0.28768 \times 0.28768 + 0 \times 0.46210 + 0 \times ... + 1.38629 \times 0 + ...$
$= 0.08276$
$V_q \bullet V_{D2}$
$= 0 \times 0.46210 + 0 \times 0 + ... + 0.28768 \times 0.28768 + 0 \times 0.46210 + 0 \times ... + 1.38629 \times 0.69315 + ...$
$= 0.08276 + 0.96091$
$= 1.04367$
$V_q \bullet V_{D3}$
$= 0 \times 0.46210 + 0 \times 0 + ... + 0.28768 \times 0.28768 + 0 \times 0.46210 + 0 \times ... + 1.38629 \times 0 + ...$
$= 0.08276$
$V_q \bullet V_{D41}$
$= 0 \times 0.46210 + 0 \times 0 + ... + 0.28768 \times 0 + 0 \times 0.46210 + 0 \times ... + 1.38629 \times 0 + ...$
$= 0$
For the query "jaguar vehicle", the cos-based similarity is:
Calculate cos-based similarity $\mathrm{sim}(v_q, d_j) = v_q \bullet d_j / | v_q | \times | d_j |$
$\cos(V_q, V_{D1}) = 0.08276 / 3.60657 = 0.02258$
$\cos(V_q, V_{D2}) = 1.04367 / 4.03707 = 0.25852$
$\cos(V_q, V_{D3}) = 0.08276 / 2.60086 = 0.03182$
$\cos(V_q, V_{D4}) = 0 / 2.88909 = 0$
According to the cos similarity, the order of relevant documents for the search-term "jaguar vehicle" is:
D2, D3, D1

Only document two contains the search-term "jaguar vehicle"; therefore, document one has the highest cos similarity value: 0.25852. Then comes document three with a cosine similarity of 0.03182 and, finally, document one, with a cosine similarity of 0.02258.

Appendix 16: A Sample Survey Result

Improving the Relevance of Search Results via Search-term Disambiguation and Ontological Filtering

Instruction:
Please judge if the following information snippets (search results) are:
R = Relevant;   P = Partially relevant;   I = Irrelevant
N = Not sufficient to make a judgement   Please mark (x) under columns R, P, I or N.

Search Term 1: Clinton
Information need: the American president William J. Clinton

INFORMATION SNIPPET/ SEARCH RESULT	R	P	I	N
1. Biography of William J. Clinton (http://www.whitehouse.gov/history/presidents/bc42.html) Brief biography of the forty-second U.S. President, Bill Clinton.	x			
2. Hillary Rodham Clinton, Senator from New York (http://clinton.senate.gov/) Official Senate site Hillary Rodham Clinton, the Democratic senator from New York. Includes contact information.		x		
3. Bill Clinton - Wikipedia, the free encyclopedia (http://en.wikipedia.org/wiki/Bill_Clinton) Hyperlinked, in-depth profile of Bill Clinton, the 42nd President of the United States. Includes notes on his early life and political career, as well as information on his presidency and 1998 impeachment.	x			
4. The Official Site of Clinton, Mississippi (http://www.clintonms.org/) Official site of Clinton, Mississippi.			x	
5. Clinton Foundation (http://www.clintonfoundation.org/) Foundation organized by former President Bill Clinton to promote the values of fairness and opportunity for all. Programs include health and HIV/AIDS, economic empowerment, leadership development, and citizen service.			x	
6. Clinton Presidential Materials Project (http://clinton.archives.gov/) Clinton Presidential Materials Project introduction page. ... The Clinton Presidential Materials Project has become the William J. Clinton Presidential Library ...	x			
7. Clinton County Iowa Home Page (http://www.clintoncountyiowa.com/) Official site featuring general information and department links.			x	
8. Clinton County welcomes you! iª Clinton County, Ohio (http://www.co.clinton.oh.us/) A growing community answering the challenges of merging rural and urban ideals. ... CLINTON COUNTY OHIO WAR TIME LOSSES/VETERANS BURIALS. Probation Staff ...			x	
9. Welcome to Clinton, Massachusetts (http://www.clintonmass.com/) The Town of Clinton's original community website - Since 1997 ... 50 great things about Clinton As chosen by our readers... The Clinton Water Department's ...			x	
10. Amazon.com: My Life: Books: Bill Clinton (http://www.amazon.com/exec/obidos/tg/detail/-/03754145767v=glance) Amazon.com: My Life: Books: Bill Clinton by Bill Clinton ... Bill Clinton discusses his life goals and how his parents met ... Bill Clinton describes his ...		x		
11. Clinton - Wikipedia, the free encyclopedia (http://en.wikipedia.org/wiki/Clinton) ... Charles Clinton (1690 ˚C 1773) French and Indian War Colonel, father of James and ... George Clinton (1739 ˚C 1812) first and third Governor of New York, ...			x	
12. Clinton, Oklahoma (http://www.clintonok.org/) Clinton Chamber of Commerce-Clinton, Oklahoma's leading business organization ... ? 2005 Clinton Chamber of Commerce ...			x	
13. OpinionJournal - Extra (http://www.opinionjournal.com/extra/?id=110004632) ... than word gets out that Bill Clinton was flying down to Washington to plan ... Behind the scenes, Clinton servitors run the Democratic Party, beginning at the ...	x			
14. Bill Clinton Jokes - Clinton Humor and Clinton Jokes (http://politicalhumor.about.com/od/billclinton) Bill Clinton jokes, political cartoons, parodies, and other classic Clinton humor. ... Political Humor> Democrats> Bill Clinton. Entertainment. Political Humor ...			x	
15. Official Websit of Clinton City (http://www.clintoncity.com/) ... Clinton has grown rapidly over the last ten years. ... Clinton City offers the finest in police and fire protection, professional court ...			x	
16. Clinton County Geneological Information (http://www.kcnet.org/~history/) ... 1870 Clinton County Census ... For those looking for a more detailed map of the Clinton County area, click here... Clinton County. Pat Lowery Family ...			x	
17. Welcome to Clinton County, NY! (http://www.co.clinton.ny.us/) Official site for the county.			x	
18. USA: biography of William Jefferson Clinton (1946 - (http://odur.let.rug.nl/~usa/P/bc42/about/clintonbio.htm) USA-project, presidents-area, biographical data of William Jefferson Clinton ... Bill Clinton was born William Jefferson Blythe IV on August 19, 1946, in Hope, ...		x	·	
19. Clinton County Government (http://www.clintoncountypa.com/) ... Welcome to Clinton County. Local Government Publications. 2006 CLINTON COUNTY RE-ELECTION SCHEDULE FOR CLINTON COUNTY ELECTED ROW OFFICES ...			x	
20. City of Clinton (http://www.cityofclintonnc.com/) find information about the history and government of Clinton, and the various departments. ... Box 199. 221 Lisbon Street. Clinton, NC 28329 (910) 592-1961 ...			x	
21. Welcome to Clinton County, Michigan (http://www.clinton-county.org/) ... Clinton County is situated in Michigan's central lower peninsula. ... governor of New York, De Witt Clinton, who was responsible for organizing the ...			x	
22. William J. Clinton Presidential Library (http://www.clintonlibrary.gov/) Extensive collection of Clinton Administration documents. Includes research facilities, exhibits, events, and educational programs on the life and presidency of Bill Clinton.	x			
23. Clinton Industries (http://www.clinton-ind.com/) ... on exacting standards, that's why Clinton Industries has been among the top ... And because Clinton handles a wide range of products, fulfilling your ...			x	
24. Village of Clinton (http://www.villageofclinton.org/) A little town with a big heart. ... On behalf of the residents of Clinton, I would like to extend a very warm and sincere welcome. ...			x	
25. Town of Clinton -- It's Summer in Maine's Dairy Capital!!! (http://www.clinton-me.us/) Clinton, ME ... Did you know that nearly 13% of Maine's milk is produced in the town of Clinton? ... The Clinton Town Office Staff will be more than happy to ...			x	
26. Town of Clinton (http://www.townofclinton.com/) Official site of Clinton, NY.			x	

Improving the Relevance of Search Results via Search-term Disambiguation and Ontological Filtering

INFORMATION SNIPPET/ SEARCH RESULT	R	P	I	N
27. American Presidents: Life Portraits (http://www.americanpresidents.org/presidents/president.asp?PresidentNumber=41) Facts, trivia, a 1969 letter to his local R.O.T.C. program officer expressing his feelings about the war, and the text to his 1993 and 1997 Inaugural Addresses.	✗			
28. Clinton, Wisconsin (http://www.clintonwi.us/) Official Website for the Village of Clinton, Rock County Wisconsin ... Search WWW Search www.clintonwi.us. free hit counter ...			✗	
29. frontline: the clinton years | PBS (http://www.pbs.org/wgbh/pages/frontline/shows/clinton) Presents a look at the Bill Clinton era. From ABC News's Nightline and PBS's Frontline. Includes interviews, photos, and anecdotes.			✓	
30. Clinton School District Homepage (http://clinton.k12.ar.us/) (Clinton) Calendar, district history, school sites, employment opportunities, ... Clinton Chamber of Commerce. Van Buren County. Van Buren County Democrat Newspaper ...			✗	
31. Clinton County Election & Voter Information (http://www.clinton-county.org/clerk/election_info.htm) ... Annual School Election (All Clinton County Schools) Members of the Board of Education ... Villages (All Clinton County Villages) State and Local Proposals ...			✗	
32. bill clinton (http://www.discoverthenetwork.org/individualProfile.asp?indid=644) ... Absolute Power: The Legacy of Corruption in the Clinton-Reno Justice Department ... Eyewitness Account Of How Bill Clinton Compromised America's National Security ...				✗
33. TLC :: What Not to Wear :: Clinton Kelly (http://tlc.discovery.com/fansites/whatnottowear/stylegurus/clinton.html) What Not to Wear ... Clinton honed his fashion sensibilities and expertise with his tenure as a ... Clinton is also no stranger to television. ...		·		✗
34. Bill Clinton - MSN Encarta (http://encarta.msn.com/encyclopedia_761564341/Clinton_Bill.html) Biographical article from the online encyclopedia Encarta. ... Bill Clinton, born in 1946, 42nd president of the United States (1993-2001), who ...		✗		
35. Clinton, IA Chamber of Commerce (http://www.clintonia.com/index.cfm) Community information, calendar of events, tourism, and more.			✗	
36. Clinton Presidential Library - Home Document (http://www.clinton-library.com/) Clinton Library, the nation's interactive tribute to President Bill Clinton, is ... Clinton Presidential Center is both an act of faith and of confidence. ...		✗		
37. CNN - Clinton: Iraq has abused its last chance - December 16, 1998 (http://www.cnn.com/US/9812/16/clinton.iraq.speech/) ... From the Oval Office, President Clinton told the nation Wednesday evening why ... Clinton also stated that, while other countries also had weapons of mass ...		✗		
38. Bill Clinton A Model Patient - CBS News (http://www.cbsnews.com/stories/2004/10/20/health/main650222.shtml) The former president is getting a little better "every day," recovering from heart surgery, and has been on the phone with advice for John Kerry. Mr. Clinton hasn't yet gotten a green light to actually hit the campaign trail for Kerry.			✗	
39. Untitled Document (http://www.clintontn.net/) ... The Clinton 12 Documentary Premier. Click here for dates and times. ... the Mission of the City of Clinton government to provide for the safety, ...			✗	
40. City of Clinton Oklahoma (http://www.clintonokla.org/) City of Clinton, Oklahoma community information and events ... Clinton is located in western Oklahoma at the intersection of Interstate 40 and ...			✗	
41. Welcome to Clinton, CT! (http://www.clintonct.com/) Information on events, local merchants, and local government.			✗	
42. Township of Clinton, New Jersey (http://www.township.clinton.nj.us/) ... Township of Clinton, New Jersey. The latest revised Windy Acres Settlement Agreement can be found here. ... The four exhibits are also available for ...			✗	
43. Clinton County, NY Genealogy (http://www.usgennet.org/usa/ny/county/clinton) Clinton County, NY: Genealogy and Local History- towns, surnames, queries, online records, discussion boards, topics, links, and more!			✗	
44. Senator Hillary Rodham Clinton: Contact Senator Clinton (http://clinton.senate.gov/contact/) ... Senator Clinton sincerely appreciates the interest of her constituents wishing ... Senator Hillary Rodham Clinton. United States Senate. 476 Russell Senate ...			✗	
45. Project Vote Smart - Senator Clinton - Interest Group Ratings (http://www.vote-smart.org/issue_rating_category.php?can_id=WNY99268) Project Vote Smart ... 2004 Senator Clinton supported the interests of the American Society for the ... in 2003, Senator Clinton voted their preferred position ...			✗	
46. Clinton County Schools (http://www.clinton.k12.ky.us/) Mission of the Clinton County Public Schools with links of district interest. ... Clinton County Schools Route 4 Box 100 Albany, KY 42602 606 387 - 6480 ...			✗	
47. Clinton, Bill. The Columbia Encyclopedia, Sixth Edition. 2001-05 (http://www.bartleby.com/65/cl/ClintonB.html) Clinton, Bill. The Columbia Encyclopedia, Sixth Edition. 2001-05 ... 12 acquitted Clinton. ... During both his terms Clinton took an active interest in environmental ...			✗	
48. Clinton Group (http://www.clinton.com/) Managing investment funds for individual, institutional, and sovereign investors.			✗	
49. Clinton County, Illinois--Home Page (http://www.clintonco.org/) Information about local government, offices, and elected officials.			✗	
50. Clinton Community College (http://clintoncc.suny.edu/)			✓	

Retrieval at: Mon Aug 21 16:00:32 CST 2006

Improving the Relevance of Search Results via Search-term Disambiguation and Ontological Filtering

R = Relevant;   P = Partially relevant;   I = Irrelevant
N = Not sufficient to make a judgement   Please mark (x) under columns R, P, I or N.

Search Term 2: Ford
Information need: Henry Ford, The founder of the Ford Motor Company

INFORMATION SNIPPET	R	P	I	N
1. Ford Vehicles: Ford Vehicles Official Site: learn about Ford cars, trucks and SUVs. (http://www.fordvehicles.com/) Learn about Ford cars, trucks, minivans, and SUVs. Get price quotes, search dealer inventory, compare vehicles, and find out about incentives and financing.		x		
2. Ford Motor Company Home Page (http://www.ford.com/en/default.htm) The corporate website for Ford Motor Company and its vehicle (car and truck) and service brands, featuring investor, career, news and media information.		x		
3. Ford Motor Company (http://www.ford.com/) Official site for the Ford Motor Company, manufacturer of SUVs, cars, trucks, and wagons. The Ford family brand includes Lincoln, Mercury, Mazda, Volvo, Jaguar, Land-Rover, and Aston Martin. Find vehicles in the interactive showroom and learn more about Ford services including financing, parts, and sales.		x		
4. Ford :: home (http://www.ford.co.uk/) ... Ford Power Products ... Ford GT. ST Performance Vehicle. Car configurator. Request a brochure. Request a test drive ... Ford Direct used cars. Accessories ...		x		
5. ......:::::: FORD MODELS ::::::...... (http://www.fordmodels.com/) Official site for the international modeling agency. Offers details of Ford offices around the world, including New York, Los Angeles, Paris, and Toronto.			x	
6. Ford Australia (http://www.ford.com.au/) Official Australian site.			x	
7. Ford Motor Company of Canada, Limited (http://www.ford.ca/) Official Canadian site.			x	
8. Henry Ford Museum & Greenfield Village (http://www.hfmgv.org/) Collection of Americana that depicts the ever-changing worlds of transportation, manufacturing, home life, entertainment and technology.		x		
9. Ford Truck Enthusiasts, 1948-2006 Ford trucks, F150, Super Duty & SUV owners community and information source. ... (http://www.ford-trucks.com/) Extensive resource for Ford truck owners featuring discussion groups, technical articles, events, and more. Find advice and information for the F-150, F-250 Super Duty, Explorer, Ranger, and other models.			x	
10. Ford - Viva o Novo (http://www.ford.com.br/) ... Ford - Viva o Novo ...			x	
11. Ford :: Startseite (http://www.ford.de/) Official German site.			x	
12. Ford Racing: Home (http://www.fordracing.com/) Offers Ford racing news, links to race results, history, merchandise, and more.			x	
13. Media.Ford.com: (http://media.ford.com/) EXECUTIVE BIO'S, PRESS RELEASES - Ford, Volvo, Mazda, Lincoln, Jaguar, Aston ... Ford snags 4 awards for concept cars ... FORD FOCUS FUEL CELL VEHICLE STARS AT ...			x	
14. Ford Foundation (http://www.fordfound.org/) Providing grants and loans to projects that strengthen democratic values, reduce poverty and injustice, promote international cooperation, and advance human achievement.		x		
15. ford motor company (http://www.mycareer.ford.com/main.asp) The corporate website for Ford Motor Company. ... Ford Motor Company was recognized as one of the top American corporations on ...			x	
16. Ford Motor Company - Wikipedia, the free encyclopedia (http://en.wikipedia.org/wiki/Ford) ... automaker was founded by an American legend, Henry Ford and incorporated in 1903. Ford now encompasses many brands globally, including Lincoln and Mercury in the ...	x			
17. Harrison Ford (I) (http://www.imdb.com/name/nm0000148) Pictures, biography, and filmography for Harrison Ford -- the mega movie star whose famous movies include the original Star Wars trilogy, Indiana Jones movies, Blade Runner, Clear and Present Danger, and Witness.			x	
18. Media.Ford.com: FORD LEADS WITH BIO-ETHANOL POWERED CARS FOR EUROPE (http://media.ford.com/article_display.cfm?article_id=21101) BIO&146;S, PRESS RELEASES - Ford, Volvo, Mazda, Lincoln, Jaguar, Aston Martin, ... FORD UNVEILS GREEN FOCUS COUP?-CABRIOLET CONCEPT, FORD IN UK TO INVEST ?1 ...			x	
19. Ford Motor Company of Canada, Limited (http://www.ford.ca/english/default_flash.asp) Ford Motor Company of Canada, cars and trucks ... vehicles (excluding Mustang Shelby GT 500, SVT, Ford GT, Edge, MKX, F-Series ...			x	
20. Ford Accessories (http://www.fordaccessories.com/) Offers Ford accessories and merchandise.			x	
21. Ford (http://www.ford.co.za/) Official South African site.			x	
22. Ford Vehicles: Ford Mustang - See pricing details, car options, V6 GT (http://www.fordvehicles.com/cars/mustang/) Official site for the popular muscle car, the Mustang. Offers photos, feature information, specs, and more.			x	
23. Henry Ford - Wikipedia, the free encyclopedia (http://en.wikipedia.org/wiki/Henry_Ford) ... As sole owner of the Ford Company he became one of the richest and best-known ... Ford, though poorly educated, had a global vision, with consumerism as ...	x			
24. The Henry Ford: The Life of Henry Ford (http://www.hfmgv.org/exhibits/hf) From his childhood through the founding of Ford Motor Company and beyond.	x			

Improving the Relevance of Search Results via Search-term Disambiguation and Ontological Filtering

INFORMATION SNIPPET/ SEARCH RESULT	R	P	I	N
25. Ford Fleet - Fleet Vehicles For Any Size Business (https://www.fleet.ford.com/) to the dedication of our people, Ford Fleet can meet the vehicle needs of any size business. ... Not at the right site? Please visit Ford.com for retail information. ...			X	
26. Ford (http://www.india.ford.com/) Official site for India.				X
27. Gerald R. Ford Presidential Library and Museum (http://www.ford.utexas.edu/) Promotes popular interest and scholarly research in U.S. history during the post-World War II era, especially the Ford presidency (1974-77).			X	
28. Ford :: Ford Team RS :: Ford Team RS home (http://www.ford.co.uk/teamrs_home) ... Ford Power Products ... Ford GT. ST Performance Vehicle. Car configurator. Request a brochure. Request a test drive ... Ford Direct used cars. Accessories ...			X	
29. Ford of Belgium (http://www.ford.be/) Online showroom van Ford Belgie met de nieuwste modellen, nieuws, dealers en Ford over Ford.				X
30. John Ford (I) (http://www.imdb.com/name/nm0000406/) John Ford (I) - Filmography, Awards, Biography, Agent, Discussions, Photos, News Articles, Fan Sites ... A Gun Fightin' Gentleman (1919) (as Jack Ford) ...			X	
31. New 2006 and 2007 Ford Cars on Yahoo! Autos (http://autos.yahoo.com/newcars/ford.html) Features information on the year's current models.			X	
32. Biography of Gerald R. Ford (http://www.whitehouse.gov/history/presidents/gf38.html) Biography of Gerald R. Ford, the former U.S. president, from the official White House web site. Includes highlights of Ford's two years as president, following the resignation of Richard Nixon.			X	
33. Ford Malaysia (http://www.ford.com.my/) Ford vehicles including cars, trucks, 4X4s and vans. Includes services for ... Ford Extended Warranty. Scheduled Service Plan. Total Maintenance Plan. Genuine Parts ...				X
34. Ford Credit - Auto financing for Ford, Lincoln and Mercury cars and trucks (http://www.fordcredit.com/) Automotive leasing, loans, and financing options from Ford Credit. Manage your vehicle finance account online, apply for credit, and get estimated payments.			X	
35. Ford | Ford Dealer | Car Quotes and Reviews | 2006 2007 (http://www.autosite.com/content/research/makesearch/index.cfm/action/SelectModel2/make_vch/Ford) Ford reviews, pictures, and invoice pricing. Get a free no-obligation price ... 2007 Ford Explorer Sport Trac Photo Gallery ... Ford keeps interest in the ...			X	
36. Ford | Free Price Quotes | Ford Dealer | Ford Car | Car.com (http://www.car.com/content/research/makesearch/index.cfm/action/SelectModel2/make_vch/Ford) Ford price quotes and reviews. Free no-obligation quote from a local dealer. ... 2007 Ford Explorer Sport Trac Photo Gallery ... Ford keeps interest in the ...			X	
37. Ford :: home :: rotating home (http://www.ford.com.ve/) Show room, modelos, caracter"ªsticas t"¦cnicas; listado de concesionarios y noticias.				X
38. Ford | Free Price Quotes | Ford Car Dealer | 2006 2007 (http://www.autoweb.com/content/research/makesearch/index.cfm/action/SelectModel2/make_vch/Ford) Ford reviews and price quotes from a local dealer. ... 2007 Ford Explorer Sport Trac Photo Gallery. Ford looks to gain traction with this sporty Explorer derivative ...			X	
39. Career Programs (http://www.mycareer.ford.com/CareerPrograms.asp) The corporate website for Ford Motor Company. ... the rapid career development you can find in our Ford College Graduate programs. ...			X	
40. Ford - Research All Models and Prices - MSN Autos (http://autos.msn.com/browse/Ford.aspx) Ford prices, reviews, used Ford classifieds, and more on MSN Autos ... The Ford Motor Company was incorporated in 1903 with ten people and $28,000. ...			X	
41. Ford Search Results (http://www.autobytel.com/content/research/detail/Ford.htm) Ford Pricing Guide - Buy your next new or used Ford here using our pricing and ... The 2007 Ford Crown Victoria is a 4-door, 6-passenger family sedan, available in ...			X	
42. Ford New Zealand (http://www.ford.co.nz/) Official site for New Zealand.				X
43. Ford Commercial Truck (http://www.commtruck.ford.com/) ... Internet Explorer version 3.0+ Netscape Navigator version 2.0 ...				X
44. Ford County, KS (http://skyways.lib.ks.us/counties/FO/) An overview of Ford County, Kansas. ... History of Kansas, first published in 1883, tells about early Ford County. ... data for Ford County online including ...			X	
45. Ford :: Accueil :: voiture neuve, achat voiture, achat auto. (http://www.ford.fr/) Le site officiel de Ford France avec nouvelles conceptions des voitures. ... Ford Power Products. Sport automobile. Championnat du monde des rallyes ...				X
46. Oy Ford Ab (http://www.ford.fi/) Oy Ford Ab ... Ford omistajalle. Rahoitus. Vaihtoautot. Tietoa Fordista. Asiakaslehti. Ota yhteytt?. Henry-takuuvaihtoautot. Luotettava ja huoleton vaihtoehto. Oy Ford ...				X
47. FORD: Summary for FORWARD INDS INC - Yahoo! Finance (http://finance.yahoo.com/q?s=FORD) information on FORWARD INDS INC (FORD) including quote performance, Real-Time ... Trading Report for (FORD) Detailed Technical Analysis + Free Market Timing Report ...			X	
48. Ford Parts - Always In Stock (http://www.racepages.com/oem/ford.html) Get your Ford Replacement Parts questions answered in seconds when you call our Customer Service Center.				X
49. Ford :: home :: rotating home (http://www.ford.es/) Gama de modelos, novedades, historia, prototipos, taller virtual, red de ... Recambios originales Ford. Llantas y neum"¢ticos. Seguridad. Talleres Independientes ...				X
50. Ford Madox Ford Society (http://www.rialto.com/fordmadoxford_society) Provides news of recent and future activities, publications, a gallery of first editions, and membership information.			X	

Retrieval at: Mon Aug 21 16:18:01 CST 2006

Improving the Relevance of Search Results via Search-term Disambiguation and Ontological Filtering

R = Relevant;   P = Partially relevant;   I = Irrelevant
N = Not sufficient to make a judgement   Please mark (x) under columns R, P, I or N.

Search Term 3: Health
Information need: How can one keep health?

INFORMATION SNIPPET	R	P	I	N
1. Medical Dictionary, Diseases, Healthy Living, Drugs & Medicines on Yahoo! Health (http://health.yahoo.com/) Provides health research, expert advice, healthy recipes, and more.		x		
2. Health in the Yahoo! Directory (http://dir.yahoo.com/Health/) health, including diseases and conditions, medications, sexual health, fitness, ... Health Sciences (36) Hospitals and Medical Centers (44) Hygiene (17) ...		x		
3. CNN.com - Health (http://www.cnn.com/HEALTH) ... More Health Video. ? Mandatory HIV testing (1:43) ? Sudden cardiac arrest (1:14) ... Time.com Science & Health. Search for jobs @ International Edition ...		x		
4. Open Directory - Health (http://dmoz.org/Health/) ... Occupational Health and Safety (684) Organizations (69) Pharmacy (3,794) ... Harvard Medical School's consumer health information, journal databases, a ...				x
5. Health News - New York Times (http://www.nytimes.com/pages/health/index.html) health news on medicine, fitness, nutrition, health care, mental health, drugs, ... Personal Health: Scientists Cast Misery of Migraine in a New Light ...	x			
6. World Health Organization (WHO/OMS) (http://www.who.int/) Directing and coordinating authority on international health work that strives to bring the highest level of health to all peoples.			x	
7. WebMD - Better Information. Better Health. (http://www.webmd.com/) Provides medical information and services for consumers, physicians, and other health providers.	x			
8. BBC NEWS	Health (http://news.bbc.co.uk/1/hi/health/default.stm) perspectives. Also entertainment, business, science, technology and health news. ... Health experts' heatwave warning. Glaxo pays $70m in price row. Patient dies ...	x			
9. MSNBC - Health News: Medical news, fitness topics and more - Front Page (http://www.msnbc.msn.com/id/3032076) ... Receive a daily update with the top health news stories and special reports ... health officials are counting on barbershops to help screen men who wouldn't ...		x		
10. National Institutes of Health (NIH) (http://www.nih.gov/) Focal point for biomedical research in the U.S.			x	
11. Health.com :: (http://www.health.com/) Covers health, fitness, beauty, wellness, and food.	x			
12. www.health.gov (http://www.health.gov/) List of governmental sites related to health issues and topics.	x			
13. Health News - AOL Health (http://health.aol.com/) Find health advice, information about diseases, diet tips, calorie and body mass ... Health, your destination for in depth information about diseases and conditions, ...	x			
14. C-Health: Your Health and Wellness Source - powered by MediResource (http://chealth.canoe.ca/) Health and wellness source with links to information on a variety of health-related topics.	x			
15. The top health news articles from Yahoo! News (http://news.yahoo.com/i/751) Use Yahoo! News to find health news headlines and health articles on weight loss, medications, diseases, aging and more. ... Sexual Health News ...	x			
16. BBC - Health (http://www.bbc.co.uk/health) In-depth resource on health, diseases, and relationships.	x			
17. Men's Health (http://www.menshealth.com/) Magazine for men containing information on health, fitness, weight loss, and more.	x			
18. AARP - Health	People Age 50 & Over (http://www.aarp.org/health/) Learn about health programs for people age 50 and over at AARP. We are dedicated to enhancing quality of life for all as we age. Information, advocacy and service.	x			
19. Kaiser Permanente: Thrive - Health Insurance Plans, Healthcare Information, Health Advice (http://www.kaiserpermanente.org/) Includes health information, members area, details of health plans, news, locations, and more.	x			
20. WHO	World Health Organization (http://www.who.int/en) WHO	World Health Organization WHO	World Health Organization 1 April 2005 -- WHO's new programme to train the next generation of health leaders has welcomed its first eight recruits this week. Over the next few years, the Health Leadership ...			x	
21. Drug and alcohol abuse, treatment, prevention at SAMHSA's National Clearinghouse for Alcohol and Drug Information (http://www.health.org/) Resource for information about substance abuse prevention and addiction treatment. Includes an FAQ on substance abuse, articles, news, and related resources.	x			
22. InteliHealth: InteliHealth Home (http://www.intelihealth.com/) Comprehensive collection of consumer health information.	x			
23. Centers for Disease Control and Prevention (http://www.cdc.gov/) Includes information on disease outbreaks, health topics, and emergency preparedness.		x		
24. Home Page - MSN Health & Fitness (http://health.msn.com/) ... MSN Videos on Health. Find a Therapist. Heart Attack Risk. BMI Calculator. Test Your Stress Level ... About Health & Fitness ...	x			
25. Join AARP: Benefits & Information	People Age 50 and Over (http://www.aarp.org/) Excels as a dynamic presence in every community, shaping and enriching the experience of aging for each member and for society.		x		

5 of 11

Improving the Relevance of Search Results via Search-term Disambiguation and Ontological Filtering

INFORMATION SNIPPET	R	P	I	N
26. C-Health : Seniors' Health (http://chealth.canoe.ca/channel_main.asp?channel_id=10) they come with their own set of health problems, as if you hadn't lived through ... View health videos about a variety of diseases, conditions and treatment options. ...	✓			
27. Breaking Health and Fitness News Stories and Video - CBSNews.com (http://www.cbsnews.com/sections/health/main204.shtml) s Health, Men&lsquo;s Health, and Health and Fitness Headlines and Information. ... Survey: Most Want Health Care Overhaul ... due to health violations. Couple ...		✓		
28. azcentral.com | health & fitness (http://www.azcentral.com/health/) women's, kids' and men's health to diet, wellness and fitness. ... condition Allergy Alternative Health Alzheimer's Disease Anemia Arthritis ...	✓			
29. Florida Department of Health Home Page (http://www.doh.state.fl.us/) Provides information about disease control and prevention, environmental health, health statistics, alerts and more.		✓		
30. U.S. News & World Report: Best Health (http://www.usnews.com/usnews/health/hehome.htm) Get health information, including our annual list of the best hospitals in ... Health News. Recent Articles. Diseases & Conditions. Allergy & Asthma Center ...	✓			
31. AllRefer Health (http://health.allrefer.com/) Health resource provides reliable and comprehensive information and news on ... Health Topics: A-Al Am-Az B C-C) Ck-Cz D E F G H I J K L M N O P-Pi Pm-Pz Q R ...	✓			
32. Discovery Health :: Discovery Health :: Homepage (http://health.discovery.com/) Offers health news and in-depth features, show information, and health library.	✓			
33. healthfinder? - your guide to reliable health information (http://www.healthfinder.gov/) Offers consumer health and human services information.	✓			
34. U.S. Department of Labor Occupational Safety and Health Organization: OSHA. (http://www.osha.gov/) Official site for the government agency that establishes protective standards, enforces those standards, and reaches out to employers and employees through technical assistance and consultation programs.		✓		
35. Health - Wex (http://www.law.cornell.edu/topics/health.html) Information about U.S. health law from the Legal Information Institute.		✓		
36. Health (http://www.washingtonpost.com/wp-dyn/content/health/) ... Health Discussions ... Scientists, health workers and activists find hope at 16th International AIDS Conference. ... South African Health Chief's Ouster ...		✓		
37. Health - Wikipedia, the free encyclopedia (http://en.wikipedia.org/wiki/Health) ... are four general determinants of health which he called "human biology" ... smoking and other substance abuse are examples of steps to improve one's health. ...	✓	•		
38. United States Department of Health and Human Services (http://www.hhs.gov/) Leading America to better health, safety, and well-being.	✓			
39. Travelers' Health | CDC (http://www.cdc.gov/travel) Includes information on outbreaks, specific diseases, recommended vaccinations, and traveling with children and pets. Presented by the National Center for Infectious Diseases.		✓		
40. Health Care, Health Care Guide, Medical Advice, Primary Health Care, Mental Health, Home Health Care (http://health.indiamart.com/) Includes general health information, news, yellow pages, and advice.	✓			
41. Excite - Health (http://health.excite.com/index/id/ap.html) Whether you're sick as a dog or healthy as an ox, our comprehensive health section can help you live a better, healthier life.	✓			
42. DenverPost.com (http://denverpost.healthology.com/) articles, womens health issues and general health information. ... Copyright Healthology, Inc., an iVillage Company providing health education ...	✓			
43. Healthcentral.com - Trusted, Reliable and Up To Date Health Information (http://www.healthcentral.com/) Providing consumer health information.	✓			
44. New York State Department of Health (http://www.health.state.ny.us/) Home page for the New York State Department of Health ... State Health Department Urges Early Identification and Appropriate Treatment for ...		✓		
45. Health:Topic (http://www.oecd.org/topic/0,2686,en_2649_37407_1_1_1_1_37407,00.html) Good health is necessary for individuals to flourish as citizens, family members, ... Scientific, Industrial and Health Applications of Biotechnology ...	✓			
46. National Library of Medicine - National Institutes of Health (http://www.nlm.nih.gov/) Extensive collection of online information for the public and health care professionals dealing with clinical care, toxicology and environmental health, and basic research.		✓		
47. Women's Health Interactive (http://www.womens-health.com/) Place for women to proactively learn about their health and health-related issues.	✓			
48. Health & Fitness Tips - Information, News, Products (http://www.health-fitness-tips.com/) Specializing in health and fitness information including weight loss, diet, and nutrition.	✓			
49. Mayo Clinic medical information and tools for healthy living - MayoClinic.com (http://www.mayoclinic.com/) The Mayo Clinic's health resource web site offers information on diseases and conditions, healthy living, drugs, and self-care.	✓			
50. Health Information - National Institutes of Health (NIH) (http://health.nih.gov/) Browse health topics alphabetically.		✓		

Retrieval at: Mon Aug 21 16:29:40 CST 2006

Improving the Relevance of Search Results via Search-term Disambiguation and Ontological Filtering

R = Relevant;   P = Partially relevant;   I = Irrelevant
N = Not sufficient to make a judgement   Please mark (x) under columns R, P, I or N.

Search Term 4: Jaguar   Information need: Information about the animal jaguar

INFORMATION SNIPPET	R	P	I	N
1. Jaguar (http://www.jaguar.com/) Official site of the Ford Motor Company division featuring new Jaguar models and local dealer information.			x	
2. One World Journeys | Jaguar: Lord of the Mayan Jungle (http://www.oneworldjourneys.com/jaguar/) A multimedia expedition into the heart of the Mexican jungle, searching for the elusive jaguar.	x			
3. Jaguar (http://www.bluelion.org/jaguar.htm) Compares jaguars and leopards and provides information about the animal's shrinking habitat and relationship with man.	x			
4. Jag-lovers - the Jaguar Enthusiasts' premier Internet site (http://www.jag-lovers.org/) Offers model pages, mailing lists, book reviews, and more for the Jaguar car enthusiast.			x	
5. Title: Jaguar Enthusiasts' Club Main Page (http://www.jec.org.uk/) Offers information on activities. Based in the U.K., but offers memberships worldwide.			x	
6. jaguars.com >> The official website of the NFL's Jacksonville Jaguars. (http://www.jaguars.com/) Official site of the Jaguars. Includes schedule, news, multimedia, photos, player information, statistics, team store, tickets, and more.			x	
7. Jaguar UK - Jaguar Cars (http://www.jaguar.co.uk/) ... Vehicles. Tools and Services. Finance. Owners. About Jaguar. Home. X-TYPE. S-TYPE. XJ. XK. Accessories ... Site Map. FAQ. Privacy Policy. Terms & Conditions ...			x	
8. Jaguar US - Jaguar USA Home (http://www.jaguarusa.com/us/en/home.htm) Jaguar USA Official Home Page ... From $62,495. From $62,495. From $75,500. From $75,500. Build Your Jaguar. Request a Brochure ...			x	
9. Jaguar AU - Jaguar Cars (http://www.jaguar.com.au/) Official Australian site for the Ford Motor Company division. Includes model specifications and general information.			x	
10. Jaguar - The British Metal Band - Home Page (http://www.jaguar-online.com/) Jaguar are a British rock band who have been very influential within the rock ... Jaguar Collectors CD Project. The band have announced an exciting project and ...			x	
11. Jaguar - Wikipedia, the free encyclopedia (http://en.wikipedia.org/wiki/Jaguar) ... a b c d e "Jaguar (panthera onca) ... The jaguar (Panthera onca) are mammals of the Felidae family and one of four " ... (European jaguar) and panthera ...		x		
12. Jaguar -- Kids' Planet -- Defenders of Wildlife (http://www.kidsplanet.org/factsheets/jaguar.html) Jaguar -- Kids' Planet -- Defenders of Wildlife Jaguar -- Kids' Planet -- Defenders of Wildlife ...		x		
13. Jaguar UK - R is for Racing (http://www.jaguar.co.uk/uk/en/vehicles/r-performance/overview/r_racing.htm) ... bred into the bloodline of every Jaguar, particularly the very special range of ... create the essence of the Jaguar breed ¨C rare, beautiful, refined, and ...			x	
14. Jag¨¹ar (http://www.jaguar.is/) Groove-oriented music with influences in funk, latin, soul, and rock.			x	
15. Jaguar DE - Jaguar Cars (http://www.jaguar.de/) ... Corporate Sales. Suche. Jaguar Weltweit. Inhalt. H?ufig gestelite Fragen. DAT Leitfaden. Kraftstoffverbrauch & CO2-Emissionen. Nutzungsbedingungen. Kontakt. Barrierefreiheit ...				x
16. Jaguar Models - Main Page (resin model kits) (http://www.jaguarmodels.com/) Jaguar Models, 12 ... Contacting Information. Jaguar Models, Inc. 18229 Railroad Street, City of Industry, CA 91748 ... We have added product listings of ...			x	
17. Jaguar CA - Jaguar Cars (http://www.jaguar.com/ca/en/home.htm) ... Request a Brochure. Locate a Dealer. Request a Test Drive. Search. Site Map. Contact Us. FAQ. Fran?ais ... X-TYPE. S-TYPE. XJ. XK. Welcome to. JAGUAR CANADA ...			x	
18. Jaguar Search Results (http://www.autobytel.com/content/research/detail/Jaguar.htm) Jaguar Pricing Guide - Buy your next new or used Jaguar here using our pricing ... The 2006 Jaguar S-Type is a 4-door, 5-passenger luxury sedan, or luxury sports ...			x	
19. Jaguar NL - Home (http://www.jaguar.nl/) Official Dutch site for the Ford Motor Company division.			x	
20. Jaguar | Free Price Quotes | Jaguar Dealer | Jaguar Car | Car.com (http://www.car.com/content/research/makesearch/index.cfm/action/SelectModel2/make_vch/Jaguar) Jaguar,Jag price quotes and reviews. Free no-obligation quote from a local dealer. ... 2007 Jaguar XK Preview. Aiming to set the luxury performance standard ...			x	
21. Apple - Apple - Mac OS X - Leopard Sneak Peek (http://www.apple.com/macosx/leopard/index.html) Sneak peak from Apple of some of the features in the next generation of their Macintosh OS X, codenamed Leopard.			x	
22. AtariAge - Atari Jaguar History (http://www.atariage.com/Jaguar/history.html) AtariAge - News, message boards, rarity guides, game database, manuals, pictures, ... Atari Jaguar with CD-ROM ... program and publish Jaguar games, and has ...			x	
23. Jaguar (http://dialspace.dial.pipex.com/agarman/jaguar.htm) Key facts and information on the jaguar's habitat, diet and status as a near threatened species.	x	·		
24. Jaguar (car) - Wikipedia, the free encyclopedia (http://en.wikipedia.org/wiki/Jaguar_(car)) ... Jaguar E-types are featured in the films The Italian Job, Robbery, The Odessa ... Harold, of Harold and Maude, had a Jaguar E-Type hearse. ...			x	
25. Jaguar (http://www.fas.org/man/dod-101/sys/ac/row/jaguar.htm) ... and tactical support aircraft, the Jaguar has been transformed into a potent fighter-bomber. ... The Jaguar strike fighter was equipped also with Magic air ...			x	
26. Jaguar (http://www.bigcatrescue.org/jaguar.htm) Jaguar Facts, Jaguar Photos and Jaguars in the news at the world's largest big ... The Jaguar and the Leopard are often confused with one another in zoos. ...		x		

Improving the Relevance of Search Results via Search-term Disambiguation and Ontological Filtering

INFORMATION SNIPPET	R	P	I	N
27. Jaguar (http://www.thewildones.org/Animals/jaguar.html) ... The jaguar (Panthera onca) is the only member of the 'big cat' family that lives ... and is about the same size as the jaguar, but it is classified as a small cat ...	✗			
28. San Diego Zoo's Animal Bytes: Jaguar (http://www.sandiegozoo.org/animalbytes/t-jaguar.html) Get fun and interesting jaguar facts in an easy-to-read style from the San Diego ... over 85 species in the jaguar diet, including peccaries, deer, tapirs, ...	✗			
29. Jaguar | Free Price Quotes | Jaguar Car Dealer | 2006 2007 (http://www.autoweb.com/content/research/makesearch/index.cfm/action/SelectModel2/make_vch/Jaguar) Jaguar,Jag reviews and price quotes from a local dealer. ... 2007 Jaguar XK Preview. Aiming to set the luxury performance standard ...			✗	
30. Jaguar - Java Access to Generic Underlying Architectural Resources (http://www.eecs.harvard.edu/~mdw/proj/old/jaguar/) ... Jaguar is an extension of the Java runtime environment which enables direct Java ... Unlike the JNI, however, Jaguar does not require copying of data ...			✗	
31. The Jaguar - Houston Zoo {N A HURY} (http://users.netropolis.net/nahury1/jaguar.htm) General overview of the species.	✗			
32. Yahooligans! Animals: Jaguar (http://yahooligans.yahoo.com/content/animals/species/6638.html) A picture and description of this animal. ... The Jaguar is the biggest and most powerful North American wildcat, and the only ...	✗			
33. New 2006 and 2007 Jaguar Cars on Yahoo! Autos (http://autos.yahoo.com/newcars/jaguar/index.html) new Jaguar pictures, specs, reviews and more from the most comprehensive online automotive site. ... Find Used Jaguar Cars Near You. Check Yahoo! ...			✗	
34. Jaguar | Jaguar Dealer | Car Quotes and Reviews | 2006 2007 (http://www.autosite.com/content/research/makesearch/index.cfm/action/SelectModel2/make_vch/Jaguar) Jaguar,Jag reviews, pictures, and invoice pricing. Get a free no-obligation ... 2006 Jaguar XJ Super V8 Portfolio Quick Spin. Preferred 10 to 1 over a corner office ...			✗	
35. Jaguar car quote, dealer prices, dealer quotes, MSRP prices, invoice prices (http://www.autobytel.cfm/content/buy/im/new/search/index.cfm/action/SelectModel/make_vch/Jaguar) Jaguar,Jag car quote, dealer prices, dealer quotes, MSRP prices, invoice prices ... Jaguar XK. ABOUT AUTOBYTEL " ... Powered by AIC - Automotive Information Center ...			✗	
36. Schr?dinger -> Site Map (http://www.schrodinger.com/Products/jaguar.html) A general purpose ab initio electronic structure package ... Jaguar Chem3D EULA. Script Center. Script Downloads. Seminar Center. June 1st 2006. May 25th 2006 ...			✗	
37. Animal Fact Sheets (http://www.zoo.org/educate/fact_sheets/jaguar/jaguar.htm) ... which includes four species of "big cats", the jaguar, tiger, lion and leopard. ... Jaguar cubs are usually born with their eyes closed, weigh about 25-29 ounces ...	✗			
38. Jaguar - Research All Models and Prices - MSN Autos (http://autos.msn.com/browse/Jaguar.aspx) Jaguar prices, reviews, used Jaguar classifieds, and more on MSN Autos ... Jaguar was founded in 1922 as the Swallow Sidecar Company of Blackpool, England. ...			✗	
39. Jaguar Performance Products, Georgia (http://www.jaguarkarts.com/) Jaguar Performance Karts is a manufacture of racing kart chassis in Georgia, ... Jaguar Performance had a record breaking season in the year 2001 and 2002 is ...			✗	
40. Used Jaguar Prices & Reviews (http://auto.consumerguide.com/Search/index.cfm/type/used/make/1608/name/Jaguar/) Search results for used Jaguar reviews. Results include car name, vehicle class, ... Jaguar was then purchased by Ford in 1989, and is now a division in the ...			✗	
41. Jaguar (http://www.co.pima.az.us/cmo/sdcp/sdcp2/fsheets/jaguar.html) ... The jaguar (Panthera onca) is the largest cat native to the Western Hemisphere. ... The jaguar can be a far ranging animal, traveling distances up to 500 miles. ...	✗			
42. JAGUAR cologne (http://www.4-fragrances.com/men/jaguar-m.htm) Jaguar ... JAGUAR BLUE Eau de Toilette Spray 3.4 oz New $48.00 $39.99. FREE US SHIPPING ON ORDERS OVER $60 ... discount JAGUAR jaguar mark 2 jaguar,cologne, ...			✗	
43. Media.Ford.com: The Products :Jaguar (http://media.ford.com/products/index.cfm?make_id=95) Ford, Volvo, Mazda, Lincoln, Jaguar, Aston Martin, Mercury, Land Rover ... Jaguar North America today announced Manufacturer's Suggested Retail Prices ...			✗	
44. Jaguar History (http://www.exoticcarrental.com/JaguarHistory.htm) Information about the history of the Jaguar. ... the company name to Jaguar. In 1948 at the Earls Court Motor Show the XK 120 Roadster was introduced by Jaguar. ...			✗	
45. J A G U A R - ?ndice (http://jaguar.edu.co/) Taller-escuela dedicado a la educaci¨®n, producci¨®n y publicaci¨®n de artes ... comercial educativo ...				✗
46. NatureWorks - Jaguar (http://www.nhptv.org/natureworks/jaguar.htm) NatureWorks ... The jaguar is the largest cat in North America and the third largest cat in the world. ... The Jaguar, unlike most big cats, loves the water. ...	✗			
47. Flickr: Photos tagged with jaguar (http://www.flickr.com/photos/tags/jaguar) Flickr is almost certainly the best online photo management and sharing ... Jaguar Luxury Automobile. Official Site-Jaguar vehicle specs, pictures, options and ...			✗	
48. Jaguar (http://www.pansophist.com/jag.htm) An owner discusses his XJ6.			✗	
49. Jaguar Printout- EnchantedLearning.com (http://www.enchantedlearning.com/subjects/mammals/cats/jaguar/Jaguarprintout.shtml) Jaguar Printout. Jaguar are medium-sized cats that live in South and Central ... As a bonus, site members have access to a banner-ad-free version of the site, ...	✗			
50. USS Jaguar (http://www.worldkids.net/jaguar) Star Trek club for kids with chat, message board, stories, and more.				✗

Retrieval at: Mon Aug 21 15:45:30 CST 2006

Improving the Relevance of Search Results via Search-term Disambiguation and Ontological Filtering

R = Relevant;   P = Partially relevant;   I = Irrelevant
N = Not sufficient to make a judgement

Please mark (x) under columns R, P, I or N.

Search Term 5: Ups

Information need: Information about how UPS (Uninterruptible Power Supply) works, key specification of UPS

INFORMATION SNIPPET	R	P	I	N
1. UPS Package Tracking (http://www.ups.com/tracking/tracking.html) UPS Package Tracking service lets you track your package across the world, including multiple packages, airmail, or freight, and offering updates on the Web or by email.			x	
2. UPS Global Home (http://www.ups.com/) Worldwide express carrier and package delivery company. UPS is a global provider of specialized transportation and logistics services.			x	
3. Cash Flow, International Trade & Small Business Lending : UPS Capital (http://www.upscapital.com/) UPS offers businesses worldwide the opportunity to integrate supply chain ... combined with the broad capabilities of UPS help enhance operations as well as ...			x	
4. UPS Careers (https://ups.managehr.com/) Job opportunities from United Parcel Services. Jobs range from package handlers, delivery drivers, and warehouse management to administration, communications, information systems, and logistics.			x	
5. UPS Calculate Time and Cost (http://wwwapps.ups.com/calTimeCost?loc=en_US) ... of, and services requested for, packages actually tendered to UPS. ... have specially negotiated rates, contact your UPS account executive for a rate quote. ...			x	
6. UPS Careers (http://upsjobs.com/) Job opportunities from United Parcel Services. Jobs range from package handlers, delivery drivers, and warehouse management to administration, communications, information systems, and logistics.			x	
7. Welcome to UPS Supply Chain Solutions (http://www.ups-scs.com/) UPS delivery solutions for businesses, providing logistics, global freight, financial services, mail services, and consulting to business customers.			x	
8. Uninterruptible power supply - Wikipedia, the free encyclopedia (http://en.wikipedia.org/wiki/Uninterruptible_power_supply) ... An uninterruptible power supply (UPS), sometimes called an uninterruptible power ... particular type of equipment, a UPS is typically used to protect ...	x			
9. APC Product Information for UPS (http://www.apc.com/products/category.cfm?id=13) ... Back-UPS HS ... Smart-UPS XL ... GUTOR Industrial UPS and DC Systems ...				x
10. RACING.UPS.COM - Home Page (http://www.racing.ups.com/) UPS Racing NASCAR teams, with current stats and standings, photos and video, details about the cars, the drivers, and the crew, and a NASCAR tutorial for racing newbies.			x	
11. The UPS Store: Packaging, Shipping, Passport Photos & Printing Service (http://www.upsstore.com/) Find out how the UPS Store can help. Track packages, estimate shipping costs, get your US passport photo, print and finish documents, purchase moving supplies & more. Find The UPS Store near you!			x	
12. UPS Community (http://community.ups.com/) ... UPS teamed up with students in Dubai to raise environmental awareness about ... UPS provided collection points for recycling waste. ...			x	
13. UPS: Summary for UNITED PARCEL SVC - Yahoo! Finance (http://finance.yahoo.com/q?s=ups) Information on UNITED PARCEL SVC (UPS) including quote performance, Real-Time ... Designers Selected to Show in the UPS Hub at Olympus Fashion Week is Available ...			x	
14. UPS Lithuania (http://www.ups-lithuania.com/) ... UPS 2nd QUARTER PRODUCES SOLID EARNINGS ON 15% REVENUE GAIN ... Neteis?tas UPS pavadinimo ir ?enklo naudojimas ... UPS 2nd Quarter Earnings Climb over 18 ...			x	
15. UPS Wireless (http://mobile.ups.com/omnisky/index.jsp) ... Welcome to UPS Wireless services. ? Tracking. ? Quick Cost. ? Transit Time. ? Drop-off Locator. Email Customer Services at. customer.service@ups.com ...			x	
16. UPS Pressroom: Current Press Releases (http://www.pressroom.ups.com/pressreleases/current/0,1088,4454,00.html) ... UPS Expands Real-World Testing of Hydrogen Fuel Cell Technology ... achievement," said Chris Mahoney, UPS senior vice president of global transportation services. ...			x	
17. UPS Sustainability (http://www.sustainability.ups.com/) ... UPS is the world's largest package delivery company and a global leader in ... Headquartered in Atlanta, UPS serves more than 200 countries and territories ...			x	
18. UPS Pressroom: Current Press Releases (http://www.pressroom.ups.com/pressreleases/current/0,1088,4402,00.html) ... The UPS Foundation in partnership with the Corporation for National and ... Press Releases. Sign Up for Email Updates. Current Press Releases. UPS Worldwide ...			x	
19. University of Puget Sound :: Home (http://www.ups.edu/) Welcome to the University of Puget Sound home page. ... 07.13.06 Harned Hall dedication to include lecture by Pulitzer Prize-winning ...			x	
20. UPS Trade Direct - UPS Supply Chain Solutions (http://www.ups-scs.com/tradedirect) UPS Trade Direct provides integrated freight and package delivery allowing you to bypass distribution centers by shipping directly to retail stores or customers' doors.			x	
21. What is UPS? - A Word Definition From the Webopedia Computer Dictionary (http://www.webopedia.com/TERM/U/UPS.html) This page describes the term UPS and lists other pages on the Web where you can ... Information about batteries used in computer UPS ...				x

9 of 11

Improving the Relevance of Search Results via Search-term Disambiguation and Ontological Filtering

INFORMATION SNIPPET	R	P	I	N
22. UPS Power Protection and Battery Backup by Minuteman - Official Website (http://www.minutemanups.com/) Line of remote-controllable uninterruptible power protection (UPS) products for telephones, computers, and data communication devices. From Para Systems, Inc.	✗			
23. UPS (http://mobile.ups.com/) ... UPS Wireless Services ...		✗		
24. the f-ups news (http://www.thefups.com/) ... F-Ups Announce Tour With Tsunami Bomb, Over It. Mar 17, 2005 "All The Young Dudes" on FUSE! ... People ask us all the time what type of music we classify ...			✗	
25. UPS (http://web.belkin.com/support/download/download.asp?category=2&lang=1&mode=) ... UPS. Desktop Accessories. Audio Video. Cables. Computer Accessories. Mice and Keyboards ... Home Office 375VA UPS With Automatic Shutdown Software. F6H375-USB ...		✗		
26. RACING.UPS.COM Race Summary Article (http://www.racing.ups.com/racing/news_results/article.cgi?file=post_20010408_20010408) Racing.UPS.com, the source for #88 UPS Racing information and The Official ... Speedway, but his third in just eight events with UPS as the primary sponsor. ...			✗	
27. THE ups DEBUGGER (http://ups.sourceforge.net/) The ups debugger for C, C++ and Fortran - unofficial home page ... 3.37 released. Archive of ups-users mailing list. ups in print. Fortran support. MP3 of ups song ...			✗	
28. UPS Careers (http://ups.softshoe.com/) ... career or a part-time position to pay for college, UPS is right for you. ... UPS kudos for being a world class employer? Find out. Welcome to UPS Careers ...			✗	
29. United Parcel Service - Wikipedia, the free encyclopedia (http://en.wikipedia.org/wiki/United_Parcel_Service) ... Historically, UPS only faced competition from USPS for the inexpensive ground ... UPS entered the heavy freight business with its purchase of Menlo Worldwide ...			✗	
30. Underground Punk Support (http://go.to/upspunk) an undergound punk distro and zine			✗	
31. OPTI-UPS Protect and Serve (http://www.opti-ups.com/) Manufactures UPS power management products.	✗			
32. UPS - UPS Manufacturers, UPS Factories, UPS Suppliers, China UPS (http://hotproducts.alibaba.com/manufacturers-exporters/Ups.html) Start here to find prequalified UPS suppliers from China and around the world ... (AVR), uninterruptible power supply (UPS), battery chargers, flashlights, and ...	✗			
33. Uninterruptible Power Supply (UPS) FAQ (http://www.jetcafe.org/~npc/doc/ups-faq.html) Frequently Asked Questions (FAQ) about Uninterruptible Power Supplies (UPSs) ... 13: Can I really count on a UPS protecting my equipment? ...		✗		
34. Howstuffworks "How does a computer's uninterruptible power supply (UPS) work?" (http://computer.howstuffworks.com/question28.htm) How does a computer's uninterruptible power supply (UPS) work? Does the computer always run from the battery? ... A UPS generally protects a computer against ...		✗		
35. The DIY (or, if you must, "Ghetto") UPS (http://www.dansdata.com/diyups.htm) How to build your own ugly and awkward uninterruptible power supply! ... contraption works in basically the same way as a normal "dual conversion" UPS. ...	✗			
36. Urban Legends Reference Pages: Rumors of War (Uniform Behavior) (http://www.snopes.com/rumors/ups.asp) Have terrorists acquired missing or stolen UPS uniforms? ... adding to their stock, former UPS employees acquiring old uniforms out of ...		✗		
37. UPS Capital Visa ? Business Rewards Card (http://www.capital.ups.com/solutions/visa_card.html) ... The NEW UPS Capital business card is a great place to begin a long-term ... The UPS Capital Visa? Business Rewards Card is offered and issued by Chase Bank ...			✗	
38. UPS - Investor Relations (http://investor.shareholder.com/ups/index.cfm) ... UPS 2nd Quarter Produces Solid Earnings On 15% Revenue Gain ... UPS, Pilots Reach Accord In Contract Negotiations ... UPS Board Sets Dividend. COLOGNE, ...			✗	
39. UPS Careers: Job Search (https://ups.liserve.com/chicago/) ... through the UPS Earn & Learn Program. Benefits (Life/Health/401K) Paid Vacations & Holidays ... One UPS Way, Hodgkins, IL 60525. Ph: 888-4UPS-JOB. ...			✗	
40. UPS Careers: Opportunities: Part-time: Job Search (https://ups.liserve.com/peakjobs.htm) ... job openings with UPS in your area. Package Handler. Search All ... UPS Global	UPS Corporate. Copyright ? 2002 United Parcel Service, Inc. All rights reserved. ...			✗	
41. The UPS Store: Locations (http://go.mappoint.net/ups/PrxInput.aspx) Search over 3,300 locations to find The UPS Store near you. ... The UPS Store? locations are independently owned and operated by franchisees of Mail Boxes Etc. ...				✗
42. UPS Selector Sizing Applications (http://www.apcc.com/tools/ups_selector/pso/rslr/index.cfm?ISOCountryCode=US) to specify your required runtime and other options, and recommend a UPS solution. ... easy way to finding the right UPS product for a single home or office ...				✗
43. Welcome To Air Cargo World -- Breaking News (http://www.aircargoworld.com/break_news/04212006e.htm) ... UPS said its freight forwarding business lost customers in the past two quarters, ... UPS has been spending money and attention on new technology for the Menlo ...			✗	

Improving the Relevance of Search Results via Search-term Disambiguation and Ontological Filtering

INFORMATION SNIPPET	R	P	I	N
44. Business Week Online: Personal Investing (http://host.businessweek.com/businessweek/Corporate_Snapshot.html?Symbol=UPS) BusinessWeek magazine: The most-read source of global ... Get Fund Prospectus. CORPORATE SNAPSHOT. UNITED PARCEL SERVICE INC CL B (NYSE:UPS) LAST. CHANGE ...			⊘	
45. UPS Israel (http://www.ups-israel.com/index.cfm) ... UPS 2nd QUARTER PRODUCES SOLID EARNINGS ON 15% REVENUE GAIN ... UPS 2nd Quarter Earnings Climb over 18% as Package Business Grows Worldwide ...			⊘	
46. United Package Smashers - The Truth About United Parcel Service, UPS and the Big Brown Turd (http://www.unitedpackagesmashers.com/) Resources and information for unhappy and disgruntled UPS customers and employees. ... plaintiffs for lawsuits against UPS for any alleged unlawful, ...			✗	
47. UPS: Headlines for UNITED PARCEL SVC - Yahoo! Finance (http://finance.yahoo.com/q/h?s=UPS) Find out the latest news headlines for UNITED PARCEL SVC (UPS) ... Designers Selected to Show in the UPS Hub at Olympus Fashion Week is Available ...			⊘	
48. UPS (Uninterruptible power supply) and DC Power systems from Powerware (http://www.powerware.com/) Power system protection, Powerware UPS, Telecom power systems and ... Site map. UPS from Powerware; Your source for UPS Power surge protectors, UPS Power ...	⊘			
49. Cover Pages: UPS OnLine Toolbox Supports XML for Tracking Shipments to Your Office. (http://xml.coverpages.org/ni2001-03-16-b.html) ... "significant enhancements" to the UPS OnLine Tools, which "offer advanced ... Announcement: "UPS Adds Two New Tools to Its Online Toolbox. ...				⊘
50. InformationWeek.com (http://www.informationweek.com/841/ups_side.htm) Logistics company redoes its infrastructure to put wireless technology to the test ... Prior to 1989, UPS was shipping 8 million to 9 million packages a day and ...			⊘	

Retrieval at: Mon Aug 21 15:54:39 CST 2006

www.ingramcontent.com/pod-product-compliance
Lightning Source LLC
LaVergne TN
LVHW042332060326
832902LV00006B/129